ness Computer
s

ONE WEEK LOAN
UNIVERSITY OF GLAMORGAN
TREFOREST LEARNING RESOURCES CENTRE
Pontypridd, CF37 1DL
Telephone: (01443) 482626
Books are to be returned on or before the last date below

Business Computer Ethics

Duncan Langford

Addison-Wesley

Harlow, England • Reading, Massachusetts • Menlo Park, California
New York • Don Mills, Ontario • Amsterdam • Bonn • Sydney • Singapore
Tokyo • Madrid • San Juan • Milan • Mexico City • Seoul • Taipei

Addison Wesley Longman Limited
Edinburgh Gate
Harlow
Essex CM20 2JE
England
And Associated Companies throughout the world

Visit Addison Wesley Longman on the world wide web at:
http://www.awl-he.com

The programs in this book have been included for their instructional
value. They have been tested with care but are not guaranteed for
any particular purpose. Their publisher does not offer any warranties
or representations; nor does it accept any liabilities with respect to the
programs.

First published 1999

ISBN 0 201 34279 0

British Library Cataloguing-in-Publication Data
A catalogue record for this book is available from the British Library

Library of Congress Cataloging-in-Publication Data
Langford, Duncan, 1944-
   Business computer ethics / Duncan Langford.
      p.   cm.
   Includes bibliographical references and index.
   ISBN 0-201-34279-0
   1. Business--Data processing--Moral and ethical aspects.
   2. Business ethics.   I. Title.
   HF5548.2.L265 1999
   174'.4--dc21   98-49323
                                                            CIP

Set in 10/12pt Baskerville
Typeset by 42
Produced by Addison Wesley Longman Singapore (Pte) Ltd.
Printed in Singapore.

For
My cousins, Nola & Lionel; my friend, Margaret Smith but,
most of all Gina and Maddy, the much loved women in my life.

And what is good, Phaedrus,
And what is not good –
Need we ask anyone to tell us these things?

ROBERT M. PIRSIG
Zen and the Art of Motorcycle Maintenance

Contents

....

CHAPTER 3
Computer use: the question of scale and other circumstances 27

CHAPTER 4
How should a business behave? 41

CHAPTER 5
Installing new computers? 56

CHAPTER 6
Practical problems 76

CHAPTER 7

Networking and the Internet 90

CHAPTER 8

The law and business computer use 112

CHAPTER 9

Support for appropriate behaviour 128

CHAPTER 10
Summary and conclusions 143

Preface

A book about business computer ethics?

This is a book for business computer users, not academic philosophers; this introduction explains why.

Background

This book grew from practical experience, and from positive reactions to my previous book, *Practical Computer Ethics*. This was the first computer ethics text in the UK intended for actual practical use by computer users rather than as a basis for philosophical discussion. A similar practical approach is used in *Business Computer Ethics*.

Some author background: I am not an ethicist, or a philosopher, or any form of abstract analyst, but a mainstream computer scientist, and businessman. My students are computer scientists and business people; and neither of these groups is noted for its tolerance of irrelevancies.

In my experience of working in the field of computer ethics, it has proved essential to build teaching and discussion around genuine issues – using real problems, and issues that actually occurred to real people. Although it is always useful in teaching, I believe that this approach is of particular importance when dealing directly with 'real world' issues – especially those issues that may be perceived, by those at the coal face, as dilemmas typically outside the concerns of an ivory-towered academic – or an author.

Computers are essential tools in today's business – but are they always used appropriately? And what does 'appropriately' mean anyway? *Business Computer Ethics* aims to find out.

Acknowledgements

I am greatly indebted to all those individuals and companies who patiently discussed ethical problems experienced with business computer systems, and, in particular, those who gave permission to use their experiences as the basis of illustrative examples. Their help was quite invaluable. Names and identifying details have, of course, been changed.

Specialist information on the 1998 Data Protection Act in Chapter 8 was largely based, with its kind permission, on material supplied by the Office of the Data Protection Commissioner (formerly the Data Protection Registrar). Chapter 8 is also indebted to *Data Protection News* for help in tackling details of the 1998 Data Protection Act.

I was grateful for the help and support of my colleagues David Bateman, Dave Beckett, Judith Broom, Roger Cooley, Barry Dean, Gillian Donaldson, Aliy Fowler, Cyril Lewis, Janet Linington, Gordon Makinson, Denise Mansfield, Judi Mayland, Marian Pitt, Jonathan Roberts, Mark Scahill, David Shaw, Brian Spratt, Gillian Waters and Christine Wilson.

We are grateful to the following for permission to reproduce copyright material:

ACM Code of Ethics and Professional Conduct reprinted from Communications of the Association for Computing Machinery, V.36:2, February 1993, by permission; Software Engineering Code of Ethics reprinted from Communications of the Association for Computing Machinery, V.40:11, November 1997, by permission; BCS Code of Conduct 1992 reproduced with permission from British Computer Society; BitLaw reproduced from http://www.bitlaw.com/internet/trademarks.html reproduced with permission from Daniel Tysver, Beck & Tysver; JANET AUP policy reproduced with permission from Joint Information Systems Committee of the Higher Education Funding Council; Computer hard disk scanning by HM Customs and Excise in posting from Vin McLennan http://www.vin@shore.net reproduced with permission; Computing service document at http://info.ox.ac.uk/rules/etiquette.html by Alex Reid, Director, Oxford Uni Computing Services reproduced with permission; Misha Glouberman http: //www.web.net/~misha/trademark.html reproduced with permission; letter from http://www.rru.com/tru/rru3.html reproduced with permission from Miles O'Neal; Business Ethics network http://www.bath.ac.uk/centres/ethical/EBEN/home.html reproduced with permission from Business Ethics Network-UK; Management Link http://www.inst-mgt.org.uk/institute/external/mansorc/prof-org.html reproduced with permission from Managing Information Centre, Institute of Management, Cottingham Road, Northampton, NN17 1TT.

While every effort has been made to trace the owners of copyright material, in a few cases this has proved impossible and we take this opportunity to offer our apologies to any copyright holders whose rights we may have unwittingly infringed.

Why do I need to read a book about ethics?

There are solid practical and professional reasons why anyone involved in the ordering, design, maintenance and, of course, use of business computer systems needs to have an understanding of ethical issues. This section tells you why.

Introduction

If you are involved in the design or use of business computer systems, this book is aimed at you, and you need to read it. A reasonable question would obviously be: 'Why?'

Computers can be misused in business, by those who are given them as business tools and by those responsible for supplying and maintaining business systems. The consequences of such misuse may be considerable, and in today's networked society may well result in a significant impact on the company. The consequent responsibility for company computer systems is potentially a heavy one. Managers clearly need a resource to assist them in this specialised task.

Let us begin by establishing the setting. Before looking specifically at business computer ethics, it is helpful to establish a firm baseline first. As business people, do we actually need to behave ethically? After all, if ethical business behaviour were generally invalid, then the specialism of appropriate business computer use would be irrelevant.

Ethics?

In order to be sure that discussion is well founded, it is necessary to start by defining terms, so this section deals – very briefly – with the general background to ethical studies. If you are not interested in how business computer ethics relates to the study of philosophy, however, you may jump to the next section.

Philosophy, as a subject, was developed by the ancient Greeks and has clearly been around for some time. 'Philosophy' itself is really an umbrella term, covering several interrelated subjects. That branch of philosophy that deals with human conduct and character is known as 'moral' philosophy – or ethics.

The subject of this book is that component of ethics which deals with personal uncertainties and conflicts of opinion: 'What choice should I take?'; 'Is this action unfair?'; and so on. It is of course possible to step further back and to ask wider questions in an attempt to analyse more general standards: 'If this action is said to be right, what does "right" really mean?' and other such queries. This larger-scale analysis is known as theoretical ethics.

The study of what moral beliefs are actually held by a society is called 'descriptive' ethics and is located on the borders between philosophy and sociology. In contrast, the prescription of authoritative standards based upon accepted norms within a society is known as 'normative' ethics, or sometimes 'philosophical' ethics.

These terms may well be confusing. Fortunately, for our purposes it is not necessary to learn them. Although it is a fascinating study, a description of the history and development of moral philosophy, or ethics, lies outside the scope of this book.

> The boundaries of the study called Ethics are variously and often vaguely conceived: but they will perhaps be sufficiently defined, at the outset ... if a 'Method of Ethics' is explained to mean any rational procedure by which we determine what individual human beings 'ought' – or what it is 'right' for them – to do, or to seek to realise by voluntary means.[1]

Why are ethics relevant to business?

Clearly, I believe that ethical behaviour is relevant not just to the use of business computers but to all business practice. There are two substantive reasons for this, both straightforward and practical.

First, ethical business practices can generally be seen as necessary, simply because today ethical behaviour is generally expected. Those concerned in the current business world, whether as shareholders, supplying companies, customers or clients, not to mention the general public and media, all have the expectation that a well-run business will behave in an ethical way.

As an illustration, it is generally expected that, regardless of any legal obligations, a business should avoid corporate lying, will be reasonably open about its business practices, and will expect its staff to maintain appropriate standards of professional behaviour. Such a visible response to perceived external expectations is the 'obvious' reason for business to behave ethically. The response is, essentially, built upon a widespread belief that behaving ethically, whether as a person or as a business entity, is behaviour appropriately built upon implicit standards of trust in business life itself. Consequently, the promotion of ethical behaviour within a business is expected to result in automatic benefits.

It may seem that this very brief description takes an unduly cavalier definition; but in treating such an approach to ethical behaviour casually, the aim is simply to speed recognition by establishing the point quickly. It is certainly not meant to deny a potentially solid basis, and appropriate justification. However, it is also essential to be realistic; how ever much of a good thing the promotion of ethical behaviour may be viewed in general, today's business does not necessarily always have the freedom to promote advancement of good works as a prime target.

In direct contrast, the second substantive reason for the support of ethical business practice is unashamedly pragmatic. It is appropriate for business to behave ethically because ethical behaviour *works* – this boils down to suggesting that unethical business behaviour tends to be successful only in the short term. Even the most cynical of business managers is likely to be persuaded of a need for ethical behaviour when presented with objective evidence. If further encouragement is necessary – ethical behaviour by a business as an *entity* surely invalidates unethical behaviour by its staff as *individuals*.

I believe that ethical behaviour is appropriate for today's business because customers, and the wider world, expect it, but also because concrete evidence shows that ethical business behaviour works. These issues are dealt with in detail later.

Why treat computing differently?

'Computer' is, of course, a very elastic term; the actual machines involved in business computer use can extend from massive office and industrial systems, at one extreme, to personal desktop machines at the other. It is hard to imagine how modern business could survive without the use of computers, and the support of networked computer systems. It can be fairly argued that computing is now essential to modern life in the developed world. As both employers and workers, we consequently experience computers either directly or indirectly in virtually all our business activities.

It may be fairly argued that, as business in the USA and elsewhere became increasingly dependent upon the use of computers and computer systems, the power and uses of business systems increased. Understandably, as computer use within business expanded, the potential for misuse also developed; as greater numbers of staff used company machines, more people were affected by their use. Consequently, the need for promotion of appropriate behaviour became increasingly important.

Computers can be an incredibly powerful tool and, like all powerful tools, as well as possessing the power to help, they have considerable capability for misuse and damage. Inappropriate use of company computers, whether as a deliberate policy or through the unauthorised actions of employees, has the potential for occasioning massive corporate damage. An appropriate computer-use policy is likely to reflect well on public perception of a company; customers and clients tend to appreciate it, as well. However, quite apart from these less tangible 'professional' aspects, there are very solid practical reasons why it makes sense for a business to have developed appropriate guidelines for business computer use.

Let us assume that a business has accepted the need itself to behave ethically and, additionally, expects its staff to behave ethically. Why, then, given such a clearly signalled overall intention, should the use of company *computers* be of particular interest? After all, they form only one part of a complex business organisation and so hardly merit special treatment?

The reason why business computers deserve particular ethical attention is basic. Whether they realise it or not, everyone working in the businesses of today's developed world experiences – and is affected by – computers in virtually every aspect of their working lives. Computers are not an add-on extra to modern business; they are its backbone.

Why is it necessary to consider the use of company computers separately from the use of other company equipment? Essentially, it is because not only are computers unique as business tools but also their use has become fundamental to the operation of most businesses today.

Today, most desktop computers and PCs are also networked – that is, they have the ability to link to other machines, usually in order to access data and other information held remotely. Such machines may sometimes be connected directly to each other, as part of an office or company computer system. Frequently, connected machines are at a considerable distance from each other, typically connected through links to a local company intranet,[2] or global systems, such as the Internet or World Wide Web (WWW). The networked machine itself may be anything from a powerful company computer with direct Internet connections to a small business machine, accessing the world through telephone and modem.

Computers are, of course, controlled and used by people. The use of business computers by individuals might graduate from small-scale personal activities, such as word processing, to accessing central company files and information, and finally moving to experience the global electronic community of the Internet.

However, widespread as computer use undoubtedly is within business, of course not every employee of every business will have direct involvement. Even without any personal use of individual computers, though, today's general experiences of computers in business are extensive. Internally, they may range from the issuing of a salary cheque to personnel records; externally, from involvement in buying an airline ticket to the use of a credit card.

The spread of global computer networking has made – and is still making – radical changes to our society. Such widely used terms as 'surfing' the Internet and 'information superhighway' emphasise the ubiquity of today's computers. Without them, present-day Western business would be impossible to sustain.

This situation leads us to two initial claims, and a conclusion:

1 Computers underpin modern business.

2 In the developed world, virtually everyone involved in modern business has either direct or indirect experience of computer use.

3 The way in which computers are installed and used is important to individuals and business.

Implications

The pace of change is rapid; computing has always been a dynamic field. New developments are constant, and the spread of technology into fresh areas is continuous. To a large extent, this expansion has always been driven by the powerful combination of market demands and technological development. A computer-based product or service, whether a computer game or a surveillance system, would normally be developed only if it was likely to sell, especially if it offered a significant technical advantage over its competitors. When attention is focused on solving a technical problem, wider effects on customers and society generally may not be given a high priority. It is therefore important to appreciate that, setting aside the demands of statute law, external issues may not be influential in the development of computer systems – within computing, the development environment is perceived as neutral.

To the public, then, the visible face of computing is a combination of radical techno-logical development and a perhaps dubious moral neutrality. Public regard for computer systems designers, builders and users is not well developed. Working with computers is perceived as lying outside ordinary experience: the necessary complexity and technical language make computer systems difficult for a non-specialist to evaluate effectively. Per-haps because of this distancing, the general public does not perceive the designers and users of computer systems as consciously making moral choices, as, for example, workers are felt to do in the field of medicine; and the image of computer specialists may be perceived as one lacking moral weight or authority.

However, most practising computing professionals would probably accept that the present professional climate does appear to support 'ethics' as a professionally relevant issue. Many of the most important indicators are certainly pointing in this direction. Since the widespread growth of business computer use in the 1980s, codes of profes-sional conduct have been revised and promoted, articles and books have been written, and conferences held. Professional issues are now even considered (by the Association for Computer Machinery (ACM), British Computer Society (BCS) and many universities throughout the world) as forming an essential part of the training of every computer scientist, although it may be true that some business studies courses still only deal with computing issues in a very limited form.

This move towards responsible design and use of computer systems is, of course, also supported to a growing degree by both the serious and popular press, as well as the pub-lic in general. The media are constantly presenting us with examples of conduct that is perceived – or at least presented – as professionally inappropriate. Of course, in this computing is not alone; even cursory study will supply further examples from other fields – financial services are a current favourite, but there are many more.

In summary, therefore, we are experiencing a situation where the widespread use of computer systems – especially networked systems – is essential to the conduct of modern business. Although the *technical* design and management of these systems will normally have been solidly based, the reasons why a system is needed, the actions that it will carry out and the manner in which it will be used may not have had the benefit of such clear analysis.

Again: two further claims, and a conclusion:

4 The design, installation and maintenance of business computer systems may not have been given non-technical evaluation.
5 Computing-related academic and professional bodies are responding to internal and external pressures to consider non-technical issues as professionally relevant.
6 Consideration of wider issues involved in business computer use is becoming necessary.

Background

Before considering suitable uses of business computer systems, and the management of their use, we must begin by clarifying what the appropriate areas are to be addressed. While the general umbrella of 'business computing' is relevant, as demonstrating our concern with all aspects of computer *use*, it is nevertheless essential to make an important early distinction. Computers do not magically appear; computer programs are not automatically neutral in values; office systems do not maintain themselves. It is therefore necessary to identify those people who are not necessarily themselves users of company systems but who are nevertheless *involved* in such use, for example in technical control and management.

Such a division, basically, allows the differences between implementation[3] and operation of office systems to be clearly distinguished. Appropriate actions differ completely between these areas; the responsibilities of staff may be radically different. As a first step, it is therefore necessary to clarify the different aspects of business computer systems involvement. We may then move on to examine actual issues, and to develop suggestions as to what may be appropriate or inappropriate conduct.

The format of this book is potentially complicated by the need to cover several related but distinct roles. The responsibilities of company executives charged with procurement and maintenance of an effective computer system may be seen as being quite distinct from the responsibilities of the computer professionals who actually provide it, and different again from the staff who will eventually use it. However, all three are interconnected, and the failure of any single part must affect the remaining two.

While we have already accepted that every business employee is likely to have at least *some* contact with computers, the actual *nature* of this contact clearly differs, depending on the nature of the employee's tasks and the level that they hold within the business organisation. While there are many possible classifications of business computer use, for the purposes of this book computer-related staff may usefully be divided into two groups. The first group, 'systems' people, contains both the responsible managers and those specialist staff responsible for technical implementation of their instructions. The second group deals with the actual 'users' of the business computer system.

'Systems' people

The first division consists of those who are actually responsible for the company computer systems. It is very important to appreciate that this section does not just include those responsible technical staff, who should possess the necessary qualifications and knowledge to successfully operate company systems. Under this definition, group members also include those responsible for the original commissioning, design and development of company computer systems. Of course, those people concerned with on-going systems maintenance are also included. For the sake of simplicity, I call members of this group *systems* people, although it must be emphasised again that they are by no means limited to specialist technical experts. Under this definition, the systems group may well also include higher executives of considerable seniority, up to and including board level.

Users

The second, much larger, division includes all those who make use of company computers, whether they are direct employees of the relevant company or not. Although members of this group may frequently have the knowledge and ability to do more than passively employ computers as tools, such use is their primary role and purpose. Members of this group are therefore defined as computer *users*.

It is important that the particular responsibilities of both systems group staff and computer systems 'users' are specifically made clear.

While membership of the two groups may (and in practice often does) overlap, the responsibilities of the two groups are so different that they are normally dealt with separately here.

Summary

Let us look again at the points established earlier in this section:

1 Computers underpin modern business.

2 Virtually everyone has either direct or indirect experience of computer use.

3 The way in which computers are installed and used is important to individuals and business.

4 The design, installation and maintenance of business computer systems may not have been given non-technical evaluation.

5 Computing-related academic and professional bodies are responding to internal and external pressures to consider non-technical issues as professionally relevant.

6 Consideration of wider issues involved in business computer use is becoming necessary.

The intention of this book is to address these points by drawing them together into a focused approach to the whole question of business computer use. There are many possible ways forward, and particular areas of emphasis that may be useful in forming a view on what might be considered as 'appropriate' use of company computer systems. Two points are of particular significance:

- The 'design gap' between technical issues and actual use;
- The ways in which modern computer systems are used, and misused.

We conclude by developing concepts to provide a series of guidelines on the responsible commissioning, design and employment of business systems.

Foundations

In identifying and addressing the issues in this book I have drawn heavily on my own experiences as a computer scientist, as well as a researcher and teacher of computer ethics. However, this is emphatically not intended as a text for academic philosophers but is instead solidly practical and specifically directed at business people and computer specialists. For this reason, I have repeatedly incorporated examples based on real issues and real problems, issues that actually happened to real people – although, of course, identifying details have been changed. I am very grateful indeed to those people and companies who gave their permission for these incidents and issues to be used as examples here.

Although you may be principally interested in, for example, the ethical implications for computer system specifications, I would urge you to read the chapters dealing with other areas, as well; it is the interconnected nature of computer systems that can lead to some of their most difficult challenges.

Why should I care about ethical problems in business computing?

This is a really tough question, a question potentially so destructive that it is probably more often whispered in the back row of lectures than asked outright. If ethics generally are too often automatically assumed to be a good thing, to question their purpose and practicalities in ·this way may be viewed – at the very least – as a grave breach of etiquette.

However, this book is emphatically not a book of philosophy, intended for an audience of ethicists. It was written with the intention that it would be *used* rather than merely providing another title to be symbolically added to a reading list or bibliography. The justification for this approach is that emphasis throughout this text is on practicalities – supported by theory, certainly, but essentially depending for a reader's attention upon continued and obvious relevance and importance to modern business practice. There are solid business reasons for acting ethically; and it is these reasons that underpin this book.

Of course, it is often easiest to respond to difficult specific questions by talking in general terms about ethical issues. However, unless we have first clearly defined exactly what these are, the approach may be a recipe for confusion – and, if handled skilfully enough, may well beg the question anyway.

The key task in responding to such a direct question is surely to ask first whether, and how, modern business computing might generate ethical issues. If this can be demonstrated, it is then essential to ask specifically why busy executives, understandably concerned with their core task of ensuring business viability, should interest themselves in such things.

To summarise: this book is intended to tackle real issues involving appropriate and inappropriate business use of computers. It will not intentionally fudge or sidestep awkward questions and issues but will attempt to meet them head on, and to resolve any consequent problems directly. Let us start by confronting the major problem, the one with which we began this section, a problem that is, potentially, so serious that it might well prevent some business and computing people from reading this book at all.

'Why should I care about ethical problems in business computing?' When you look more closely, it becomes clear that there are actually three parts to this question:

1 Are ethics relevant to business?

2 Are business computers relevant to business ethics?

3 Should we worry?

The first is certainly the defining issue – in any discussion of ethics and business, it is clearly necessary to begin by judging whether or not ethics are actually *relevant* to business. To look at the situation in a contrary 'frame': if after consideration it is decided that ethics are in fact irrelevant to business practice, then there is no point in pursuing the topic further. This would mean that nothing is unethical in business, so whatever uses are made of business computers must, automatically, be warranted. This extreme argument surely cannot be justified. However, if we do decide to accept that ethical issues are indeed of some relevance to modern business, we must then face the second issue, concerning the relationship, in a business context, of computers to ethical issues. Are computers always impartial, or do they, potentially, offer the possibility of ethical misconduct?

While debate here may last a little longer, it should soon be clear that computers can indeed be used inappropriately, if 'inappropriately' is taken to refer to uses that act against commonly held ethical views. To take two random examples: a computer is surely used inappropriately when a computerised payroll is manipulated to cheat staff of part of their salaries, or if computer-generated invoices are changed to reflect negative values, thus crediting a customer instead of charging them.

Finally, if the contention that computers may be used inappropriately is also accepted as valid and appropriate, we come to the clincher – why should we worry?

Let us begin by examining the relevance of ethical problems to the business field. As this issue is dealt with in more detail later, for our present purposes we may simply say that the relevance of ethical issues to business may be demonstrated by reference to personal and professional codes of conduct. For the pragmatic, there is also a practical justification based upon empirical evidence – generally, people prefer to do business with those who are perceived as ethical.

Second, it is clear that the misuse of virtually any resource can create ethical problems, the essential point here being that tools of all types may be used for immoral, as well as moral, ends. For example, a hammer is necessary for driving nails but might also be used in an assault. The degree of potential harm may of course bear a functional relationship to the original activity – a heavy hammer may drive nails faster and further, but it is more dangerous when used as a weapon. Similarly, while a gun may be used legitimately, it is potentially dangerous; a more powerful weapon is likely to be more dangerous, and so on. Given the significant part played by computer systems in modern business, the use of a powerful computer can be no exception to this rule.

So we may assume that it is possible for a machine used to support and promote business – a computer – to also be used in an unethical way. However, why should we care?

What can an appreciation of ethics give to a business professional? There are many reasons, which naturally vary in significance from individual to individual; many are described in the following chapters.

Three incentives that may be particularly important to you are:

- *Trust*: an individual or business known to operate under a consistent ethical code is one who can be relied upon.
- *Security*: being aware in advance of the implications of your actions guards against unexpected outcomes.
- *Comfort*: this is admittedly subjective; but peace of mind is probably the most important benefit of all.

Discussion points

Each chapter ends with a series of points, intended to form the basis for a class or seminar discussion on the issues raised in that chapter. They should not be considered until after the chapter, and any relevant case examples, have been read and thought through.

All questions have been carefully chosen to encourage debate, and they are primarily intended to encourage thinking about the issues. This may mean that questions are not necessarily capable of producing definitive answers.

1 What do you understand by 'ethics'? Write down three or four words that you feel appropriately describe the subject, and, if possible, compare them with the views of others.

2 How might your definition of 'ethics' relate to your role (actual or potential) within business?

3 Can you think of any reasons why *you* should act ethically?

4 Can you think of any reasons why *others* should act ethically?

5 Are there any differences between your answers to the two previous questions? Why might this be?

Notes

1 Sidgewick, *The Methods of Ethics*, 1874, quoted in *Computer and Information Ethics*, Weckert, J. and Adeney, D., Greenwood Press, London, 1997.

2 An 'intranet' can be thought of as a company-specific, cut-down version of the World Wide Web; Intranet pages viewed electronically can be accessed only from company-owned machines and are not available to the outside world. In most other aspects, though, they look exactly like typical WWW pages.

3 By 'implementation' I mean a process that begins with a managerial discussion on computer system purchase and concludes with the system's technical installation.

2

Business computing – and ethics

Why should ethics be relevant to business computer design and use? What actually *is* 'business' computing? This chapter establishes the background to such questions by examining wider issues involved in the uses of computers within business. Starting with an analysis of the relevance of ethics and computers to business, it moves on to look at ways in which companies of different sizes might respond to pressures to misuse computer systems, before moving on to define ways in which unethical conduct may occur. It concludes with an examination of justifications for ethical behaviour in the use of business computer systems.

Introduction

Most business people are naturally aware of public and social pressure for them to act in an ethical and responsible way. Such pressure is widespread in most areas of today's society, and the professional use of computers has not been exempt from such demands. Responsible computer-focused organisations have responded by developing and introducing new codes of professional conduct, as well as by revising old ones. Appreciating the fundamental role played by computers in business today, many large companies have also introduced specific rules and guidelines for the appropriate management of their company computer systems.

However, just how relevant are ethics to business use of computer systems? If your company uses efficient computers running productive software, do you really need to spend limited and expensive resources worrying about additional issues? This question may seem particularly relevant when the issues being considered form no part of any technical problem, and indeed may well appear peripheral to the main purpose of your business. This chapter directly addresses these problems. It faces the unwelcome truth that, in a cut-throat world, the competition does not always play by professional rules, and examines the disadvantages, as well as advantages, of ethical behaviour.

It is first relevant to consider how 'unethical' business practice is typically determined. There is, of course, input from trade and professional organisations, teaching, and business literature. Nevertheless, many firmly held defining opinions – essentially, 'what makes ethical behaviour in business?' – were originally developed empirically. Based upon common human experience, such general ethical rules are often intuitively obvious to business person and customer alike. Such generally accepted classifications are clearly of considerable help in identifying potentially unethical behaviour.

As the range of resources available to modern business developed, the potential range of both ethical and unethical behaviour has increased dramatically. It is no longer possible to rely solely upon common human experience in evaluating behaviour, because much current business practice lies beyond it. For this reason alone, it may no longer be practicable to define ethical behaviour in business without reference to other specialist fields. If this is so, I suggest that, to modern business, computing may well be the most important of these 'external' fields.

We now move on to consider these and related questions and in the process attempt to determine why the use of business computer systems may be overdue for ethical analysis and oversight.

What is 'business' computing?

The task of defining exactly what is meant by 'business' computing is by no means straightforward. One complication is that there exists no single type of computer or computer system that must be used by business people, because the nature of properly designed computer systems is to change and adapt to specific needs. Surely, though, at least the widespread use of IBM-compatible PCs must allow for some generalisation? Unfortunately, for an analyst attempting to draw general conclusions, in business computing even physically identical computers become quite different in appearance and use when dissimilar applications (software) are employed. Even software carrying out similar tasks on physically identical computers may be totally different in appearance, and perhaps in function, too. Consequently, there can be no easy global definitions.

In this context, the task of developing a usable definition is both complex and perplexing. However, while acknowledging the complexity of the subject, for the purposes of this book I take as a workable definition of business computing 'any activity using computers that is undertaken by business'.

Even after such a generalised line has been drawn, the position is further complicated by consideration of the important issue of *scale*: clearly, the computing needs and responsibilities of a large corporation are very different from those of a small corner store. Potential ethical problems involving the use of business computers understandably reflect this difference.

Finally, practical use of the systems is not the only relevant issue. The actual *material* processed by business systems – all 'data' entered and generated – differs greatly. This is important, as the nature of data held on company systems must affect the uses to which it may ethically be put. For example, a list of names and addresses held on computer and used by a bookshop to mail invoices and statements is surely acceptable. However, if an identical list of names, addresses and invoice details were secretly examined and correlated to determine which customers were buying 'suspect' literature, the ethical position is very different, and the need for ethical consideration clear. Such issues need attention.

Ethical business computer use?

Let us begin by asking what is perhaps an obvious question. Why, either as business people or as individual members of society, should we be interested in computer ethics? Why, indeed, should the use of computers be of particular interest to you, or anyone else?

The reason is actually very straightforward. Whether those concerned actually realise it or not, virtually everyone living in the developed world must interact in some way with computers.

It may be fairly argued that, as business in the USA and elsewhere became increasingly dependent upon computers and computer systems, the potential for computer misuse increased. This possibility has not been overlooked in computer literature.[1] The specialist field of computer academia is therefore no longer limited to technical areas and now, for example, contains many articles and books on 'professional issues', while specialist academic conferences on the ethics involved in computer use have been held in Europe, the USA, and beyond. There are no signs of this expansion of relevance slowing; indeed, professional issues are now considered by the key setters of professional standards in international computing, such as the Association for Computing Machinery (ACM), Institute of Electrical and Electronic Engineers (IEEE) and British Computer Society (BCS), to form an essential part of a computer scientist's training. Formal accreditation of many computer science courses now depends upon it. Most – but by no means all – universities teaching computer science now believe that consideration of the use to be made of a computer does not end with the solution of technical problems.

The implications of such 'technical' appreciation of the importance of wider issues in computer use are clear. However, while computer scientists may promote the concepts of ethics in the development and design of computers, how may we consider applying such a view to the employment of computers within business?

How is inappropriate computer use relevant to business?

Let us begin by marking out some territory and clarifying the issues. First, it is important to face facts: the environment in which we work is governed not by ethical textbooks but by commercial realities. Specifically, the modern business world places continual pressure on individuals, and the businesses that employ them, to succeed. Success may sometimes appear to be made easier by bending or breaking the 'rules'. While, if challenged, we would probably all claim to know what is meant in this context by the term 'rules', a universally acceptable yet precise definition is in fact quite hard to determine. However, for the purposes of discussions here, I define such 'rules' as 'written or unwritten expectations of ethical behaviour'.

While a commonly understood code of anticipated behaviour may certainly exist and even be generally recognised, it is by no means automatically followed by everyone. Indeed, if one looks around and seriously examines many common business practices, it often seems that such 'rules' are, as Hamlet said, 'honour'd more in the breach than the observance.' This is an important point to understand. Realistically, then, it is essential to appreciate that we live and, especially, work in a world where people are able to act unethically – and frequently do. How ever much we might prefer to live in some ethical alternative universe, it is necessary to accept that current circumstances are unlikely to change.

In the 'real world' – the one actually lived in by business, if not by academics – is it therefore realistic for any firm to compete adequately with unethical rivals without first sharing their morals?

Most executives and managers who have seriously considered the implications of initiating or supporting 'official' ethical practice will probably admit that similar questions have occurred to them. Is there perhaps a down side to the development of formal company codes of conduct, codes intended, for example, to govern use of company computer systems? At the heart of such concern is a basic fear: would strict adherence to an ethical code result in suicidal tilting of a previously level, if unethical, professional playing field?

The use of networked company computer systems, together with the widespread use of personal computers, is very much a part of the way modern business operates. The ways in which computers are used are consequently an integral part of this problem.

Size issues

While some aspects of potential computer misuse are equally probable whatever the size of the concerned business, there are also varieties of risk that differ as the size of the concerned company changes. Although the relationship of company size to the use of computer systems is discussed later in more detail (Chapter 5), some general conclusions are relevant here. I will therefore now look briefly at four typical levels of business computing, before moving on to identify common and specific areas within a company where ethical difficulties may arise.

Level one

This is the smallest scale of business computing – a typical implementation of a level one company would be a corner store. All business tasks, including use of the computer, are likely to be shared. The computer will be used as a simple tool, often simply for letters and maintaining stock and financial records. At level one, specially written computer software is generally unknown; instead, there is a total reliance upon packaged, commercial software. Because at this level computer skills are uneven – most users are typically self-taught – specialist knowledge of computers and computer systems use is unlikely. At this level, there is also potential for the use of inappropriate equipment and software, often as a result of financial pressures. It is probably more common in level one companies for some software to be 'pirated', i.e. illegal.

Level two

Here the business organisation is larger, and level two companies usually find it possible to nominate a specific individual to look after their company computers. However, the selected member of staff may well have other, possibly conflicting, duties. Typically, they are also likely to pick up knowledge as they go along, rather than being qualified on appointment, or able to undertake specific training. If more than one computer is owned, computers may be either used as individual machines or networked.[2]

Actual computer use will obviously depend upon the type of business, but typical level two companies cover most aspects of business activity. Their reliance is still likely to be on packaged commercial software, although some specialist computing material may be produced 'in house'. If so, such locally generated software may well fail to comply with industry software standards, or even to meet the requirements of relevant computer legislation.

Typically, both job description and task definitions of a level two computer manager are likely to be vague; within the company, there is also potential for the use of inappropriate equipment. There may be difficulty in co-ordinating use of machines, particularly if the company is growing in size, or has recently grown. Companies at level two normally have no formalised policy concerning computer use.

Level three

At this level, a business is large enough to employ a designated computer specialist, who will be given the task of setting up and maintaining company computers. However, the *status* of this person may not necessarily be high, and consequently their ability to set enforceable rules for the use of company computer equipment may be limited. Without the interest and involvement of senior management, it is very probable that the task of a level three computer specialist will be defined in purely practical terms. It is fatally easy for senior managers to think of their computer specialist as simply being employed to keep company computers running efficiently.

Level four

From this level, the company will have at least one team of computer specialists. The role of their team leader will ideally be considered a senior one in the general management hierarchy – although this is by no means assured. Given the involvement of knowledgeable specialists, an enforceable company policy on computer use may be possible, but implementation will depend upon the individual concerned. A computer manager who concentrates purely on technical issues is likely to leave an ethical 'gap' in company computer use policy.

Without specific training or direction, the actual users of company computers may also act unethically, either because they do not know or appreciate the potential consequences of their actions, or because their use of company systems is not adequately policed.

Divisions

Demands on management to determine computer-related policies tend to develop as the number of terminals and size of the computing task grows, but there are a number of common issues among the four groups. A need for company computers to be used responsibly, and of course within legislative requirements, remains whatever the size of a company. It is therefore important to appreciate that, even at the level of the smallest business, there is room for an official policy on computer use. In its simplest form, this may be no more than a verbal understanding between the two or three company members, but everyone should be aware that such requirements exist, and of the importance of keeping to them.

However, as the size of a company, the number of its computers, and the complexity of its computer systems grows, there is need for an 'appropriate use' policy to be made explicit. Reliance on individuals remembering verbal agreements is obviously inappropriate with larger numbers of people. This does not merely mean that a written policy needs to be created; it is clearly insufficient for a new appropriate computer use policy to be developed, written and then filed. Once the policy has been created, it must be actively promoted. It is essential for the expectations of the company, both of its computer managers and of employees who use computers, to be made quite clear to everyone concerned.

As was briefly mentioned earlier, I contend that there are two principal ways in which an ethical oversight of computer use may appropriately be divided. These concern the actual *manner* in which computer systems are employed within a business, and the *use* that is made of company-owned data. Each area is addressed individually below.

The tasks of business computing

Some years ago, most companies owning computers were large, and all made use of an often highly paid team of computer specialists. These select individuals appeared to live in expensively air-conditioned office suites, where they acted as acolytes, tending a multi-million dollar computer. What these computer specialists actually *did* was viewed as necessarily incomprehensible to a non-specialist. Times have changed. Today, in very different circumstances, a powerful computer sits on the desk of most executives, while many even carry a portable machine. Delegating computing tasks to a remote person in a white coat is no longer possible; everyone in business today is expected to possess the ability to use a computer.

However, this gain in productivity and access by individuals may have been at the expense of expert knowledge. Someone who is using a computer as just one business tool among many may lack the specialist experience to realise when their tool is being used inappropriately, or not to its full potential. It is also true that even rules that have worked well in the non-electronic world may not easily transfer to computer-based operations.

Essentially, computers are used in business to solve problems. An individual manager, focused on use of a computer for the task in hand, may understandably lack specialist awareness of wider ethical issues. Even if a computer manager is aware of the importance of such questions, time for proper assessment is unlikely to be available without the encouragement and support of senior staff.

Naturally, individuals who work for a business are expected to behave ethically. However, an obligation for employees to act ethically makes for a corporate responsibility and as such should be considered in the same way as other corporate responsibilities. For example, in an organisation of any size it may be impractical, as well as inefficient, to encourage multiple ways of responding to telephone requests from customers, particularly when clear company procedures are possible. A similar approach may be applied to computing matters: it would then be important to decide, as a matter of policy, what the company considered to be appropriate use of its computer systems.

Development of a company philosophy on computer use is not a job to be delegated down the corporate ladder but one to be defined and published from the top. Only then can a company be confident that all steps have been taken to eliminate unethical or questionable practices.

Data considerations

Consideration of data use by business computer systems falls into two distinct, and equally important, categories. First is the *nature* of the data – what is it, why was it collected, what uses are made of it, and so on. A second, less visible, category is frequently overlooked. It concerns appropriate authorisation for *access* to company data. Exactly who are the members of staff authorised to view and use company-held information? What restrictions, if any, are placed upon distribution of data to others? This section briefly looks at these points.

Of course, the differing natures of modern businesses is reflected in their data needs. The arrival of cheaper computer systems and the greatly reduced cost of data storage have allowed even small companies to engage in collection, collation and analysis of data in ways that were not previously practical or affordable. While smaller-scale companies may be content with simple electronic recording of transactions, larger firms are likely to require increasingly sophisticated data collection and analysis.

Increasingly, specific needs are met by additional data being expressly collected, beyond the recording of normal information generated by the business itself. As an example, consider the use made of swipe card technology by supermarket chains. Information on the spending patterns of individuals is of obvious potential benefit to retailers. However, credit card companies, who collect this information automatically as part of their trading, understandably refuse to release it to third parties. (The ethics of access to data are discussed below.) To circumvent this block, individual customers are now encouraged to apply for 'personal' swipe cards by the expectation of gaining discounts. These cards are processed whenever a purchase is made. Regular use potentially provides a store chain with very detailed who-buys-what-when data, which may subsequently be analysed to provide marketing information impossible to obtain otherwise. The *actual* use made of this data is, however, uncertain. Participating companies that I have asked refused to give details, even under a non-disclosure agreement.

I do not suggest that the issue and use of 'user loyalty' swipe cards are inevitably unethical, but the potential for misuse of such data is clear. This example illustrates the importance of responsible managers considering the ethical issues raised by collection of data *before* permission is given for collection. At the very least, analysis of the justification for the collection, consideration of the explanation given to data subjects and the use to be made of the collected information should be made.

Discussion on the usage of data leads on to the second point – what access will be made to company-held electronic information? Here, legal issues may become relevant and may affect the way in which businesses are able to use collected information. (Legal issues are discussed in Chapter 8.) In some countries – the UK is an example – *all* those intending to collect personal data must first be registered with a national authority. Even when registered, though, in the UK personal data collected for one purpose may not automatically be used for another. Additionally, such data may not be kept beyond the need of the original project; individuals whose details are held by a company have the right to obtain a copy of the information at nominal cost. The rights of data subjects have been further increased under provisions of the new 1998 Data Protection Act, discussed in detail in Chapter 8.

While qualified computer personnel may be well aware of the legal issues surrounding computer use, those people working for a small business and who have been given the additional task of looking after company computers may well have no knowledge of specialist legal matters. It is here that the need to act ethically is paramount. Consideration of the rights of others should prevent circulation of confidential information, for instance; because even if this were not illegal, it is likely to be unethical.

Ethics are bad for you?

We will now look at ways in which the involvement of ethics in computer business use may appear inappropriate. Before going on to describe examples where ethical behaviour appears inadvisable, though, a word of explanation.

I am sure that most people who believe deeply in the importance of ethical professional behaviour have sometimes been tempted to at least put a 'gloss' on its benefits. Indeed, going further, it might be thought sensible to deliberately avoid examples, such as those described below, that appear to disprove the thesis. However, such a course is not sensible – or, of course, ethical.

Consequently, as I have described elsewhere,[3] I feel strongly that it is essential, especially when talking to those as yet inexperienced in the area of professional ethics, to be both accurate and truthful. Although on occasions this can be difficult, it is the only way to promote ethical behaviour effectively. It should consequently be kept in mind that, when describing inappropriate behaviour, I am not in any way intending to advocate it.

What is 'unethical' computer behaviour?

The compilation of a massive list of potentially unethical computer uses may appear both tempting and simple. Regrettably, however, any serious attempt to provide a comprehensive register of inappropriate computer behaviour must be doomed to inevitable failure. The reasons for this are purely practical – uses of computers in modern business are so widespread that, even if generating such a list were possible, it would inevitably increase in size far faster than it could be read.

While a comprehensive list may be unrealistic, it is perfectly possible to illustrate the problems of unethical computer behaviour through the use of appropriate models. To do this, I have selected four areas of business as representative examples, intended to illustrate groups of wider problems. As usual in this book, the four examples should not be taken as being in any way exclusive. They merely represent some illustrations of the range of possible 'unethical' behaviour in business computer use.

For the purposes of discussion, then, let us assume a commercial organisation called UnEthical Inc., which produces widgets for sale to the public. If observance of computer ethics might be counter-productive, just how might its computer systems potentially allow an unfair trading advantage to UnEthical Inc.?

The areas to be considered are:

- General practice
- Controller power
- User responsibility
- Company responsibility.

General practice

The first section considers the relationship of computer use to general business practice; after all, business has historically used many tools, of which computers are only the most recent. A general understanding of what is considered as appropriate business behaviour is consequently of long standing. It is both logical and appropriate to consider the use of computers within this frame.

Controller power

A second area looks to the way in which control of computer systems may convey inappropriate power to the controller. Simply because computers allow their business owners to define both purpose and task, there is the potential for 'global' misuse; and also the possibility of personal misuse by the individual who is given charge of a business computer system.

User responsibility

A further section considers the responsibilities of an individual user – someone who is given use of a company computer as a part of their job. The direct responsibilities of such a user may be clear, but the increased potential for inappropriate actions that control of a computer (particularly an Internet-connected computer) may provide are in practice very considerable.

Company responsibility

Finally, when considering the responsibilities of users, we must not ignore the responsibilities of business itself. It may be easy to overlook, for example, that computers are very good at collecting and analysing data. Once information has been collected, there is consequently a clear need to use such electronically stored material reasonably, and to protect stored information from other, inappropriate, uses.

These four illustrative areas are now dealt with in more detail, under the following additional headings:

- Transferability
- Using super-user powers inappropriately
- Misuse of user powers
- Inappropriately using information.

General practice – transferability

Not all computer misuse is necessarily directly and uniquely related to computer use. While it is perfectly possible to transfer to the employment of computers ethical stand- ards and expectations accepted as being appropriate in the wider business world, less savoury items may also be transferred. For instance, it is perfectly possible to 'computer- ise' business practices that have already been considered unethical in an earlier, non- computerised form. It is certainly true that actions that have previously been condemned as unethical do not and cannot become magically acceptable just because a computer is now involved.

From a time long before computers were invented, business has always attempted to maintain appropriate standards of conduct. For example, advertising claims made about products are expected to be reasonably accurate. If a widget has a battery life of less than 10 hours, claiming in a magazine advertisement that it has a 40-hour life is not ethical (and, of course, may be illegal, too).

If UnEthical Inc. involves a computer in its publicity campaign, perhaps by publishing favourable but incorrect information electronically on the World Wide Web, its behav- iour would naturally be just as unethical as it was in the past, when it may have used a traditional paper publication. However, because of the much larger potential audience available through electronic publicity, such a false claim may nevertheless result in considerable extra business. One example is the so-called 'pager scam', where an unscrupulous company used computers connected to the Internet to publicise a 'free' pager. Other, very common examples are the numerous 'get rich quick' pyramid schemes broadcast on the Internet by news and e-mail. Most people who have had expe- rience of using the Internet are alert to the possibility of such false claims and tend to automatically dismiss them. However, with a potential Internet audience in the millions, fooling even a small percentage of users can bring large rewards.

Controller power – using super-user powers inappropriately

Someone who is responsible for administering and maintaining a computer system is known as a 'super-user'. The actual users of a company system may not appreciate that, in order to do their job properly, administrators have to be allowed sweeping powers over a computer system. Indeed, the power that a systems administrator, as super-user, has over 'their' machine is virtually infinite. They can access any data passing through the machine, they can monitor, create and destroy files, and, in particular, they automati- cally have the ability to electronically 'become' any of their users and are then able to behave as if that person's data were their own.

Clearly, once they have been given the ability to act in this way, any sort of external monitoring and control of a super-user is very difficult indeed. For example, should the administrator of a company computer system decide that they would like to examine anyone's confidential electronic files and records, they would normally be able to do so without the unfortunate owner even being aware that it had happened. It is also clear that, should the company *itself* decide to instruct a super-user to act in this way, there is the possibility of very considerable problems.

Once a company computer system is established, it can naturally be programmed to undertake many different tasks. A reasonable assumption to make would surely be that such programming will normally be legal and ethical – but this is not always the case. For example, supermarkets owned by UnEthical Inc. offer each customer a plastic card; as described earlier in this chapter, these cards claim to give a small percentage discount on purchases. Considerable and specific personal details are requested by UnEthical Inc. before the cards are validated; cards must then be presented at each supermarket transaction. At that time, computers read customers' data from their cards and automatically match it with product information from the tills.

Detailed profiles of customers, including when, where and what they buy, may then be built up without anyone outside the company knowing anything about it. This accumulated personal data might be used internally by UnEthical Inc.; copies of it may even be sold. Although such actions are unethical, they are potentially very profitable – but they would be quite impossible without the power of skilfully programmed business computers.

User responsibility – misuse of user powers

Users themselves, once authorised to use a company system, must to a considerable extent then be trusted to use it appropriately. Trust is particularly important if the company system is connected, through a wider computer network, to the expanded world of the Internet. Electronic mail originating from a company site is normally identified automatically, using a kind of electronic letterhead. Employees who use company resources to propagate individual views and opinions may consequently be perceived by the outside world as representing the official views of their company. Further, by misusing the Internet, employees may potentially cause considerable trouble and expense to many thousands of people, who may then understandably identify the unfortunate company as being responsible for their problems.

Once an individual has been authorised to use any sort of company system, they are normally expected to use it ethically. For example, if an employee were to be allowed the use of a company telephone for their work, contacting premium chat lines on it would be considered inappropriate by most companies. Interestingly, in contrast, use of a company computer to play games, or to connect to Internet news groups, is quite frequently tolerated, if not officially sanctioned. Of course, while a company must pay for its business connection to the Internet, an employee of the company normally does not. This situation, where individuals are allowed free access to the Internet, holds a real potential for misuse. For example, running an individual, personal, business in addition to working for someone else is not an unheard-of activity for employees – but what if an employer's connection to the Internet is used to publicise and promote such a private firm, free? Company financial controls are generally tight, and for an employee to get their company to pay for print advertisements for a private company would be very improbable – but it is certainly not unknown for an employee to attempt to piggy-back their own electronic business on that of their employer in this way.

Company responsibility – inappropriately using information

It may happen that someone finds an unethical use for legitimate information that is stored electronically – a list of customers, for example. An unethical individual might easily make use of this information for other purposes – perhaps to send out flyers for another business. Similarly, access to computerised personnel records could be misused to privately obtain the unlisted home telephone number of a member of staff – and so on. The purpose of storing data electronically is to allow it to be accessed easily – a business that is the owner of such information clearly has a responsibility to be certain that such access is appropriate and ethical.

Apart from data collected by analysing spending patterns and customer details from its supermarket cards scheme, UnEthical Inc. circulates compulsory enquiry cards to all its customers – an UnEthical widget cannot be registered for warranty unless the card is completed and returned. Why were these particular questions asked – and what use will be made of the data? Customers may assume that all questions on company registration cards are always necessary and appropriate, and that the data collected will never be applied inappropriately. However, this may not always be so. One US company turned over data on wealthy customers to a political organisation, allowing specially written mail shots to be very accurately directed. Another used analysis of computerised personnel records to distinguish individuals with 'inappropriate' spare time activities. These people were then gradually 'released', in the cause of smooth company running.

Incidentally, on a personal level, I would strongly advise that, whenever you are faced with a requirement for personal information, that you look very carefully at the request. It is always well worth considering the uses to which, after collection, your personal information may be put. If the eventual use is not clear, it may be wise to think hard before providing data.

In this section, I have briefly described four areas in which the use of computers may present potential problems, and looked to see whether a business might, by misusing its computer systems, obtain a competitive advantage.

As will be seen from these examples, there are many ways in which computers and computer systems, together with data stored electronically, may potentially be misused. Frequently, such misuse may appear to give a direct or indirect commercial advantage to the concerned company. Does this mean that, where business computer systems are concerned, unethical behaviour is as inevitable as it is profitable?

Why acting unethically does not work

Fortunately for my argument, there is evidence to show that, although unethical behaviour does indeed sometimes appear beneficial, there are strong practical, as well as philosophical, explanations why it may not function as a regular strategy.

Some reasons why this may be so are discussed below:

- Short-termism
- Company image
- The law and professional standards
- Personal feelings
- Employer pragmatism.

Short-termism

For supporters of ethical behaviour in business, there is good news and bad news. The bad news – acting unethically sometimes *does* work. The good news is that it tends not to work for long. The reason why is bound up in the nature of *trust*, which may perhaps be best illustrated by looking first at relationships between individuals, rather than companies.

Consider casually meeting someone – call him Mr A – who offers you the chance to buy into a new investment opportunity. 'Give me £100,' he says, 'and in seven days I will return you £150. I guarantee it.' What stops you diving for your wallet or purse? Of course, you might consider the proposal to be too good to be true and the 'guarantee' consequently worthless. However, if Mr A appears trustworthy, and phrases his offer intelligently, we might just possibly consider the enormous potential profit, and risk our £100. We might do this once; but, if it did not work and Mr A took our money, we would be very unlikely indeed to trust him twice.

This illustrates a basic human assumption, one that is frequently, and unconsciously, made in both personal and business transactions. Despite the views of professional cynics, until proof is received to the contrary, most people are assumed to be trustworthy. However, once given proof or experience of dishonesty, it is impossibly hard for companies, as well as people, to be persuaded to return to a trusting state.

For this reason, short-term unethical behaviour can indeed work. However, what if we have purchased an UnEthical Inc. widget, understandably expecting the advertised battery life of 40 hours, but the widget's battery goes dead after only four? One thing is reasonably clear – we are certainly unlikely to believe future UnEthical Inc. advertisement claims. Once fooled by a widely published Internet claim, we will not return to that supplier – and so on. Unethical conduct of this sort carries its own limited shelf life.

Company image

Closely related to the above point is the issue of *image* – which I define as the view taken of a business by its customers and the wider world. A business that is considered to be lacking in ethical scruples is likely to have a poor external image. How do potential customers who have not directly experienced a company's behaviour normally decide for or against dealing with it? Their decision is certain to be based, at least partly, upon their perceptions of the company image.[4] It follows that a company that decides to act unethically should be aware not only of the possible effect on present customers but also of the effect on those who might potentially become customers in the future. The wrong sort of image may make all the difference to success.

If the introduction of ethical computer systems does not come about naturally, a pragmatic business management team might therefore decide to act ethically, simply in order to promote a positive company image. The alternative, to act unethically but attempt concealment, has disadvantages that are as major as they are obvious.

The law and professional standards

As well as the need to be aware of what the public may think of a company, there is a clear need to act within the law. In recent years in most developed countries, there has been a growth of computer-related legislation, reflecting a growing awareness on the part of government and public of the potential risks involved in computer use. This area is discussed in detail in Chapter 8, 'The Law and Business Computer Use'.

Demands of professional codes of conduct have been added to formal legislation. In the area of business computing, such codes of conduct describe the behaviour generally accepted to be appropriate for computer professionals. Seeking to persuade employees to act outside the law is clearly foolish. Attempting to convince professional computer staff to ignore their profession's formal codes, in order to act unethically, may be equally unwise.

Personal feelings

Although it is not something easily quantified, in business terms, there is no doubt that considerable personal anxiety can be caused to an individual working within a setting whose ethical philosophy does not match their own. I have not yet found a case of an unethical individual made uncomfortable by working within an ethical setting, but I have certainly been made aware of a number of opposite examples. This topic is considered in Chapter 9.

Once a business is seen as representing the sum of individuals who make it up, the importance of considering the personal feelings of employees and company officers becomes clear. The beneficial effects of working within an ethical setting may be intangible, but empirical evidence suggests that they are nevertheless real (Singer 1994).

Employer pragmatism

Considering the effect of unethical working practices on employees leads us directly to question a surprisingly basic assumption, one that is frequently made when discussing the unethical behaviour of a company. Although commonly viewed and discussed as a single unit, such an unethical company must, by definition, be staffed and controlled by individuals who lack ethical scruples, and who are encouraged in this attitude by their employer. Although, as we have seen, unethical behaviour towards customers and others might potentially benefit the company, might there be other effects of this behaviour? For instance, what makes such unethical-to-others individuals decide to act ethically towards their *employing* company? Once officially encouraged to disregard ethical standards, what is to prevent them from taking advantage of their employer, as their employer is encouraging them to assist in taking advantage of others? After all, in an environment where unethical conduct is general and approved, it is hard to see how such conduct could reasonably be condemned.

Unethical working is therefore demonstrably inappropriate. On practical grounds, because it is likely to work only over short periods, and because the effect on the public image of an unethical company is likely to be unfavourable. Additionally, there is a risk of breaking the law, or professional codes of conduct. Finally, and perhaps most importantly, the effect of working unethically is likely to be detrimental to employees.

Conclusion

Ethical behaviour is generally considered appropriate for business. However, in this chapter I have examined some of the disadvantages of ethical behaviour, using business computer systems as a focus for discussion. Perhaps unfashionably, I have stressed the importance of admitting and recognising the apparent attractions of unethical behaviour to business, and have accepted that such behaviour may indeed appear to produce benefits.

Nevertheless, despite such apparent benefits, there are strong practical as well as moral reasons why failure to behave ethically is disadvantageous for business. An ethical company is more likely to enjoy a solid reputation, to attract and keep customers, and to have a more contented workforce – while there may be unanticipated disadvantages in encouraging unethical conduct.

I have also examined the uses that may be made of computer systems by businesses of varying sizes, and have proposed that there are ethical issues common to all. As the widespread use of computers is a comparatively recent phenomenon, we have not yet had time to build up the expectations and traditions that govern the use of more established business tools. I suggest there is a case for the establishment of a series of rules for the appropriate use of business computers.

Business computer ethics are very far from a luxury. Just as computer systems themselves provide the foundation for modern business, an appreciation and understanding of computer ethics provides the bedrock on which successful business computer systems are built.

All companies, of whatever size, should consider their use of computer systems. If a policy on computer use has not already been developed, it is not just sensible but *essential* that urgent consideration be given to the ways in which systems are currently being used. Clear guidelines need to be in force, both to support staff and to ensure that appropriate use is made of computer systems for which the company is responsible.

Discussion points

The following points are intended to form the basis for a class or seminar discussion on the issues raised in this chapter. They should not be considered until after the relevant sections have been read and thought through.

As all questions have been carefully chosen to encourage debate, they are primarily intended to encourage thinking about the issues and are not necessarily capable of producing definitive answers.

1 In your business role, are you aware of pressure to act in a certain way? Identify areas from which pressure may be coming. (If you are unaware of any pressure, think again.)

2 Once you have identified specific areas, attempt to define *why* you are being pressured. (Pressure may be applied in both negative and positive ways.)

3 How would you define 'business' computing?

4 Why should you be concerned with the ethics of business computer use?

5 Why should you not be concerned?

6 Consider your answers to the above two questions. How are they different, and how are they similar?

7 What do you understand by a 'professional code'?

8 Write down three examples of what you believe to be inappropriate uses of business computer systems. Discuss your examples with others. Are there any similarities between them?

9 What differences do you think the size of the company owning or using business computer systems might make on the inappropriate uses in your examples?

10 In what ways might *data* held electronically be misused? Again, write down several examples and discuss them with others. How are they different, and how are they similar?

11 Have you ever met (or even known about) a computer 'super-user' in your company or another? Why might their role be difficult to police and manage?

12 In a group, discuss ways in which you feel the unethical use of company computers might work. What might make such behaviour unprofitable?

13 If your employer asked you to act unethically for commercial advantage, would you feel more or less likely to act as an unethical employee? Discuss.

Notes

1 For example, Myers, C. (ed.) *Professional Awareness in Software Engineering*, McGraw-Hill, London, 1995.

2 Networked – that is, they have the ability to link to other machines, usually to access data and other information held remotely. Such machines may sometimes be connected directly to each other, as part of an office or company computer system. More frequently, however, connected machines are at a considerable distance from each other, typically connected through links to global systems such as the Internet or World Wide Web (WWW).

3 *Practical Computer Ethics*, McGraw-Hill, London, 1995.

4 'Image' is closely concerned with 'goodwill', but they are not the same.

Computer use: the question of scale and other circumstances

When deciding appropriate guidelines for the use for business computers, it is essential to bear in mind the circumstances under which the computers are used and maintained.

This chapter discusses the development and general environments of business computer use and identifies areas of potential ethical difficulties. After discussion of the issues of scale, it concludes with five suggested rules for the appropriate use of business computers.

Development of business computer use

Setting aside specialised business computer uses, such as the control of automated production machinery, it is reasonable to assume that the core *tasks* for which most businesses employ computers are likely to be broadly similar.

Traditionally, business computers have always been used for the basic large-scale maintenance tasks of business – typically, stock control, payroll management and general accounting.

For many years after their first use in business, computers were large in size, and very expensive. Their use was understandably restricted to very large companies, which were able to afford the high purchase and maintenance costs involved. Additionally, persuading a large, 'mainframe' computer to undertake even simple tasks was a non-trivial exercise and invariably needed the skills of highly trained programmers. This restrictive and costly approach inevitably meant that a typical business computer was normally accessed only through intervening technical specialists, as in Figure 3.1.

Figure 3.1 Large computers in business

A user who wished to process data – or, more probably, a department with justifiable computing needs – would in this scenario pass on their request, in an appropriate form, to the specialist computer staff, who would then be responsible for efficient and appropriate completion of the task. After some time the output would then be passed back, by the computer staff, to the department or individual who originated the request.

The monolithic computing departments of the 1950s and 1960s gradually disappeared, but it was not until the advent of easily programmable microcomputers in the late 1970s that the spread of business computer ownership beyond large companies really began.

However, although computer power has grown spectacularly, and small computers are now widespread, by no means all business applications are run on PCs. Even today, for most companies of any size, 'heavyweight' applications, such as payroll, are likely to be run by specialists using large computers. While large computers may be used, though, they may not actually belong to the company concerned. Sometimes, particularly in the case of payroll management, tasks involving heavy processing may well be farmed out to a specialist firm rather than undertaken directly by the business itself.

This scenario – where a task requiring the power of a large computer is passed on to a specialist department within a company, or to a specialist firm outside it – may be viewed as the traditional model of computer use. In this model, the responsibility for employing the power of the computer appropriately lies with specialists who are working closely with it, and who are employed specifically to do so. They are very likely to be professionally qualified computer scientists, and nowadays an essential part of their training is likely to include knowledge of the ethical implications of computer system use.

Current position

Today the general label of 'business computing' has changed. It no longer conjures up images of vast air-conditioned rooms containing large computers with spinning tape spools, probably tended by intimidating men in white coats. More realistically, the term now tends to be accepted as describing the use within a company of large numbers of individual microcomputers, typically, but by no means exclusively, PCs. These physically small computers may of course be used as independent, stand-alone machines, but in most businesses today computers are normally networked, and consequently able to draw upon and contribute to centralised information resources. This produces a very different scenario within business.

First, vastly reduced costs have led to a greatly increased number of computers being used in business. Their physical distribution throughout the business organisation is consequently much wider. It is also true that the range of business tasks now undertaken by computers is hugely expanded.

Second, as is clear from Figure 3.2, the technical management of networked microcomputers is very different from the 'traditional' model of mainframe computer use. Here we see the effects of direct control of individual computers by individual users. Those wishing to use a computer no longer have to pass instructions on to a controlling specialist but instead have the ability to carry out work directly themselves.

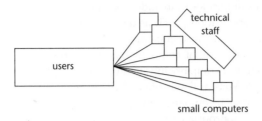

Figure 3.2 Small computers in business

Computer use within business today

Traditional specialist computer work of course continues, but it is undoubtedly true that in the past ten years more general computing within business has opened up remarkably widely. Business computing is clearly no longer the exclusive preserve of computer specialists using large, expensive machines. This is largely through greatly reduced costs, and because, quite apart from basic, 'number crunching' work, many additional business uses, previously uneconomic or even impossible, now exist as mainstream tasks.

The immense spread of personal computers throughout business means that many successful modern companies do not actually possess any computer that is larger or more powerful than a conventional PC. Is it therefore reasonable to suggest that such companies consequently have no need to employ specialist computer workers, and that they need not consider the way in which their machines may be used? Clearly, no. While the tasks of computer specialists may be radically different within today's business, as long as business computer systems need to be appropriately maintained and used, there is still a necessity for the employment of knowledgeable specialists.

It is particularly important, therefore, to appreciate that employment of specialist computer staff is not restricted to those companies owning or using large mainframe machines. The maintenance of all company computers, and in particular the establishment and maintenance of a company network, does still need the continuing services of computer specialists. This remains true even if the company network consists solely of microcomputers.

There is still a need for technical support for most business computing, particularly in a typical business that employs networking for its microcomputers; but such technical support and oversight is far less direct and visible than before. It is possible, for example, for a networked business system to be set up by an outside operator and then left to non-specialists to run and maintain, calling in outside help only when serious problems occur. In these circumstances, the appropriate use of company machines may have been given little consideration. When problems occur, identification even of technical responsibility may be far from clear.

Summary

It is important to keep in mind the point that, in normal practice, business microcomputers are actually operated directly by those needing a computer's help. Typical illustrative uses within most businesses include (word processing) together with employment of other (standard applications) such as (databases) and (spreadsheets) As we have seen, such basic functionality may be complemented by the introduction of internal networking, allowing the introduction of company-based electronic mail. Business computer systems may also include a company intranet, which is simply a contained company version of the World Wide Web, and may often also extend to the provision of full Internet access. I maintain that such company networks need appropriate on-going direction and supervision, as well as appropriate technical design and management.

We therefore have a situation where it is no longer possible to address 'company computing' in simple, monolithic terms. Company computers fall into at least two distinct groups. One consists of traditionally large (in power, if not in size) 'mainframe' machines, supported by specialist staff; the second group contains a much larger number of far smaller, cheaper and more widely spread personal microcomputers – potentially used by staff with no specialist training. Large 'whole company' tasks, typically 'number crunching' ones (such as the task of payroll processing, described above) may understandably still tend to remain the preserve of powerful mainframe computers, and attendant computer specialists. In contrast, individual employee tasks, such as word processing and personal access to company data, are generally carried out on individual PCs by individual users.

Categories

In order to consider what ethical responsibilities lie upon those responsible for company computer systems, we must first break down the monolithic concept of 'business computing' into more rational divisions. As a first step, we may assume that computer use can generally be defined as falling within one of two principal groups. These are:

- The employment of specialist staff to operate and maintain large, expensive and very powerful 'mainframe' computers;
- The provision of smaller 'microcomputers' to assist the work of employees who are not necessarily themselves computer specialists.

Clearly, the tasks and responsibilities of these two groups are very different. To be effective, the managerial responses of a business employer need to reflect this difference.

Essentially, therefore, when we are considering the definition and specification of 'appropriate behaviour', we may safely assume that the majority of today's computerised businesses are able to define their uses of company computers under either 'mainframe' or 'microcomputer' headings. Analysis of the special responsibilities of staff working under these headings are addressed later in this chapter.

Definitions

For the purposes of this analysis, employees in the groups discussed above who are working with company computers may be defined as:

1 Those developing networked computer systems for business.
2 Those company employees (or employees of a contracted firm) who maintain 'company-wide' computer-assisted tasks.

3 Those employees who maintain company networks and individual microcomputers (PCs).

4 Those employees who use company computers, but who do not themselves necessarily possess specialist computer knowledge.

There is the possibility of a fifth group, containing those individuals, working at a higher level within a company, who are responsible for developing a computer use policy. Essentially, these are the people who choose to purchase computers, define what their specifications should be, and how and for what purposes they should be used. Although it would arguably be relevant to include their role and responsibilities here, the specialist accountability issues raised in consideration of this group are discussed in Chapter 5, which looks in detail at the installation of new computer systems.

Treatment of issues with wider application

Before beginning this analysis, a further word of explanation. It is unrealistic to view ethical issues as in some way contained and able to be carefully analysed in separate watertight compartments. If they are relevant at all, ethical business practices must, by definition, underlie all aspects of business practice. For this reason alone, there must inevitably be a degree of overlap when attempting to examine different areas of business computerisation individually.

As with many other facets of business analysis, it is first necessary to establish, and of course continue to maintain, an appreciation of the wider context within which we are working. Such context setting is particularly relevant when considering the business use of computers. The complexity of modern business, and the huge range of potential tasks that may potentially be dealt with by computer systems, inevitably means that there are multiple levels of potential computer use that need to be examined.

Due to this complexity, this book may sometimes appear in different chapters to approach broadly similar issues from different directions. Although this may result in an apparent overlap, such 'double coverage' is actually quite deliberate and is intended to ensure that, whether a reader has approached the text through linear reading or by specific directed reading of particular topics, important questions are adequately covered.

When considering issues in the business use of computer systems, therefore, similar points to those relevantly addressed elsewhere may sometimes be applicable. Rather than inserting a distracting series of internal references, such issues will normally be dealt with directly, if more briefly than elsewhere.

Issues of scale

The question of responsibility and appropriate behaviour within company computer use is further complicated, particularly by issues of scale. So far in this chapter, we have assumed that all companies using computers are functionally identical. However, while similarities certainly exist in the employment of technology by most modern companies, it would clearly be foolish to assume that all computer use in every company is indeed identical, compatible – or even, frequently, at all comparable.

Leaving the question of ethics aside for a moment, let us take as an initial example the need to tackle those practical problems inherent in computerisation. Such issues must inevitably be faced by every business that aims to use computers; the resultant operation is naturally one in which particular computer-specific demands are inevitable. Once the implementation issues are seriously considered, though, it is obvious that the ways in which the logistical resources of a large company are employed to overcome problems must, inevitably, be very different from similar procedures intended to resolve the problems of a small business.

It is obvious that the purchase of one computer will be radically different from arranging to buy several thousand – the appropriate handling of software requirements is similarly different. Arranging for the appropriate distribution of computer-related tasks, the setting-up and implementation of specialist training, and much else, all change when company sizes are disparate. Clearly, too, the efficient organisation of thousands of employees has to be a very different matter from the techniques used when managing half a dozen. Similarly, differences of scale are relevant when we are considering suitable approaches to the consideration of ethical issues.

When considering the issue of scale, we must in particular discuss:

1 Appropriateness of computer use
2 Decisions on software purchase
3 Decisions on computer purchase
4 Decisions on staffing.

These headings are addressed in more detail below.

Appropriateness of computer use

Early in my computing career, in the late 1980s, I acted as a specialist consultant to small businesses that wanted to become 'computerised'. They were usually small manufacturing companies, or businesses involved in wholesale sales. (Once, for two never-to-be-forgotten months, I acted as computing consultant to a chain of pubs). Frequently, I was brought in only after large sums had already been spent on the purchase of computer equipment – equipment that sometimes proved to be of very little practical use to the purchaser.

These purchases were not solely due to the (always impressive) activities of computer sales staff. Often, it seemed, senior managers had made major purchasing decisions based on the most flimsy of supporting evidence. Computing and computers were then considered 'trendy', and if competitors were believed to have already made the jump to computerisation, this alone was often felt to be a sufficient justification to buy. It was a good time to be an independent consultant. The expensive mistakes that I observed then, and specifically the lessons I learned from them about business purchase of computer systems, remain valid and are still important today.

The rules given in the following section are relevant whether you are yourself making a purchase decision, or whether you are responsible for advising an employer or client.

When considering the appropriateness of computer use

Often the decision to purchase new equipment or extend an existing system may be accepted without debate; after all, computers are continually becoming faster and more efficient, so it is natural to assume that a newer model of computer will automatically bring speed and efficiency to company processes. While this may well be so, it is a major error to assume, without appropriate investigation and analysis, that this must always be the case.

For example, the introduction of new machinery could mean that there is a need for additional staff training, and perhaps the associated production of supporting handbooks or other educational material. Depending upon the number of staff concerned the additional costs involved may easily offset the advantages of improved computer performance. It may also be that a new system or changed system may be unnecessary, or might bring unexpected problems.

A company network was replaced with a new system. During the installation it was discovered that electronic monitoring of some computer use was now practicable – the duration of individual employee connections to the Internet, for example, and even the content of downloaded files, could be invisibly recorded. This facility was not at the time known to senior management, although the system default was for such recording to take place. At a later date, the stored recordings were accidentally discovered (the sheer volume of secret recording had led directly to a consequent need for increased storage): much anguished debate then took place at high level in the company over what use, if any, should be made of the data.

The secretly recorded data was eventually deleted, allegedly without being studied, and monitoring was discontinued; but discontent within the firm continued for some time.

RULE ONE: *Never automatically assume that buying a new computer, or extending your current computer systems, will always be appropriate.*

When considering the purchase of a new computer or computer system, first clarify the immediate question. For example, what are the particular task or tasks intended to be carried out by the new computer? If there is a current problem, exactly how will the purchase of a computer resolve it? Once the objectives are clear, it is sensible to investigate whether alternative methods – *especially* those using existing methods and equipment – may not actually be more effective in achieving the desired objective. It is much too easy to assume that new technology will always and automatically provide a better solution. Often, of course, it does; but it would be a serious error to assume that an improvement following introduction of new computers is always inevitable. There can be expensive exceptions.

Figure 3.3 sets out a path that may be followed when assessing and identifying a task that might appropriately be computerised. It is designed so that the questions and responses hold good whatever the scale of the investigation – whether there is just one, simple, task or the prospective implementation of a completely new company-wide system.

It will be clear from examination of the diagram that there may well be need for recursion here – there is often a need to obtain more data and reconsider issues in the light of new information. While re-evaluation will obviously take time, a policy of review can repay any extra time that it takes many times over. Appropriate computer use, in particular, is helped by such further examination encouraging the identification of possible *ethical focus points* (EFPs).

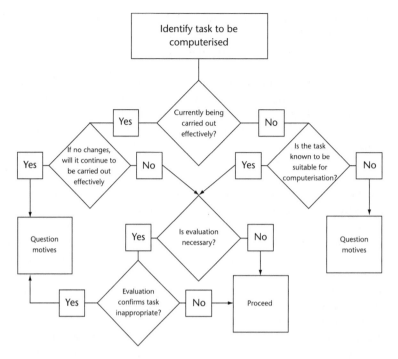

Figure 3.3 Computerised task identification

EFPs identify particular issues, problems or potential conflicts that might justifiably be considered as 'ethical'. Essentially, EFPs describe problem issues that are specific and relevant to business systems development without necessarily being a part of the technical decision-making process.

One example of EFP identification followed the potential replacement of outdated computers in the accounts department of an insurance company. Although the replacement was totally justified (the existing computers had been in place a long time), concerned staff were able to demonstrate a potential problem. Gradual changes to the current company software, over a period of some years, actually meant that proposed replacements would not have been able to continue to support several much-appreciated processing short-cuts.

In this example, the company concerned learned of these potential difficulties before the introduction of the new replacement system. Had its discovery been delayed until later, the effects would undoubtedly have cost a considerable sum, through both direct costs and related staff problems.

Decisions on software purchase

It is perhaps unfair to suggest that the purchase of software is frequently driven by an earlier decision on the purchase of computer hardware, but there is no doubt this may still happen. It is appropriate, then, to begin with the second of this chapter's rules:

RULE TWO: *Software leads hardware. Always make sure that software exists which will meet your needs – before considering an appropriate computer platform.*

Ignoring this rule can lead to considerable problems. Some years ago, on its start-up, a design studio in London spent many thousands of pounds in buying PC computers. Shortly afterwards, the company discovered that, at the time, the best software for its needs ran only on Apple Macintosh machines. This 'inappropriate computer' problem was compounded by the fact that none of their three newly appointed specialist designers had ever worked on, or even used, PCs. The subsequent learning curve was horrendous and the feelings of the highly paid specialist staff incendiary. Interestingly, the choice of machines had been made by financial specialists, who had not looked beyond what they saw as a small saving on capital expenditure.

It is clearly important, *before* purchase, to be certain that off-the-shelf, packaged software will appropriately meet company needs. An associated point, relating to the use of packaged software, lies in the importance of maintaining product-licensing conditions. Purchase of a single software package does not allow for copying and use on more than one company computer. Indeed, it is virtually certain that such behaviour is expressly forbidden. For example, *The Times* reported (on 14 April 1997) that a two-and-a-half-year jail sentence was handed out to Curtis McLean, of the Vogue Computer Company, for supplying forty-six unauthorised copies of Novell NetWare to Wandsworth Borough Council Education Department.

Although it may appear to be a tempting way of saving money, the duplication of software in this way is potentially illegal, and almost certainly unethical too.

Following attendance by a senior staff member at a lecture on business computer ethics, one large company instituted a survey of the packaged computer software held on its computers. Exact results must remain confidential, but the overall picture revealed an incredible 70 percent of software held on the computer hard disks of individual staff had been copied, rather than purchased, and was therefore illegal.

Interestingly, while much room on staff hard disks was obviously taken up with business software, they also contained much games software – that is, programs that had never been officially purchased or approved by the company that owned the computers. In the event of an external investigation, however, the company would nevertheless have been responsible for any illegally held material.

Another example concerned a fairly small company that knowingly made use of 'unofficially' duplicated commercial software in order to save costs. A senior manager was extremely indignant when he found that several members of staff had taken home copies of company word-processing software for their own use. During a fairly lengthy discussion, he remained quite incapable of seeing any reason why they might have felt justified in doing so.

Not every company buys only packaged software. Larger companies often request specialist software to be written for them, but this is not an exclusive prerogative of big business. I have known owners of the very smallest firms sometimes spending much time and energy in writing their own bespoke applications. The issue of cost-effectiveness in specialist software development is clearly relevant here, although it lies outside the scope of this book.

Essentially, before the purchase of computer software, the same requirements criteria should be met as before the purchase of any other business material. The additional problem to be considered with computer software lies in its potential for EFP risks. Beyond the immediate question of whether the initial purpose will be served by this specific purchase, the question 'will a suggested software choice lead to wider issues or problems?' needs to be considered and addressed.

Decisions on computer purchase

My own experiences, mentioned earlier in this chapter, show how company computer hardware may sometimes be purchased without adequate preparation. While it is probably unlikely, in today's economic climate, that many businesses are prepared to sign cheques quite so freely, it is still true that within many companies, a full cost–benefit analysis of computer purchase may lack a wider, appropriate usage, dimension. Such consideration is, however, essential.

It is also important to restate Rule Two, this time from the perspective of hardware, rather than software, purchase.

RULE THREE: *Software leads hardware – never buy hardware (or recommend the purchase of hardware) before making quite sure that software exists that will meet your needs – and that will run on that platform.*

In my research within business, probably the most important issue to emerge concerning hardware purchase was compatibility. This was followed very closely by widespread amazement at the rapid depreciation in the value of computer hardware. Depreciation lies outside my brief, but problems of compatibility are certainly relevant.

Generally, it is easier for a company of size to work with computers that are compatible, the term 'compatible' being defined as being able to share software, data and, perhaps, peripherals. There are two schools of thought here. One maintains an absolute insistence on every section of the company using identical computers, while the other points out the advantages of allowing specific computer hardware to reflect local needs. As we will see in Chapter 5, external imposition of purchase requirements may well carry unexpected disadvantages, too.

It is clearly ridiculous for different parts of the same company to be unable to exchange data with each other; and, of course, the advantages of bulk purchase apply to computers just as much as to anything else. However, there are also advantages in variety. Fortunately, even the initially dissimilar Macintosh and PC computers are increasingly compatible, while the advent of Internet and intranet software for networked company machines can go a considerable way towards meeting the requirement for data compatibility.

Decisions on staffing

Here we are concerned with at least two important issues. One relates to those technical staff, mentioned earlier in this chapter, who are responsible for the supply, installation and maintenance of company computer systems. The other concerns the staff who *use* company machines as part of their everyday jobs.

Technical staff

As is discussed in more detail in Chapter 6, it is essential for technical staff to be aware that more than technical issues are relevant to their work. While their natural focus has clearly to be on technical problems, management support must be provided to enable awareness of the wider effects of their work.

Joe, who was computer network manager for a large travel company, was asked to help to implement a new group scheme whereby specialist office groups in the networked head office shared pertinent files. The intention was that material of relevance to one group was not inappropriately distributed to everyone. Joe's implementation went rather further: his changes also allowed all the files belonging to every group member to be open to every other group member. The effects can be imagined: personal files, for example, were suddenly vulnerable to oversight, copying and distribution. Although the changes were rapidly reversed, their effects were still felt almost two years later.

Joe solved a technical problem perfectly; his changes fully met the brief he had been given. However, his ignorance of wider issues that were relevant to his work reflected the attitudes of the group of technical staff to which he belonged. In the travel company at that time they were seen, and saw themselves, as having little or nothing to do with people who made use of 'their' computer system. This distancing attitude is sometimes known as 'technical isolation'.

The relationship of a company's own management to its technical staff, and particularly the officially encouraged perception of their tasks, is potentially of considerable importance in overcoming technical isolation. The problem is not solely an internal, technical one, though; it is particularly important that other managers are also aware of wider implications that may be involved in technical work. The general relationship between the technical and operational side of a business is clearly of significance here.

As the size of a company decreases, the amount of resources that it may be able to devote to computer systems support generally diminishes too. However, it is necessary that the importance of a smaller technical team is not misunderstood; the necessity for appropriate use and management of a computer system is unrelated to the physical size of a network.

When the size of the employing company makes it impossible to allow even one person exclusive systems maintenance responsibility, the need for company awareness of the effects of technical change is even more important – it is very easy to overlook social issues when striving under pressure to maintain a technical service.

RULE FOUR: *Those technical staff responsible for computer systems support and maintenance must be encouraged to always consider wider issues.*

Users of company systems

Of course, apart from consideration of those who maintain computers and computer systems, it is also relevant to consider those who use company machines. Employee use of company computers must be appropriate – but how is 'appropriate' to be defined? Unfortunately, no global definition is possible. While some activities, such as the use of company machines for illegal activities, are clearly to be condemned, exactly what may be defined by a specific company as 'appropriate' must clearly vary according to local and industrial circumstances.

Every company is faced with responsibility for the actions of its employees, so it makes sound sense to determine, *in advance of any problems*, just what may be considered an appropriate use of company computers.

For instance, a small company, having to pay for an Internet connection over a standard telephone line, is likely to have a firm definition of what it considers appropriate Internet access by its staff. A large business, however, with many direct Internet connections, is likely to take a different view of what may actually be very similar staff access; and so on. However, when considering definitions of appropriate usage there are certain points that should always be considered as relevant. These points, which basically ensure legal, decent and appropriate computer use, are discussed fully in Chapter 8.

Once senior management has agreed what it considers to be a solid and workable definition of appropriate use for their company, this information must be fully distributed throughout the business. It is never sufficient for a policy just to exist; it must be actively promoted, and no member of staff should be able to justifiably claim ignorance of its content.

RULE FIVE: *All companies should make their expectations of computer use by staff clear. All staff need to be certain that their use of company computers is legal, decent and appropriate.*

Conclusion

In this chapter we have discussed the general circumstances in which company computer systems may be used, and have examined a number of ways in which problems may occur.

Beginning with a brief examination of the development of early business computer use, which suggested that virtually all tasks originally undertaken by business computers involved large, mainframe machines, operated by specialist staff, we then moved to look at the very different position today.

Nowadays, the use of microcomputers is widespread throughout modern business. It is important to appreciate that business microcomputers are generally operated directly by those needing a computer's help rather than being operated by specialist computer staff. This distinction has obvious implications for the appropriate management of business microcomputer use. It was also mentioned that, apart from typical applications such as word processing, the functionality of modern business microcomputers may be complemented by internal networking, a company intranet, and frequently the provision of full Internet access.

We then examined two principal groups of staff involved in business computers, those of technical employees, responsible for introducing and maintaining computer systems, and 'users', those members of staff who actually have a computer on their desk. A more detailed division of business staff into four sub-groups was then made:

1 Those developing networked computer systems for business.
2 Those company employees (or employees of a contracted firm) who maintain 'company-wide' computer-assisted tasks.

3 Those employees who maintain company networks and individual microcomputers (PCs).

4 Those employees who use company computers but who do not themselves necessarily possess specialist computer knowledge.

After a discussion of the treatment of issues with wider application, the chapter concluded with a more detailed examination of the issues of scale, considered under four main headings:

1 Appropriateness of computer use
2 Decisions on software purchase
3 Decisions on computer purchase
4 Decisions on staffing.

Examination of these headings resulted in the listing of five important rules, which, for convenience, are detailed again below.

The five rules of Chapter 3

RULE ONE
Never automatically assume that buying a new computer, or extending your current computer systems, will always be appropriate.

RULE TWO
Software leads hardware. Always make certain that software exists that will meet your needs – before considering an appropriate computer platform.

RULE THREE
Software leads hardware – never buy hardware or recommend the purchase of hardware before making quite sure that software exists that will meet your needs – and that will run on that platform.

RULE FOUR
Those technical staff responsible for computer systems support and maintenance must be encouraged to always consider wider issues.

RULE FIVE
All companies should make their expectations of computer use by staff clear. All staff need to be certain that their use of company computers is legal, decent and appropriate.

Discussion points

The following points are intended to form the basis for a class or seminar discussion on the issues raised in this chapter. They should not be considered until after the relevant sections of this chapter have been read, and thought through.

1 How does the use of large, mainframe computers differ from the use of desktop microcomputers?

2 How might this make a difference to company computer use policies?

3 Why is the job of a technical computer support person important to the appropriate use of a business computer system?

4 List some ways in which you feel a business computer might be misused.

5 How might opportunities for misuse increase if a single business microcomputer is networked?

6 How might opportunities for misuse increase if a single business microcomputer is connected to the Internet? (See also Chapter 7 for discussion on potential Internet-related problems).

7 Do you feel that the responsibility of a company for appropriate use of its computer systems differs for the actions of a member of its technical staff and an 'ordinary' user?

8 If so, why? If not, why not?

4 How should a business behave?

What are acceptable standards of 'computing behaviour' within business? This chapter looks at possible descriptions of appropriate conduct, as well as examples of good and bad computer-related behaviour. The chapter begins, though, by taking another look behind the generally accepted promotion of ethical behaviour appropriate for business computing.

The promotion of ethical use of business computer systems is based upon what is, when considered, a fairly major assumption – 'acting ethically is good'.[1] Although precise definitions of 'good' and 'bad' in this context are probably infinitely debatable, the basic sentiments behind the suggestion appear widely entrenched. However, is it necessarily true?

Definitions

A reasonable starting point is to examine the background to the current position. This may be summarised fairly simply as an assumption that for a business person to act ethically is 'good', while for one to act unethically is 'bad'. What, though, does this actually mean – and where do such concepts come from? As with many areas of experience with which we may be unfamiliar, it can help to understand new issues by appropriately considering experience from another area of activity.

Consider, for example, a computing manager who uses their job to steal software and equipment; or who, in order to gain promotion, pretends to possess knowledge that they do not actually have. Such actions are classified as (unprofessional) under BCS (British Computer Society) and ACM (Association of Computing Machinery) codes of conduct. However, although they certainly involve business computing, both examples could readily be adapted to other areas of business with only very minor changes.

Most professional codes of conduct consequently incorporate definitions of 'unacceptable' behaviour for their members, definitions that actually reflect wider opinions that are generally held within society. The assumption here is that an action that is *normally considered unethical does not become acceptable* because it is considered from a specialist viewpoint – in this case, when the behaviour in question is considered as an aspect of business computing.

A team member was working on the development of a new product. A colleague had left for the day, but the worker wanted to refer to some printed notes left in a locked desk drawer. Most people would accept that, in order to get the notes, it would not be appropriate to break open the desk. What, however, if the worker had the ability to hack into the office computer system, and access the original file that generated the printed notes? Is breaking into someone's electronic office comparable to breaking into a physical one?

Here, accepting the personal privacy of employees as a fundamental right would mean that both desk and directory should be left strictly alone. Using a computer does not convey any special right to ignore normal standards of behaviour.

As such examples illustrate, within the field of computer use, as elsewhere, 'professional' definitions of appropriate behaviour tend to begin by applying 'general' standards of ethical behaviour to specialist circumstances. In our case, analysis of such problems then clearly permits responses developed elsewhere to be appropriately applied within the field of business computing.

Briefly, then, whether or not their actions are explicitly proscribed by any relevant professional code, it can be concluded that users of a business computer certainly risk being labelled 'unethical' if their actions do not comfortably fit within the perceptions that wider society has of appropriate behaviour.

Of course, not all uses of business computing offer opportunities for such a straightforward comparison. Given the essential nature of new technology, there must, inevitably, be specialist areas of professional computer use, areas that have no natural corollaries in the wider world and cannot therefore be measured and judged against pre-existing external standards.

As the variety of potential uses of computers within business is huge, it is clearly impossible to give a definitive list of possibilities here. However, examples might include an employer's ability to use 'smart' ID badges (which allow tracking of an individual's activities) to generate data for confidential analysis of employee behaviour; or the possibility of monitoring the speed of computer keystrokes in data entry. Neither are actions with a predetermined label that may be easily transferred from a different area of experience.

It is also important to appreciate that the driving force of developing technology lies behind many decisions that are taken in the business use of computers. When a development becomes technically possible, understandably there is often pressure to make profitable use of it. As well as awareness of existing issues, therefore, it is also necessary to appreciate that business use of computers additionally presents *dynamic* problems – what was technically impossible yesterday becomes attainable today, and may be common practice tomorrow. For obvious reasons, such potential uses may need special consideration.

For example, development of specifically targeted mail shots has for many years been a familiar business technique. However, the specially issued magnetic 'savings' cards – such as those urged on their customers by major supermarkets – permit the collection and collation of additional information. Today, mail shot targets may be selected following computerised analysis not just of actual purchases but also of spending patterns over time, perhaps additionally matched against specific shopping locations, and even, potentially, with other people who might be shopping at the same time. The resultant shift in emphasis may well need examination.

Individual businesses could benefit from the encouragement of a suitably progressive professional or trade association – it is in this area that there is perhaps the greatest need for corporations to act together in defining and agreeing appropriate behaviour. As informed authorities, they are well placed to observe and potentially to influence new business development.

The final line of definition concerns legality. Although there are exceptions – totalitarian states such as Nazi Germany are obvious examples – it is reasonable to assume that if an action is demonstrably illegal, it may generally be classified as 'unethical'. However, the reverse is not necessarily true. While in slow-moving areas of activity the definition of 'illegal = unethical' may be quite sufficient, the world of modern computing is very much a special case.

Importantly, in the developed world the legislative process involved in establishing new statutes is normally lengthy. Understandably, therefore, this inevitably means that most, if not all, current laws are customarily well behind many of the possibilities inherent in current technology. For this reason alone, when considering the categorisation of business computing issues, what is, strictly speaking, 'legal', cannot automatically be taken to be 'ethical'.

There are consequently at least three major areas of potential conflict in the definition of ethical standards for the use of business computers. First, there is the transference of standards that have previously been applied in other areas. Second, there are 'new' standards, introduced following technical development, and potentially guided by professional and trade organisations. Ultimately, although this can by no means be considered as definitive, there is the role played by statute law in defining what may be considered 'legal' behaviour.

The apparently seamless concept of 'ethical' behaviour within business practice may therefore be potentially composed of at least three different elements. In reality, however, the situation is probably even more complex.

Even if the moral aspects of ethical behaviour are accepted as clear and obvious – an assumption that is by no means incontestable – what of the practical advantages? There are undoubted benefits to ethical conduct, but there are also potential disadvantages. Moreover, even if we assume that acting ethically *is* good, would it be reasonable to ask, good for whom? The continued wider promotion of ethical behaviour may encourage the cynic to rephrase the statement: 'if *they* act ethically, it's good for *me*.'

As this book is intended for an audience of professional business and computing people, rather than for philosophers, it is not appropriate to pursue the philosophical aspects of the problem further here. We may assume that there exist issues of ethical definition open to debate without necessarily taking part in such debate ourselves. However, those who are interested may find that some of the specialist philosophy texts in the Bibliography are of interest.

Business computer use

We now move on to look more specifically at what may be described as 'inappropriate' business computer use. It may be helpful, for the purposes of analysis, to divide the broad field of potentially 'unethical' behaviour in business computing into three substantive categories:

- Individual behaviour
- 'Public' behaviour
- Company behaviour.

While this division is relevant to our discussion, none of the three headings should be thought of as definitive; they are intended principally to encourage debate rather than to establish rules. For this reason, and to help generally with understanding, both a theoretical appreciation of the headings and practical testing of them are recommended. The application to actual, 'real world' examples of such definitions is particularly valuable.

For instance, in the questions at the end of this chapter, it is suggested that examples of potentially 'unethical' behaviour in business computing are first identified or imagined, and then an attempt is made to categorise them under the three headings. To help with this later analysis, possible categorisation of issues should be kept in mind while reading this section.

Individual behaviour

This category contains those actions and potential actions carried out by individuals acting in a way that directly concerns their own professional work. Such behaviour is distinct from work-related actions that attempt to influence or direct others, or actions carried out when an individual is acting as the representative of a company.

While many employees may feel that all their actions while at work should be the sole responsibility of their employers, this is emphatically not so. Delegation of personal ethical responsibility to someone else, although clearly tempting, is not possible. An unethical action cannot be magically transformed simply because someone is being paid to carry it out. Indeed, it could be said that while at work an individual's ethical responsibilities are in fact greater, as the implications of professional actions must be considered in addition to personal actions.

An accounts department clerk was asked to copy-type customers' financial data from a printout into the company accounts system. The data had been changed, by hand, apparently to reflect an increased liability to her company. She did not ask anyone whether this was appropriate, assuming that it was not her responsibility. However, a later request was clearly illegal, and she refused to carry it out. Her manager then expressed surprise, saying that she had never complained before. To her, this assumption of her agreement to act inappropriately was the most upsetting part of the experience.

The clerk believed herself to be an ethical person, but as her ethical behaviour did not initially appear, it was assumed by her manager not to exist. Of course, both she and her manager had been selective about their perceptions, she in deciding the appropriateness of what was asked, and the manager in the interpretation he placed on her agreement to follow instructions. Their actions illustrate a basic human attribute – it is very easy for us to see only what we wish to see and to ignore unwelcome information. In this case, anomalous requests by a manager were refused only when their inappropriate nature became impossible to ignore.

The example also underlines the need for individuals to take a wider ethical view. In the longer term, keeping quiet, and taking on board 'impossible' tasks, could well lead to serious problems. These problems would probably not be helped by a defence of 'only following orders'.

Alternative responses to the same situation can allow direct comparison of the effects of 'ethical' and 'unethical' behaviour. A classic combination of such a wrong/right answer is the (composite) case of computing students interviewed by a major UK bank. Asked in interview about knowledge and skills, one was unremittingly honest and admitted freely to areas of ignorance and poor performance. In contrast, his more cynical colleague started off by reading the interviewer's notes upside down. She then deliberately gave what she felt were all the right responses, whether or not they were accurate. In an ethical world, honesty would have been rewarded; but would anyone really be surprised to hear that a job offer went to the cynic?

Such examples illustrate the potential of ethical actions that can apparently backfire, resulting in an unwelcome outcome. Similarly, acts that might be judged 'unethical' may appear to lead to undeserved success.

'Public' behaviour

In this category I include actions that, although they are not necessarily directly related to the professional work of the individual, are intended to have an effect on others. An example would be a specialist who writes a letter to the press giving expert views on a matter of general importance.

A professional software engineer of considerable experience was working in an area of substantial industrial decline. Some years previously, the region had been the subject of an investigative programme. The engineer had been interviewed and his opinions sought on what might be needed to attract 'high-tech' companies to the area. In the interview he gave a frank assessment of what he felt were poor practices of large companies in the implementation of new technology. He now considers that this interview made him a 'marked man', leading to the eventual loss of his job.

Nothing the engineer had said was untrue; indeed, he later stressed that many of his points were actually rather weaker than those he had frequently heard made by colleagues in general conversation. What was different, of course, was that those conversations were in private. Once the admittedly honest answers to questions had been expressed publicly, a very different view was taken of them. Would he perhaps have faired better if he had lied or remained silent?

A member of a large insurance firm was a keen user of computers and made full use of a computer that his company had given him for work at home. Although he could have made use of company links, he personally paid for an Internet connection through a private Internet service provider (ISP), which allowed him a World Wide Web (WWW) site. He used the site as a platform for both his private and professional views.

However, the employer objected, feeling that, even though no mention of the company was made directly, its public image would be affected by the site. Any employee using a public platform to express unmoderated views on the insurance industry was felt undesirable. The loaned computer was retrieved and a 'heavy hint' given that terminating the site would be wise.

Further discussion, however, revealed this as an example of an inappropriate official reaction. The responsible manager, acting without consultation, had not attempted to distinguish between use of the Internet and ordinary publication, and had, as he thought, played safe by imposing an automatic ban. The restriction was based on historical concern, apparently originating over employees once having used company letterheads for private correspondence. Although such blanket restrictions may appear sensible in the short term, they are unlikely to prove a substitute for a reasoned official policy. In this case, the ruling was eventually reversed at a much higher level in the company following a general debate over official and private Internet use.

As I have suggested elsewhere,[2] ethical conduct cannot be turned on and off like a tap – a professional who acts ethically does so in all circumstances, not just in surroundings where their ethical views and actions are unlikely to create problems. As the first example above illustrates, though, following through on ethical beliefs may not be without difficulties. The example probably also demonstrates that professional people speaking publicly need to be aware of the dangers of naiveté.

Company behaviour

Not all professional actions are concerned with individuals acting as individuals. Every business is necessarily composed of people who act on its behalf; if inappropriate, their actions may lead to the company itself being guilty of unethical behaviour.

A London company was invited to tender for a computer-related engineering job. However, its quotation was deliberately pitched at an uneconomically low level. Once the client business was firmly committed, 'unexpected' charges and expenses were discovered – and the final price charged was substantially higher than the initial quotation. The action was defended as being in the company's best interests: 'after all, we would not have got the contract otherwise.'

Here, the end may at first seem to justify the means. If a company cannot attract business, it must close – and who would want that? Initially, this point may seem valid; but employees of competing, ethical, companies, who were honest about the costs involved in a contract quotation, would probably disagree.

A consultant was telephoned when leaving the office. A client company was holding a board meeting and wanted to confirm an earlier provisional quotation. The consultant did not have immediate access to his computer and felt that he did not have sufficient information. After 'some pretty rapid thinking', he decided to say that he could not respond until the next day, when he knew the information would be available. His company lost the contract.

The consultant believed that he was acting ethically by not responding until he was certain that the figures he would be confirming were accurate – but, if he had responded immediately, the contract may well not have been lost. He is still unsure whether he was right to act as he did. There have apparently been debates within his firm, too.

As a final example of the apparent benefits of unethical behaviour in business computing, consider the following response to a common problem:

A member of a company sales team was given the task of using a computer for analysis in order to produce a definitive list of customers for a special sales promotion. Due to unexpected difficulties, however, the work had gone much more slowly than anticipated. Failure to complete the work on time would not only lose a much-needed bonus but would almost certainly result in serious loss of professional face. For these reasons, analysis was deliberately cut short, and the final list of customers was not checked or evaluated in any way. This meant that it was probably both incomplete and inaccurate. However, the senior manager, who was ultimately responsible, remained unaware of the decision, so penalties were avoided.

Whatever we might wish, our experience is likely to confirm that both individual and corporate 'unethical' behaviour often *does* seem successful, while actions that appear ethical may have led to unwelcome results. Most people who have experienced 'real-life' business computing for any time will probably have experienced cases similar to these examples. Empirical evidence, at least, is likely to prove that acting ethically does sometimes seem to work against the best interests of both individuals and companies. Can it therefore be true that ethical conduct may indeed be bad for you, even if, in abstract, it may be good for the wider community?

Acting unethically does not work

However, acting unethically does not work. Some reasons why this may be so were discussed in Chapter 2 under the headings:

- Short-termism
- Company image
- The law and professional standards
- Personal feelings
- Employer pragmatism.

Essentially, the short-term nature of unethical behaviour may be because the social and business framework of our society is built upon a presumption that certain social rules are, generally, valid. One of the most fundamental of these rules is the assumption that most people normally tell the truth. There are of course circumstances when truth is relative, when a 'white lie' may be appropriate, when a partial truth is acceptable. Generally, though, we normally tend to believe that most statements are broadly true.

Such a state of affairs is naturally very tempting to those who are prepared to lie. After all, if you believe Ripoff Software when it says that 25 hours of work took 50 hours, why should the business not make extra profit? Such an (undoubtedly unethical) action may work once or twice. However, once evidence emerges of the true state of affairs, and word of it gets around, things are likely to change. Once doubt is cast upon a professional judgement, the balance of belief reverses rapidly. The assumption then becomes that while everybody else normally tells the truth, Ripoff Software normally lies. After that, even if its statements are currently truthful, it is likely to be disbelieved.

It is for this reason that despite all the short-term advantages of lying, society still assumes that truth is the norm. I suggest that the lesson is directly applicable to unethical conduct.

The way in which public perception can be influenced by the activities of both individuals and companies provides a further incentive to act in a way seen as ethical. This is the issue of 'image'. The public image of a company is carefully cultivated, often at considerable expense. How this image is viewed by the public can reinforce or destroy it. The same is true of an individual professional.

Consequently, an ethical public image, reinforced by advertising and word-of-mouth support from clients or customers, is a powerful asset to any company or specialist. Repeatedly acting in an ethical manner will gradually reinforce this image, but a single act of unethical behaviour could potentially destroy it.

To a lesser extent, individual workers are also affected by the image held of them by both their employer and co-workers. An image seen as reflecting an 'unethical' individual is likely to result in negative behaviour from colleagues, if not in formal action from the employing firm. Interestingly, the reverse is also true: even if the ethical employee is working within an 'unethical' environment, empirical evidence suggests that they tend to be regarded favourably by colleagues.

In a democratic state, there is of course a general duty on the part of individuals and companies to make certain that all their actions are within the law. The relationship between statute law and the appropriate use of business computers is, as described above, not an easy one to define. While accepting that it may seem ethically necessary to disobey laws seen as 'wrong', fuller discussion of the issue unfortunately falls outside the area of this book. However, it is surely reasonable to assume a relationship between legality and ethical behaviour, and to conclude that a company or professional who acts illegally is likely to suffer.

A small company was faced with an urgent need to complete the processing of its computer-based accounts, but vital staff were away on sick leave. A worker who had previously been involved in the task had left its employment although was still in touch. The worker was informally approached, and in return for an under-the-counter cash payment agreed to continue the work without the agreement, or even the knowledge, of their current employer, who was also paying for their time. This was possible through a very unofficial electronic linking of computers in the two businesses.

In this instance, actions were clearly illegal as well as unethical, as was made clear when the arrangements became known. The legal issues may have been settled, but the ripple effects of the unethical action on both the company and the individual continued for some time.

Ineffective

So far in this chapter, we have looked at three levels of involvement, examining why, in practical terms, unethical behaviour might prove ineffective. While it is true that there can be no guarantee that unethical behaviour will always prove a poor long-term choice, there is substantial evidence to suggest that this may often be so.

Perhaps controversially, however, it has also been suggested that such behaviour is not necessarily and inevitably dysfunctional. Those who support the wider application of both general ethical expectations and formal rules should accept this situation and not deny the apparent short-term advantages to be gained by acting unethically. Indeed, such a denial might itself be considered as unethical, thereby demonstrating the very point it is attempting to disprove.

Despite the apparent advantages to be gained by the unethical use of business computers, a solid professional career can only be founded on the bedrock of ethical personal conduct and beliefs. Today's manager needs not only to be aware of ethical issues but also to be prepared to respond properly and appropriately to them. The users of business computer systems should always act responsibly, following their own ethical beliefs, the expectations of society, and the regulations of professional organisations and statute law. They cannot afford to do otherwise.

What are acceptable standards of 'computing behaviour'?

So far we have been looking at general examples of business computing, using them as illustrations of wider points. We will now move to examine more specifically what may be meant by 'acceptable' and 'unacceptable' behaviour. This process will begin the gradual accumulation of descriptive rules covering appropriate business computing behaviour. These rules will be listed in the text as they arise and collected at the end of this chapter.

A key factor in the consideration and classification of inappropriate business computing behaviour is the concept of *knowledge*. The probability of inappropriate action is greatly increased when those involved are unconcerned, or unaware, of the effects of their actions on others. Essentially, when the wider population – of company, industry and public – lacks knowledge of any computer-related actions that will affect them, there is potential for concern.

Of course, there are many absolutely sound reasons why matters should be kept dark. An all-purpose seal of 'commercial confidentiality' is often applied to prevent wider distribution of information, even within the same company; and it is clearly inappropriate, as well as totally impractical, to suggest that the general broadcasting of information is always necessary. Nevertheless, it must be accepted that, as a rule, the greater the degree of secrecy concerning an action, the greater the risk of that action having unanticipated consequences. Additionally, disregard for consequences can follow should those responsible believe that, whatever the consequences of their actions might be, they will remain personally unidentified. An example is relevant here.

The personnel office of a fairly large company kept, as is normal, computerised records of its employees. However, for 'historical reasons' material in these particular records was not just collected directly, from employee interviews and application forms, but was continually enhanced from a wide variety of other sources. Some of these sources were anecdotal, and much of the additional information was almost certainly inaccurate. However, as no one other than a few senior managers – who found the information very useful – and the personnel office manager himself knew of the system, it continued for several years.

Interestingly, the system was known unofficially as 'enriched' personnel records. It was not until an outside consultant learned of the existence of the records, and advised the company that it was in breach of UK legislation, that matters changed. Even then, nothing actually happened until the outside consultant's initial verbal report had been officially confirmed in writing. From first to last, though, those most concerned – the company's employees – knew nothing of the system. Had they done so, is it likely that the practice would have continued for quite so long?

A large distribution business had several sites in different locations, all linked electronically. Much use was made of electronic mail. The administrator of the system had developed an excellent installation that worked well; perhaps in consequence, his staff were frequently under-employed, with time on their hands. Unknown to anyone, one member of the technical staff began to monitor electronic mail, particularly mail to and from senior managers. He was able to do this because the monitoring of electronic mail was electronically possible, while the possibility of it actually happening remained inconceivable to most staff.

In this case, the outcome was particularly unfortunate, the illicit monitoring coming to light only after an apparent blackmail attempt on a female member of staff. Had the ability of systems support staff to read anyone's electronic mail been known throughout the company, greater care may well have been taken – although that does not excuse the supervision failure of the systems support manager.

Incidentally, as a general rule, it is always wise to assume that everything you send electronically may be published and distributed; without explicit security encoding, there is seldom such a thing as secure electronic mail.

Rules of appropriate conduct

RULE ONE: *Employees affected by the operating of business computer systems should always be made fully aware of the likely effects and implications of such use.*

A further instance of the importance of knowledge concerning the operation of a business computer system lies further afield. Clearly, the manner in which business computer systems are used may well affect more individuals than those employed by the company itself. Although they are unlikely to have any direct responsibility for the computer systems, and indeed may not even know of their existence, they might still be affected. Company responsibility in these circumstances may be less obvious, but issues of wider accountability are by no means hypothetical.

Those potentially affected by the use of company computer systems are in three main groups:

1 Those businesses or individuals who have commercial dependence on the company – for example, suppliers of raw materials.

2 Those businesses or individuals on whom the company is dependent – for example, customers.

3 Members of the wider public.

Examples of inappropriate conduct involving each of these groups follows.

Group 1

As is generally known, a company supplying components or raw materials to another may in some circumstances be considered dependent upon that customer. For example, a bulk purchaser may demand special discounts; invoice payments may be deliberately delayed; and so on. Might this dependency relationship potentially be exploited?

The following example, which has of course been changed to prevent identification, may appear complicated, but it is worth studying carefully as it demonstrates how computerised data may be misused.

Company A manufactured machine tools and purchased its components from a variety of different suppliers. A fairly complex computerised database was built, into which all known details of both suppliers and components were entered. Information about the original source of components was one of the items entered, so, if the company supplying Company A had actually purchased an item elsewhere, this data would be entered (if known, obviously).

After the system had been in operation for some time, the computerised data was extensively analysed. Among other results, it appeared that 45 percent of components from one supplier, Company B, had actually originated elsewhere. A direct approach to the original supplier would have allowed a small cost saving to be made. However, instead, Company A's buyer used the information to force Company B into granting a larger discount. (The threat was that other Company B customers, once made aware of the data, would desert them.) This worked so well that the threat was extended to other component suppliers. Some smaller companies were intimidated into passing over internal data directly. I was not able to learn to what other uses the data was put, or indeed of the full extent of the Company A database.

Clearly, this is by no means a typical example; hopefully, few companies are prepared to take data collection to quite these lengths.

Those original suppliers who were inadvertently providing information to Company A were unaware of the use to which it would be put. If Company A's intentions had been more widely known, it is very probable that it would have been unable to continue its actions.

A similar case, albeit on a smaller scale, involved a business that requested additional (and normally confidential) company and product information from suppliers as a condition for placing orders. Rather than making use of this information itself, though, the undeclared intention was to collate and sell it.

RULE TWO: *Those businesses or individuals who have commercial dependence on a company and may be affected by the operating of its business computer systems should always be made fully aware of likely effects and implications.*

The second group to be considered consists of those businesses or individuals on whom the company is dependent.

Group 2

Customers may be the unwitting source of much electronically held data. Of course, because data is held electronically does not necessarily mean that it is held inappropriately, but I suggest that, as an essential step in the commissioning of any new technical software, possible developments and analysis of wider issues be considered.

One relevant example concerned the establishment by a group of associated companies of a private computerised credit rating index. The contents of this index were built up from the formal and informal experiences of each member company; the results were shared and used to judge the appropriateness of allowable credit. In its essentials, such a system may well have been totally legal and proper, but this particular implementation added the personal financial details of company officers to the records of their firms. No one outside the group knew of the existence of the database, or that the information in it was 'pooled' from various sources. It was therefore possible for individual companies to informally and unwittingly pass to one firm information of considerable interest to another.

It is not just personal details of this sort that may be inappropriately recorded, of course.

A mail order company kept computerised records of all those who had purchased goods from it, categorised under a variety of headings. Customers were unaware that these lists were periodically sold on to other companies, resulting in an on-going distribution of junk mail.

Although the use of the Internet is dealt with specifically in Chapter 7, one aspect is particularly relevant here. The propagation of 'junk mail' is one of the down sides of Internet use. Companies concerned with junk mail buy and sell huge lists of individual e-mail addresses, using them in a similar way to the above example. Of course, the accuracy of this information is not guaranteed. Consequently, a recent twist is to include in electronic junk mail a note that the target's name will be removed from lists if they e-mail a reply requesting removal. While in theory this sounds like an excellent idea, the actual effect is simply to confirm that the e-mail address of the prospective customer is accurate – and to ensure that this correct address is then included in the circulating lists.

RULE THREE: *Those businesses or individuals upon whom the company is dependent, and who may be affected by the operating of business computer systems, should always be made fully aware of likely effects and implications.*

The final group consists of members of the public.

Group 3

It is often difficult to consider members of the public when designing or implementing a specialist business computer system. After all, they are very unlikely to be involved in the design process, their views are not likely to be sought in the development process, and their responses to the implementation may be hard to judge. Nevertheless, it is important to take these wider issues into account.

An example of what can happen when commercial issues are considered in isolation occurred in 1993, when a bizarre case from Sweden was reported in the international press.[3] It appeared that an elderly person had, apparently, died in 1990 but had lain undiscovered in her apartment for more than three years. During this time, 'computers received her pension and automatically paid her bills.' It was only after the landlord had made repeated efforts to gain the occupant's permission to renovate it that police were called to break into the apartment, and discovered the body. Presumably, had the landlord not wished to renovate the home, the automated pension and bill payment might have continued indefinitely. Clearly, wider issues were not considered by those responsible for the computerised business systems involved in payment of both the unfortunate woman's pension and her utility bills.

Members of the public may be affected by many other computer-related activities, too. In the USA, for example, Lotus (a computer software company), using information supplied by Equifax (a credit bureau), produced Marketplace, a searchable CD-ROM intended to assist targeted direct mailing. Comprising information on over 80 million households, it included not just consumers' telephone numbers and addresses but also details of gender, age, marital status, shopping habits (for over one hundred products) and even estimated income levels. Information contained in Marketplace was certainly accurate – it was taken directly from consumer credit files. The CD had entered production before a widespread adverse reaction resulted in its withdrawal.

Marketplace touched a raw nerve among consumers, and took on a broad symbolic significance in the debate over electronic privacy. When Lotus offered to delete data about anyone who called or wrote, it was flooded with about 30,000 requests. Consumers learned about the product through widespread news reports.

... Marketplace also became one of the hottest topics on the computer networks linking technology students and professionals. Complaints and protest letters were posted and copied on hundreds of networks. Opponents circulated Lotus's phone number and the electronic-mail address of Jim Manzi, its chief executive officer. 'If you market this product, it is my sincere hope that you are sued by every person for whom your data is false, with the the eventual result that your company goes bankrupt,' declared one letter to Lotus that was posted on several networks.[4]

A statement on the cancellation of Marketplace by Jim Manzi, Lotus CEO, indicated that the decision resulted from consumer concerns and 'the substantial, unexpected additional costs required to fully address consumer privacy issues.'

The case of Lotus's Marketplace is relevant on several levels, not least because it shows that an effective consumer backlash might be co-ordinated through use of the Internet. It is interesting, too, that Marketplace offered small businesses a low-cost entry into targeted direct mailing, a marketing field previously reserved for large companies. In this context, wide accessibility to data, by raising the profile of the exercise, may have proved a significant disadvantage.

RULE FOUR: *Those who may be affected by the operating of business computer systems should always be considered. If appropriate, they should be made fully aware of likely effects and implications.*

We can now summarise two general points, based upon the four rules so far described.

First, responsible use of business systems is a concept that cannot take place without prior thought and planning by responsible management. It is unlikely to be sufficient merely to assume that employees and staff will act appropriately; help and guidance must be given to ensure that their behaviour is in accordance with company policy. This also demands that a company policy must first have been established and its existence made clear to all concerned members of the company.

Second, the potential effects of business computer use will not be limited to those using them directly, or restricted to the responsible company. It is therefore insufficient to limit concern over responsible use to internal effects – it is *essential* that wider issues are also considered. These issues may relate to effects on suppliers, customers and, a group frequently overlooked, the general public.

These points will be mentioned again later as we draw together other such issues into a prototype code of conduct for the appropriate use of business computers.

Rules of appropriate conduct

RULE ONE
Employees affected by the operating of business computer systems should always be made fully aware of the likely effects and implications of such use.

RULE TWO
Those businesses or individuals who have commercial dependence on the company and may be affected by the operating of business computer systems should always be made fully aware of likely effects and implications.

RULE THREE
Those businesses or individuals upon whom the company is dependent, and who may be affected by the operating of business computer systems, should always be made fully aware of likely effects and implications.

RULE FOUR
Those who may be affected by the operating of business computer systems should always be considered. If appropriate, they should be made fully aware of likely effects and implications.

Discussion points

The following points are intended to form the basis for a class or seminar discussion on the issues raised in this chapter. They should not be considered until after the relevant sections have been read and thought through. As all questions have been carefully chosen to encourage debate, they are intended primarily to encourage thinking about the issues and are not necessarily capable of producing definitive answers.

1 Stealing computer equipment was used as an example of an action involving company computers and was defined as 'inappropriate' because similar actions in other areas were so defined. Can you think of additional examples?

2 Improper use of data gathered by 'smart badges' was given as an example of an inappropriate action that would have been impossible without the use of a company computer. What other such actions can you think of? What makes the use 'improper'?

3 Apart from any possible practical advantages, why might responsible company managers need to consider new developments in technology?

4 Does 'illegal' mean 'unethical'? If so, why? If not, why not?

5 'Unethical' behaviour in business computing may be divided into three substantive categories. Define an action that might be classified as belonging to the first group, individual behaviour. Is appropriate behaviour within a company different from behaviour at home? If so, why? If not, why not?

6 When might it be appropriate for a member of staff to challenge the instructions of a manager?

7 How might the private views of an individual employee affect their company? What circumstances might make it reasonable for an employer to restrict the private expression of an employee's opinions?

8 Consider why acting unethically might not work, and list your points. How might these reasons be expressed in a code of conduct?

9 A business computer is being used inappropriately. First consider whose responsibility this might be and then try to find reasons why this might not be so. Pick another group at random and repeat the exercise. What might this tell you about assessment of responsibilities?

10 You are asked to express your views on computer use at a public meeting, held outside work hours. Why might your employer need to be consulted? Why might they object?

11 You continue with your plans to speak; what reasons might you put forward to justify your actions?

12 You are responsible for a company computer that is devoted to stock records. A supplier asks you to copy some files for them and offers a confidential 'bonus' to do so. The copying would be invisible – nothing will be missing from the company system, and no one would know. What are your reactions?

13 What are your *personal* views on the appropriateness of the information intended for Lotus's Marketplace CD-ROM?

14 You are manager of a direct marketing organisation. Do your views on the Lotus CD differ? If so, how – and, more importantly, why?

Notes

1 A more general discussion of this area was made in Chapter 2, and, although understanding of this section does not depend upon reading the earlier chapter, it is recommended that Chapter 2 is studied before reading this section.

2 *Practical Computer Ethics*, McGraw-Hill, London, 1995.

3 See the *Los Angeles Times*, Sunday, 19 September, 1993.

4 From the *Wall Street Journal* of Wednesday, 23 January, 1991.

5

Installing new computers?

This chapter looks from several differing perspectives at some of the potential problems involved in the installation or modification of a company computer system.

Introduction

When examining the role of computers within business, issues of scale are not only relevant but also of considerable importance. In this chapter, we look specifically at potential problems in business computer systems installation, considering matters from three different company size perspectives. As discussed elsewhere, however, there are common questions and issues in the installation of all new business computer systems, whatever the size of the commissioning company. After consideration of individual cases, therefore, the chapter examines the case examples in relation to each other, with the intention of bringing common issues together. As usual, the chapter concludes with a series of questions, based on the case illustrations, to provide a useful basis for class discussion or individual consideration.

Three fictional companies are described, each representing a typical level of business computer involvement. The first is EthiComp Marketing, Inc., which employs 9500 people. The second, Defective Televisions, is a small chain of electronic appliance shops; while the third, Mom&Pops, is a local convenience store. The cases are intended to be considered together, as they combine to demonstrate the relationships between potential problems at different company sizes, but each illustration may also be examined individually.

Although descriptions of these companies have been developed from actual examples, for this exercise the specifics of the example businesses are not important. If it helps in following or discussing the issues, do replace these company examples with others that may be better known to you. The essential intention of the approach taken in this chapter is, simply, to discuss what is appropriate for the computer systems used by a business of a particular size, uncomplicated by any 'real world' specifics that would be involved in a particular market or location.

Finally, it should be stressed that, while the problems encountered and described in this chapter are typical, and real, those companies used as case examples are not intended in any way to depict any actual corporations or enterprises. The unfortunate fictional businesses are actually built up from amalgams of a number of different examples, drawn from a large variety of different businesses.

Although all the difficulties described here have actually happened to someone, I sincerely hope that no single company will ever suffer from all the problems experienced by these three firms in their efforts to install a new computer system.

Case example 5.1

• • • • • • • • • • • • •

A large business – EthiComp Marketing, Inc.

When considering the implementation of business computer systems within a large corporation, responsibility may potentially fall on several groups of people. They are likely to include responsible senior executives, managers given the task of managing installation, technical staff who will actually carry out the necessary practical work, and, finally, the software and equipment suppliers. All carry a degree of responsibility for the eventual system, although all must appreciate that this responsibility is a shared one.

Consider Figure 5.1, representing the principal groups typically involved in computer systems purchase for a large company. It will be seen that the hierarchy of the company is represented by the three blocks representing senior managers, divisional managers and technical staff, with the addition of an 'extra' external category, representing the suppliers of computer and networking equipment. All these groups carry important responsibilities for determining an appropriate new computer system for the company.

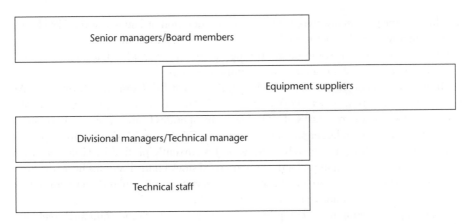

Figure 5.1 Hierarchy

It is particularly important to understand that, even though other individuals within a group, and of course other groups, may carry partial responsibility for an implementation, this does not in any way permit *personal* abdication of accountability.

Equipment and software suppliers

Suppliers of equipment may not be considered relevant to a discussion on business computer systems installation. However, this is a mistake. Consideration of the issues will rapidly show that suppliers of hardware and software have a considerable influence, both on the type of equipment to be installed and on the way in which it may be employed. For efficient and balanced practice it is necessary that this external influence – which is not necessarily harmful – is appreciated by client businesses.

Although there are clearly limits to the freedom with which a sales person is able to recommend computer hardware or software, it is essential that the degree to which they can be trusted to provide solid and reliable advice is both known and acted upon by a commissioning company.

This is an issue that is likely to be particularly significant when considering the risks to smaller companies, which may not possess sufficiently knowledgeable technical staff to appropriately vet the claims of sales people. It is still necessary, however, for even a large company to make certain that a comprehensive and relevant specification and purchase brief is developed, and to ensure that the responses of prospective suppliers are always appropriately vetted.

For example, similar or even identical computer equipment is frequently available from several sources, but the cheapest supplier may not always be the most appropriate choice. Commissioning purpose-built software is a potential minefield, especially for a company that lacks the internal resources to provide detailed requirements specifications, or to appropriately evaluate submitted software.

The ethics of computer equipment sales staff, although arguably relevant, unfortunately lie outside the scope of this book.

Company description

To illustrate the potentially complex need for consideration of issues at several levels of a large company, as well as between different categories of staff at the same level, it will be helpful now to work, in some detail, through a specific example of a large company approaching the task of installing a new computer system.

For the purposes of discussion, we will study the firm of EthiComp Marketing, Inc. We will assume that it is an unexceptional, reasonably large concern, which employs 9500 people, 150 of whom are office staff. The company operates from two sites, a fairly small head office and a much larger warehouse complex. EthiComp Marketing, Inc. operates in the area of reselling and merchandising, and is currently profitable. However, when we first consider the company, elderly computerised stock control systems have, for some time, been thought to increase overheads unnecessarily, as well as playing a major part in difficulties over maintaining appropriate stock levels.

EthiComp Marketing has a computing division, reporting to the company's technical director, Jason Pitt. Despite its grand name, the computing division's chief task has always been seen as purely practical – basically, its purpose has always been to keep the company computer systems running. Members of the team had never been concerned with anything beyond maintenance and technical issues.

Implementation

After a request from Jason Pitt, the technical director, the company's board discussed the issue of a replacement computer system. It was a brief meeting, and discussion on the item relating to the purchase of the new computer system was short. Essentially, Pitt had previously informally requested a figure of £750,000 for 'a new system'. Before this meeting, he and the financial director, Bill Zabrinkov, had met and informally settled on an overall cost of £500,000. As both Jason and Bill were in agreement, this expenditure was given rubber-stamp approval by the board. There was no discussion on anything beyond the financial issues involved. Most seriously, there was no consideration of the possibilities of improving the present system, or the implications of a replacement computer system on current working practices, the potential knock-on effects of a changed system, and, in particular, results of the inevitable disruption and changed routines on staff.

What happened next?

The selection of a software and hardware supplier was carried out purely on price, the successful tender coming from a new company with aggressive sales techniques but little experience in this area. The chosen computer system was a complete replacement for the existing one, and, according to the supplier, would easily combine the original stock control functions of the old system with the addition of networked electronic mail, Internet connections and a host of further potential benefits.

However, these and other additions were appended individually at a late stage to long-standing original plans. These plans had assumed that the existing system would remain in place, at least until a new system had proved itself. These original assumptions were discarded without publicity by the new supplier, largely on cost grounds. In the event, for a variety of practical reasons, development and installation were piecemeal, reflecting a changing mix of current plan and current availability. Before work started there was no clear overall specification, which, among other problems, led to unexpected technical incompatibilities between sub-sections of the final system. The final specification (which went through several iterations, even after it had been officially completed) actually 'evolved' to justify officially piecemeal decisions that had already been informally made and implemented.

EthiComp had no policy on appropriate use of its computers, and there were no plans for one to be developed. Consequently, there was no consideration of the wider effects that the introduction of a new system might have, for example on employee behaviour.

For whatever reasons, the eventual cost of the new computer system to EthiComp Marketing was more than double the original estimate. In addition to this 'actual' cost, due to repeated system failures (and other problems described below) there was also a considerable related loss, particularly of sales and production.

Middle management

Middle management had played no part in the decision to replace the existing systems. There had been little prior discussion at any level, and, although it had been known informally within the company for some time that the computer system would eventually change, the final implementation decision was widely seen as having been made hastily.

This background meant that, at best, middle managers were not committed to the change; at worst, there were serious internal conflicts between departments, principally over allocation and deployment of appropriate resources. These conflicts led inevitably to major disagreements and continuing 'turf wars' over needs for personnel and equipment. For example, some managers insisted on new computer equipment for reasons of status rather than any specific technical need.

In one instance, a particularly awkward head of department was, after continuing loud and aggressive arguments, given permission to upgrade their departmental computers, despite there being no technical justification for doing so. Although this single concession was supposed to be confidential, once the decision had been made word of it flew around the company. Other intransigent managers grew even more uncooperative, while those managers who had previously avoided involvement began to complain, and to seek renegotiation of their earlier compliance.

Staff

Staff involved in areas where the new system was to be introduced had not been advised of its purpose, or involved in its development. Word quickly spread that the real intention of introducing a new computer system was to save money through subsequent staff cuts, and that introduction of the new system would inevitably lead to massive lay-offs. Although the company was not unionised, a series of small strikes occurred, and for a time the risk of a complete labour withdrawal was considered very real. There were also major problems even among staff who were prepared to work in establishing the new system, largely due to lack of information and appropriate training.

Moreover, once the system had been introduced and was running, it became clear that it was, in parts, quite unworkable. As one middle manager commented later, 'I could have told them it wouldn't work – but no one ever asked me.'

Still further staff problems were caused by the new electronic mail system, which had been a much-promoted advantage of the new networked computers. While it was eventually officially denied that any such actions would take place, the discovery that all electronic mail could be invisibly monitored, and electronically checked for suspect keywords, understandably led to much anger.

In the absence of specific guidelines, some staff made improper use of the new system. One member of staff ran a money-making personal web site from the company computer; another regularly accessed the customers database, extracting lists of prospects, which were passed on to a competitor.

Staff morale plummeted. There was considerable absenteeism and high employee turnover, neither of which was restricted to the affected areas of the company.

Customers

EthiComp Marketing's customers suffered both from a deteriorating service (due to technical difficulties) and from further continuing problems related to staff attitudes. Suppliers also experienced the effects of technical problems, while the heavy drain on EthiComp's cash flow delayed bill payments, leading to further supplier difficulties. A senior member of staff later described the expensive new system graphically as a 'running sore' that dragged down and corrupted everything it touched.

Although eventually in place for just under two years, the new computer network never really worked to everyone's satisfaction. When EthiComp Marketing was taken over by another company, the computer system was finally scrapped completely.

There is much room for discussion on this case example. Many of the actions taken by EthiComp and its supplier were clearly inappropriate; to be charitable, other problems may have been unforeseen. Some difficulties were brought about by concentration on the practical results to be expected from the new system, ignoring any consideration of the likely wider effects. Such inappropriate focusing is an important issue, not only for what may be seen as intangible 'ethical' reasons but also for solid business ones. After all, the new system proved not just extremely costly but also very bad for business.

It is suggested that this example is discussed in detail. To help discussion, a summary of some relevant points. The EthiComp system:

- was introduced without proper planning
- was introduced without discussion, particularly at 'worker' levels
- lacked a realistic budget
- lacked a clear advance specification
- lacked any analysis or appreciation of its effects on staff
- implementation changed inappropriately under pressure
- lacked any company 'conditions of use' policy
- lacked appropriate information
- involved no planned staff training.

In a company of any size, there are at least three possible levels that can be used to direct consideration of these issues:

1 *Top level*: the senior executives who actually run the company.
2 *Implementation level*: those managers who are given the task of organising and implementing the decisions.
3 *Staff level*: those individuals who are given the actual job of carrying out and supporting the changes.

We may also consider adding

4 *Employee level*: those workers who will be affected by the changes, even if they are not directly concerned in the implementation.

We will return to these points after considering two further examples of business systems implementation.

• • • • • • • • • • • • • • • • • •

A medium-sized business – Defective Televisions

When considering companies of medium size, we may take a similar approach to the one used for EthiComp. The main differences are probably that specialist computing staff are likely to be thinner on the ground and the chain of managerial responsibility shorter. Technical staff may well report directly to non-technical managers, who will consequently be less able to appreciate any specialist issues.

As will be seen from Figure 5.2, another effect of the different managerial balance that must be considered is that, without a specialist computing group, the influence of an equipment or software supplier may well increase.

Consideration of the section on equipment and software suppliers earlier in the chapter is also relevant here. The involvement of external suppliers and potential suppliers may well be more intrusive at this level, particularly if they are involved directly with senior managers, as indicated in Figure 5.2. Of course, whatever the size of the commissioning business, it is always true that external pressures from a supplier or a potential supplier always need to be anticipated.

In smaller companies, there is also the possibility that members of the workforce may feel more able to contribute directly to any debate on changed systems, either through unions or staff associations, or directly, through line management. Whether this is true or not, it is at least arguable that the shorter the chain of responsibility, the more responsive it is likely to grow.

Company description

Defective Televisions is a chain of eleven electrical appliance shops. These shops were originally operating independently but, over a period of years, were gradually bought up by a long-standing holding company, Defective Radio, which controlled several other such retail chains. Each Defective Television unit has between ten and twenty staff, who are mostly involved in sales. Although the group buys centrally, the local computer systems of Defective Television were not compatible with that of Defective Radio, or indeed with each other, and managing stock was consequently very difficult.

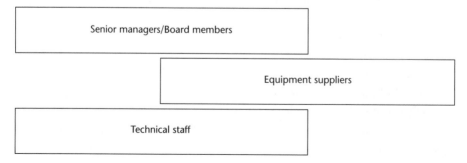

Figure 5.2 Hierarchy of a smaller firm

Two engineer members of staff had the task of maintaining Defective Television's computers, but their job was seen, in the words of one engineer, 'as simply connecting wires and plugging-in components.' Although company headquarters of Defective Television were fully networked, the existing computer systems in the shops were not connected. Each unit still operated largely independently. For example, although each Defective Television sales unit had to submit regular statistics to head office, the production of these statistics (on paper) involved different and incompatible computer systems, driven by incompatible software.

Implementation

The decision to implement a new, networked computer system for Defective Television was taken at a board meeting of its holding company, Defective Radio. Although there was a Defective Television representative on the parent board, they were not asked for any preliminary information; the decision was taken pragmatically, in order to bring the whole group electronically into line. For this reason, the choice of computers and software reflected that which was already in use in Defective Radio's headquarters, and in other subsidiaries. No detailed study had been made of any special needs of Defective Television or of its individual units; apart from its stock control functions, the new software was principally intended to provide statistical information on unit operations for head office analysts. While the local workload would inevitably increase as a result of the changes, there was little or nothing that could be seen locally as providing any commensurate benefits.

What actually happened?

The supplier, who provided both equipment and software, was chosen centrally and was physically located at a considerable distance from the installation locations. The supplier's work was largely effective, although the number of machines at each location had not been properly considered; each unit had been allocated three networked computers, but the volume of work, and consequent need for computer use, varied greatly between sites.

The imposition of new computer terminals without detailed local planning also meant that a number of terminals were sited inappropriately – for example, in areas to which the public had access, or where the machines could not be properly secured. When local managers complained, the official response was to introduce a long and complex password protection sequence to the system. This was certainly cheaper than extensive relocation of machines, and, used correctly, this measure would probably have provided adequate security. However, in practice, it took so long to go through the new accessing process that individual users tended to leave themselves logged on to the system for lengthy periods, completely defeating the purpose.

Initially, the system was planned to use ordinary telephone lines to establish its networked links between sites. In use, however, it was rapidly found that this method had serious flaws – for example, telephone numbers were engaged, the bandwidth of the link was low, and modem problems were experienced. A system that had worked well when installed in a large single building became unbearably slow when operating with a much greater volume of data over a wider area. In an attempt to improve matters, piecemeal modifications were introduced, which further complicated the task of staff trying to understand the workings of the system.

Finally, due partly to these problems and partly to poor financial planning, the original budget was soon exceeded. Company financial controls were tight in the Defective Radio Group, which, when a budget was exceeded, inevitably meant that expenditure was automatically frozen. Freezing was in place for three months. During this time, computers were delivered but could not be connected; repairs were hard to organise, and even special staff who, it had been planned, would act as facilitators of the system – at head office – could not be employed. The financial freeze inevitably led to massive further difficulties.

Management

The various layers of company and inter-company management in the parent company, Defective Radio, and its subsidiary, Defective Television, created considerable difficulties. Senior managers, who were based at the group's head office, tended to make broad decisions for the whole group, leaving lower-level managers in their associated companies to concern themselves with details of implementation. This inevitably meant that opportunities for feedback on the viability of proposals were few, and comments difficult to make. Valid objections, which might have been known at lower levels in the organisation, consequently failed to reach senior decision makers. It was also true that sometimes group decisions were introduced that, although broadly appropriate across the board, caused major problems in individual local cases.

Although, in theory, as a company Defective Television was able to make autonomous decisions, and for minor issues this happened regularly at a local level, in practice, company-wide decision making was seriously discouraged, both by official ruling and by a long-standing culture of dependence. Those managers who were directly responsible for Defective Television also sat on the board of the parent company, so it may have been harder for them to maintain the necessary objectivity.

Within the Defective Television company itself, local managers had not been involved in either the decision to install networked computers, the choice of machines, or the choice of software. Several were consequently obstructive; most found reasons for making the installation difficult and were not motivated to make the system, once installed, a success.

Staff

No plans had been made for staff training, and although each store was provided with a printed computer manual, the manuals had originally been written for another group company. They were also thick and intimidating, and were generally not seen by staff as being either helpful or accessible. Lack of knowledge of the new computer systems inevitably led to numerous errors, particularly in data entry. The lack of any immediate benefits to local staff from use of the computers led directly to a lack of motivation and a widespread reluctance to enter data. Many staff simply found the new machines too difficult to use; others, perhaps more experienced, found that it was possible to reboot the computers to run games software.

The system was eventually fully installed but within weeks was rendered largely obsolete by the introduction of another idea – integrated electronic tills.

Again, this example has included many points that may be used to provoke discussion. While liberally criticising Defective Radio's management, it is important to appreciate that none of the decisions, how ever disastrous they may have proved, were *intended* to provoke problems. Each option was chosen in the belief that it would result in an improvement to Defective Television's use of computers, and hence its operations. We will refer to these issues again later in this chapter.

• • • • • • • • • • • • • • • • • • • •

• • • • • • • • • • • • • •

A small business – Mom&Pops

When considering appropriate use of business computer systems in a small company, it is always necessary to be realistic. This is particularly important when considering ways in which smaller businesses may implement changes and introduce new business tools. Although computers are accepted as useful tools for all levels of business, in most larger companies they have devoted specialists who maintain them and who may be seen as being responsible for the effective and appropriate use of company machines. The case is clearly likely to be very different within a small company, where, typically, every member of staff is likely to be expected to cover several different jobs, tasks that in a larger organisation would probably be considered to merit several different employees. However strongly a specialist computer scientist might feel that all business computers need particular oversight, for purely pragmatic reasons this is very unlikely to happen in a small business. It is therefore worth keeping in mind that a business situation where a small number of individuals each has to carry out a series of different jobs may give rise to some unique problems.

When considering the role of business computing, chief among these problems is the potentially serious influence of the equipment supplier. As will be seen from Figure 5.3, the decision hierarchy of a small firm is potentially very different from that of a large one, especially in the role of a supplier. This is basically because, through a potential lack of specialist knowledge on the part of the business, an equipment supplier may inappropriately influence the choice of both hardware and software.

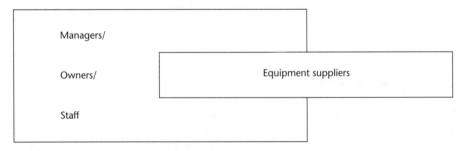

Figure 5.3 Hierarchy of a small firm

In my days as a freelance computing consultant to business, I was repeatedly surprised to be called in, at a late stage, to advise on what could be done with equipment that had been purchased, often at a high cost, without any clear purpose. Usually, a sales person had convinced the owner of the advantages of a high-powered new computer system, sometimes without ever moving into specifics. Although undoubtedly an excellent affair for the sales person – and, it has to be admitted, for a computing consultant – this was inevitably bad news for the unfortunate business.

Even assuming that a suitable computer system is supplied and installed, though, a further potential problem is the difficulty faced by a small business in obtaining appropriate software. It is seldom open to a small business to commission bespoke software; it must choose from off-the-shelf packages and hope that its needs will be met by commercial software that is, understandably, aimed at a broad market. In these circumstances, it may be tempting to copy software illegally – thus obtaining so-called 'bootleg' software. Sometimes an unscrupulous dealer may offer such software, complete with photocopied manuals, in an attempt to clinch the sale of a computer system; sometimes an individual will see a program that they like on a friend's machine and casually seek a copy. Despite the frequency of its use, the legal and ethical position concerning such software is very clear. It should never be used.

Reasons for a total embargo on illegal software are legion, but the example of one small firm makes an ideal illustration. When brought out in lectures and discussions, I have found that this example has helped the most pragmatic of small business people to see the disadvantages of bootleg software. I will call the central character Harry. Harry is a small businessman who wrote me a long, aggrieved e-mail seeking support in his complaints.

Basically, to save money, he had for some time used a 'bootleg' software package for his company accounts. The software company that had unwittingly supplied Harry with his earlier package had recently introduced a new version of its accounting software, which looked a big improvement. Harry had 'borrowed' disks from a friend and copied the new software on to his hard disks. However, when he attempted to copy over his data from the original package, 'it all went pear-shaped'. Lacking any manuals, and carrying out the operation entirely by guesswork, Harry managed to wipe vital company data. (Yes, he did have a backup; but it was, unfortunately, six months old.) Harry firmly believed that the disaster was not his fault, feeling strongly that the software firm ought to have made it clear that there was a risk of data being lost during the upgrading process.

When I asked, diffidently, about the fact that he had not paid anything for the software, he said that he was quite justified in 'checking it out' before paying for it. (He assured me that he had, of course, intended to pay for it eventually.) Whatever you may feel about his morals, Harry certainly ended up paying a high price for his 'free' software.

Company description

Mom&Pops is a corner store, run by two partners, with help from two part-time staff. The turnover is not large, margins are small, and the business has never owned a computer. Jake, one of the partners, saw an advertisement for a computer system and was most impressed, feeling that it would be a great asset to the business. He had visions of smoothly integrated accounts, beautifully printed correspondence, typeset advertise-ments and even an Internet presence, which he felt was certain to attract a wider customer base.

Implementation

The two partners initially telephoned a computer dealer, who sent a sales person to visit them. After a single hard-talking session, they agreed to purchase a top-of-the-range PC, together with laser printer, modem, CD-ROM drive and other peripherals, together with a quantity of packaged business and games software.

What actually happened?

The new computer was delivered and physically connected together by the dealer. However, no training, particularly in using the business software, was offered – or was indeed available. Learning how to operate the computer and its different software pack-ages proved to be a slow and painful task, and one that took valuable time away from the everyday needs of the business. Data entry, especially, was found to be particularly time-consuming. The cost of the purchase, as a percentage of total business costs, was considerable and was in no way recouped by any related advantages. Indeed, after the computer purchase, overall costs went up, both directly, through interest charges on the equipment, and indirectly, through time lost to learn its use and to maintain it. The business was soon faced with a stark choice: of continuing to attempt to integrate the new computer system into its operations: or to cut its losses by reverting to its former manual system.

Understandably, I would hope to report invariable success in business computer use but, sadly, although the Mom&Pops partners did continue to try hard to use their com-puter system, they failed, and the business closed. Of course, there are many pressures on small businesses, so there may well have been other reasons for the bankruptcy. However, one of the partners, speaking sometime later, blamed 'that <expletive> computer' for all their problems.

Why did failure occur? Some relevant points. The Mom&Pops system:

- was introduced without proper planning
- lacked a realistic budget
- lacked any analysis or consideration of its effects on staff
- implementation changed inappropriately under pressure
- lacked any 'conditions of use' policy, which affected use
- lacked appropriate preparation and information
- lacked planned staff training.

• • • • • • • • • • • • • • • • •

What should have happened?

By now, we are seeing a degree of congruence between the different case examples. Although the effects of scale are important, there are underlying aspects of computer system use that are common to all three implementations.

Generally, when considering the implementation of a new office computer network, it has to be accepted that it is virtually impossible to draw a consistent dividing line between professionally appropriate issues and those normally addressed by a competent systems analyst (whose role is described below). It is also true that the introduction of any new policy or change in existing practices within any business brings the possibility of related difficulties. Sometimes, too, a change that is itself relatively innocuous may act as a focus for previously existing conflicts.

There are therefore solid reasons why the extension of ethical behaviour to the area of office computing should not be contentious. Full consideration of the issues usually shows that there are sound business reasons why acting appropriately is the wise choice.

As we have seen, an important difference between larger and smaller businesses lies in the possibilities of independent advice, or internal specialist advice, being available for larger companies. Such a specialist, involved in the investigation and planning stages of a larger business computer systems implementation, is known as a 'systems analyst'.

Systems analysis

Essentially, the job of a systems analyst is to carry out an effective investigation of the needs to be met by a computer system, and to produce accurate and suitable recommendations that may then be used as the basis for system design. If such analysis is carried out appropriately, then it is far less likely that there will be either practical or ethical problems with the resultant system. It is not sufficient simply to leave everything to a systems analyst, though. Not all new installations can be initiated after systems analysis; and, even if they are, knowledge of what is considered by systems analysts to be professionally appropriate can only be of help to the commissioning client.

It is important here to clarify the distinction between valid technical decisions and ethical ones. While the two often overlap, there is no certainty that a systems analyst who is following a focused technical brief will automatically take into account any wider, ethical issues. Clearly, too, unless relevant points are specifically made clear to an outside consultant, identification of any ethical issues that potentially may be involved in the local use of a computer system must be more difficult.

For this reason, I strongly suggest that a company using the services of a systems analyst, either directly or through the contracting of a specialist systems design consultancy, gives thought to the wider issues that may influence the design of a new system. This information should be passed directly to the specialist, who should then be able to incorporate the material into their development of a final specification.

The practical steps to be taken by a systems analyst in investigating and making appropriate technical recommendations lie outside the scope of this book. Fortunately, though, good specialist texts are available for those interested in learning more of the role of a systems analyst when a new computer system is being considered (some are listed in the Bibliography). It is tempting, but inappropriate, to duplicate such material here.

Ethical analysis

We will be looking at the case examples in this chapter particularly to identify those areas where introduction of a new computer system threw up non-technical problems, or what

I call *ethical focus points* (EFPs). EFPs identify particular issues or problems that might justifiably be considered as 'ethical' – that is, those points that are specific and relevant to business computer systems development without themselves necessarily being part of the technical decision-making process.

Emphasis on the importance of non-technical issues to system development is necessary particularly because there is often considerable intimidation surrounding the making of technical decisions within business. Those who are perceived by technical staff to lack appropriate qualifications or experience are frequently sidelined and their views dismissed as reflecting irrelevant issues.

Jake was an accountant with a large industrial company. He was told that a new financial computing system was being introduced but was not given any opportunity to influence design or purchase decisions – his input was limited to specific issues relating to financial analysis. Jake felt that the new system might make unrealistically high demands on staff and was especially concerned over the need for specialist data entry. His views were ignored 'because they knew I wasn't a computer person'. Later events proved that he had been right and the systems analysis people wrong.

In this case (which was actually rather more complex than the summary indicates) an 'in-house' development team was responsible for developing the original computer specifications and for drawing up detailed plans. Despite all those concerned being employed by the same company, there was still a considerable gap between specialists and other staff, and no attempt was made to identify possible EFPs. Additional case examples, involving systems development using an outside agency, indicate an even greater potential distance between technical and non-technical staff.

Problems may also arise when technical staff are not involved in system specifications:

A small industrial company purchased a very expensive networked computer system, based largely upon a vice-president's assessment that it would be appropriate. After six months of failure and an (at least) 25 percent cost overrun, it was discovered that the responsible vice-president had no relevant knowledge or experience. The selection was defended, though, as having been based on existing company purchase guidelines, which was true. (The guidelines had been drawn up and intended for raw materials purchases.) The company now views technical purchases as needing specialist knowledge; the vice-president is still in post.

This example demonstrates a need for specialist technical knowledge in management or, at least, management readiness to seek and accept specialist advice. It is also necessary to evaluate the views of technical employees, whose views may be sometimes be dismissed, appropriately as inconvenient.

Discussion on adequate external oversight of specialist computing staff resulted in one disagreement at board level between two vice-presidents of vast seniority, one technical, one non-technical. The argument actually ended with the ultimate dismissive comment: 'Why should you care anyway – you – *user.*' 'User', in this case, referred to the employment of computer services. The comment still clearly still rankled even years later, when it was told to me.

Finally, quite apart from potential (yet very real) direct benefits, it is important for staff morale that their views are considered seriously. The canvassing of non-technical opinions at all levels must not be considered as simply a public relations exercise.

Analysis of case example 5.1

Let us now go through the case of EthiComp Marketing, Inc., identifying the possible EFPs that may have led to the subsequent problems. Some of these points overlap with effective systems analysis, because effective systems analysis must always consider and appreciate non-technical issues.

Consider the (limited) processes shown in Figure 5.4, which sets out a model of consultation open to EthiComp. Each box in the figure represents a part of a possible consultation and discussion process. EthiComp did dispose of much potential interaction; apart from the board discussions, therefore, all of the illustrated stages are potentially dispensable if the risk is felt to be justified.

What, then, is significant about the figure? First, it is important to appreciate that all connections are two-way and potentially recursive. This means, for example, that the views of 'managers' are both sought by and feed into the 'initial investigation'. Such a double connection allows managers' views to influence the actual shape of the subsequent investigation.

Second, the integration of individual views into the model of appropriate initial investigation is assumed. Essentially, this approach stresses that the opinions of staff are not to be sought as a bolt-on cosmetic extra to facilitate PR but are fundamental to the technical investigation itself.

Other relevant issues will be clear from a study of the figure. For example, consideration of the plan at board level is preceded by a technical feasibility study. Board views may feed back into modification of the study, and so on. It must, however, be appreciated

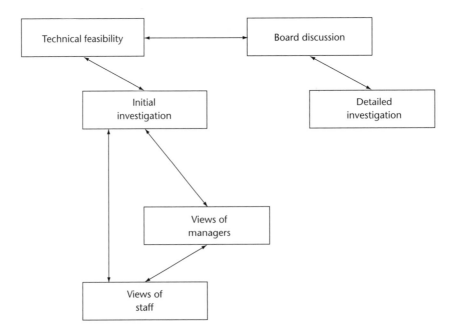

Figure 5.4 Suggested implementation cycle

Table 5.1

What should be done	Who is responsible
Initial research	
• appropriate systems analysis	Relevant managers Internal or external specialist staff
• staff knowledge and attitudes	Training/staff development Line managers
• 'selling' the case for change	First, 'sell' managers; then Training/staff development Internal publicity – e.g. newsletters
Evidence for the board	
• financial	Relevant board members, drawing on appropriate investigation and records
• background	Specialist research
• projection	Development team

that this illustration is necessarily limited – in particular, in every implementation local issues will undoubtedly need to be considered. Such issues are likely to be unique and may only be clear to those on the spot. It is also true that if no one is seeking to identify them, even essential local points may be missed.

Constructing a table along these lines (Table 5.1) can be of considerable help when planning the implementation of a business system. It allows potential EFPs to be identified and demonstrates clearly and visibly a determination to involve the opinions of staff and managers in the development. While I am unaware of any current academic research supporting the point, I have been told repeatedly by managers that staff who feel they have been involved in a decision-making process are more ready to accept the results. Interestingly, this conclusion remains true even though the consulted members of staff might strongly disagree with the eventual outcome.

The case of a company the size of EthiComp is almost certainly atypical; within a large organisation it is much less likely that the implementation of a massive new computer system would take place without adequate preparation. How ever unlikely it may be, though, such activities certainly do occur. The experiences of EthiComp during the implementation cycle of the project are more frequent, however. It is undoubtedly important to continue to maintain wider perspectives.

In the case of EthiComp, any initial discussions that took place concerning the new company computer system were strictly limited. It was not clear whether the technical director actually discussed the specification (as distinct from the cost) with anyone outside his own department. What the system should or should not do was certainly never debated, while the wider issues of appropriate use were not even considered. Quite apart from any wider problems, too, the new scheme was technically flawed, and these flaws were materially assisted by a shifting specification. It is viewed as proverbial by systems analysts that an elastic specification inevitably leads to expanding costs. EthiComp certainly provides an interesting example of business computer system installation.

Analysis of case example 5.2

Figure 5.5 sets out a model of consultation open to Defective Radio. It will be seen that this diagram differs from that for EthiComp, partly due to the smaller scale, and partly as the board discussions, which determined the shape of the new system, were carried out by a different company. Those processes in the figure that are directly concerned with Defective Television are therefore flagged.

The figure again demonstrates how the initial stages of the implementation might have been considered. While a direct link between the technical feasibility process and the Defective Radio board is possible, it is clear from the diagram that local investigation prior to discussion is appropriate. Consideration of EFPs, as an essential part of this process, would certainly include at least the potential problems of disparate local units, and, in particular, consideration of local need.

While top-down, management-driven systems design has much to recommend it – especially to managers – there are likely to be both direct and indirect benefits from consideration of a different perspective. Employees' views can play a significant part in this process.

Analysis of case example 5.3

Finally, Figure 5.6 considers the rather different implementation processes that are potentially involved in the small business of Mom&Pops. Here only two people were involved in making the decision, so the forum for investigation is obviously far smaller. Nevertheless, it is still essential to carry out an effective investigation of both the technical and non-technical aspects of the proposed new business computer system.

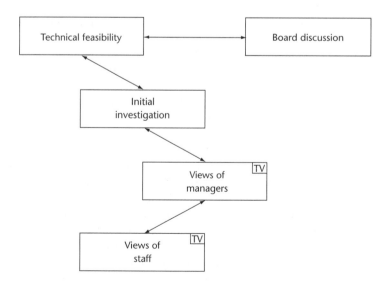

Figure 5.5 Suggested consultation cycle, Defective Radio

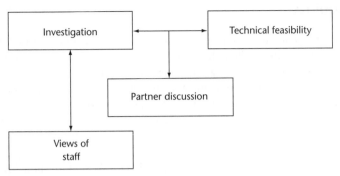

Figure 5.6 Suggested implementation cycle, Mom&Pops

EFPs that are likely to show up in an investigation of this type more probably involve the technical practicalities. This is particularly true when, as in the example, no members of the company possess any specialist computer knowledge at all. Even so, relevant information that may come from employees should not be overlooked. After all, a system may be technically appropriate but, in practice, unnecessary.

Conclusion

In this chapter, we have looked at the issues involved in the introduction of three very different business computer systems. The first involved a large company and demonstrated the importance of appropriate planning. Such planning should ideally involve all levels of staff and result in a solid implementation design that should not change inappropriately under pressure. Establishing and maintaining a company 'conditions of computer use' policy was also mentioned, as was the need for appropriate staff training and support. The second example of a smaller company carried these points forward and additionally showed that there was a particular need for attention when a parent company made decisions for a subsidiary. Finally, the smallest business demonstrated the potential vulnerability of a small company to external pressures, in this case from a computer sales person with unfounded promises of benefits.

We can now bring together some of the more important issues discussed in this chapter.

1 Decisions concerning business computer systems need not, and almost certainly are not, exclusively technical.

2 If non-technical issues are relevant, then the views of non-technical staff are potentially relevant, too.

3 If non-technical issues and the involvement of non-technical staff are relevant and appropriate, then time and space must be provided to enable presentation *and consideration* of such views.

4 Such presentation may usefully take place at all levels, but it *must* take place at the top.

Discussion points

The following points are intended to form the basis for a class or seminar discussion on the issues raised in this chapter. They should not be considered until after the relevant case examples have been read and thought through. As all questions have been carefully chosen to encourage debate, they are primarily intended to encourage thinking about the issues and are not necessarily capable of producing definitive answers.

Case example 5.1

1 With whom do you think EthiComp's technical director, Jason Pitt, should have discussed his proposed new computer system?

2 Identify at least *three* different groups who could justifiably be involved in the implementation of EthiComp's new computer system.

3 What specific implementation points do you feel should have been discussed with each group, and why?

4 What general implementation points do you feel relate to the EthiComp system?

5 What general implementation points do *not*, in your view, relate to the EthiComp system? Why?

In the case example, financial director Bill Zabrinkov reduced the initial estimate for the new system by a third, saving the company £250,000.

6 Zabrinkov felt that making this saving was a good decision. What reasons can you see for agreeing with him?

7 Setting aside the advantages of hindsight, what reasons can you see for *disagreeing* with him?

8 You are financial director Bill Zabrinkov. You are approached, before the board meeting, by technical director Jason Pitt to talk about the new computer system. What points do you feel it would be appropriate for you both to discuss?

9 What points do you feel it would be *inappropriate* for you both to discuss?

10 At the board meeting discussion over the new computer system, what issues do you feel should have been covered?

11 'There are too many middle managers to consult them all.' This is true. What do you suggest?

12 What should happen if EthiComp cannot afford extensive training for everyone?

13 Halfway through implementation, there is pressure to modify the system. You are in charge. What do you do? Why?

14 What do you *not* do? Again, why? (To respond to this and the previous question, it helps to first make a list of likely pressure points, and then your responses to each. Remember, what is an appropriate response may differ between different pressure points.)

15 What lessons have you learned from the EthiComp system installation?

Case example 5.2

1 You are a board member of Defective Radio. List at least *three* different things that you need to know before making a decision about a new computer system for your subsidiary, Defective Television.

2 You are representing Defective Television on the Defective Radio board. It is considering installation of the new computer system. What points do you feel it is important for you to make?

3 As an ordinary board member (i.e. not representing Defective TV), would your position be different? How?

4 You are manager of a Defective TV shop. What part do you feel you should play in the decision?

5 You are an employee in a Defective TV shop. What part do you feel you should play in the decision?

6 Why might Defective Radio justifiably insist on its plans being fulfilled?

7 List the *non-technical* points that you feel may affect the Defective TV plans. Which of these do you feel may be the most important? Why?

8 What lessons have you learned from the Defective TV system installation?

Case example 5.3

1 You are a partner in Mom&Pops. A computer sales person assures you that buying a new computer will make your company money. What *non-technical* questions might you ask? Why?

2 As a partner in Mom&Pops, what do you feel you need to know before ordering computer hardware? Are these questions different when considering ordering software? If so, how are they different? If they are not, why not? (Think about the differences between hardware and software.)

3 What reasons can you see that might have persuaded Mom&Pops to continue its use of the new computer system? Why might these objectives not be valid? (Not all possible reasons were mentioned in the study.)

4 What reasons can you see that might have persuaded Mom&Pops to *discontinue* its use of the new computer system? Why might these objectives not be valid?

5 What lessons have you learned from the Mom&Pops system installation?

6

Practical problems

General discussions on the broad ethical implications of company computer systems naturally have their place. However, should you be given responsibility for the installation or operation of a company computer system, or even experience non-technical problems in the use of one, practical help can be useful. This chapter therefore looks at a variety of ethical problems with business computer systems. Beginning with the aids to the identification of ethical problems, it moves on to describe some actual problems involving business computers from a variety of perspectives. The chapter concludes with a series of practical suggestions and help with the development of an 'appropriate use' policy.

Definitions

Personal ethical code

An obvious question – just what *is* an 'ethical' problem in the establishment or use of a business computer system? In order to answer this query, we first need to look in more detail at some of the elements dealt with in earlier chapters.

So far we have discussed the concept of ethical issues within business computer systems from a variety of different perspectives. Although earlier chapters have used a number of actual case examples, much of the related discussion has been in general terms. While we have considered several issues of importance to those concerned with business computing, there has been, so far, no attempt to define just what an 'ethical' issue might be. This omission has been deliberate. Without an appreciation of the background, attempts to define what may be an 'ethical' problem in business computing are often potentially confusing. There was a need to avoid such confusion by establishing some main points before entering the potential minefield of ethical issues identification. However, definitions are necessary, and the time has come to try to establish them.

First, it is probably useful to clarify what is *not* an ethical issue. Ethics are concerned with an individual's beliefs and are therefore hard to define globally, but it is still possible to make some general points. A useful rule is that an ethical question can be considered as one that addresses beliefs, rather than convenience. For example, not wanting to work late because an employer is forcing regular unpaid work may be an ethical problem; refusing a special request to work late through fear of missing a favourite television programme may not be. Because ethics are founded on belief, not opinion,[1] individual views about ethical issues tend to be deeply held. It is also unlikely that ethical beliefs will change frequently. If an action is therefore appropriate on Monday, it is still likely to be appropriate on Tuesday – unless, of course, new information has come to light.

The greatest difficulty for anyone attempting to deal with the practical implementation of ethical issues is the virtual certainty of disagreement between individuals. While such disagreement may perhaps be founded upon the bedrock of personal beliefs, many personal convictions are often unformed and may never have been properly thought through. Ill-founded disagreement between individuals may not survive discussion and analysis, but too often in the modern business world there is insufficient time for adequate discussion and analysis.

In summary, an issue is less likely to be an ethical one if the individual views that define it are:

- primarily concerned with convenience
- founded on opinions, not beliefs
- casually modified, or frequently changed.

As they are founded upon individual beliefs, there must inevitably be a large grey area around a wider definition of ethical issues. Discussion and analysis may be useful. As always, the individual must take personal responsibility for drawing an appropriate line. For these reasons, when considering issues that may potentially have an ethical component, it is important to have first clarified – in advance of any disagreements – what your own personal beliefs may be. What, for you, is ethical behaviour?

This is a key criterion, and it is essential for individuals to have given thought to a range of general issues in advance of any specific problems. Having a firm hold on what, for you, is appropriate behaviour can make all the difference in identifying and responding to potential difficulties. However, while knowledge of your own ethical beliefs is crucial, it is also necessary to be careful how you express them, and particularly to be aware of the dangers of *inappropriately* imposing your own standards on others.

When presented with a problem situation, such as one that appears to have an EFP (ethical focus point), it is important not to rush to judgement; further reflection may well alter the picture radically. Here the issue is concerned with allowing time for reflection – admittedly, not always easy in today's business world. However, it should be appreciated that, as ethical issues are potentially complex, they may well need additional time for analysis. When dealing with the technical possibilities inherent in company computer systems, it is particularly important to take sufficient time to ensure a clear understanding of what may be involved.

Briefly, ethics – also known as 'moral philosophy' – are potentially very much focused on personal beliefs. It is consequently necessary for individuals concerned with working ethically to begin by first establishing or confirming their personal 'baseline' of belief. This baseline, which defines the core of an individual, will, among much else, define appropriate actions *for them*. All external ethical codes, whether they are developed by employers, industry or even the state, must serve these personal beliefs or they, and the individual, will fail.

What does this mean in practice? Essentially, I suggest that it is vital for business people themselves to have a concept of what they personally feel is ethical behaviour. Without such a 'personal' perspective, against which personal and professional actions can be measured, it may be virtually impossible for anyone to behave ethically consistently, whatever their business role.

This assessment, which prevents any final reliance upon external definitions of appropriate conduct, may well prove disturbing. In the circumstances, though, a feeling of unease is perfectly understandable. Many people do feel distinctly uncomfortable when placed in a situation that forces them to draw upon their individual, as distinct from their business, personality. However, simply because an assessment may feel uncomfortable does not, of itself, signify that it is inappropriate and should be ignored.

In this case, it may be generally argued that behind all responsible business behaviour lies a clear understanding of what is personally appropriate. Knowledge of what is appropriate must always be relevant to business conduct, and this awareness should underpin all business behaviour. If an individual has no clear internal understanding of what is appropriate or inappropriate personal behaviour, they cannot possibly establish or judge the conduct of others. It is therefore essential for those concerned with the appropriate use of business computer systems to have a clear comprehension of what, for them, is appropriate conduct.

'How do I tell whether an issue is an ethical one or not?' At the risk of sounding unscientific, it may help if I conclude this section by passing on a personal finding. Although comparisons with other problem cases, analysis and discussion all help, what seems to work best in identifying ethical issues is what I call the 'feeling factor'. For example, consider a proposed action, or course of action. There may be no actual evidence, no obvious cause for concern; but does it *feel* right? When you think it through, are there areas, how ever ill-defined, that worry you? If so, there may be grounds for further analysis, and there may well be an ethical component to the issue.

While this approach is based upon considerable personal experience and many discussions with business people, the technique does admittedly still appear very subjective; but, in practice, it also seems to work!

Finally, do not overlook the advantages of a straightforward approach. Lockheed Martin Corporation of Bethesda, Maryland, recommends a quick quiz to staff faced with a potential ethical problem:

When in doubt, ask yourself

- Are my actions legal?
- Am I being fair and honest?
- Will my action stand the test of time?
- How will I feel about myself afterwards?
- How will it look in the newspaper?
- Will I sleep soundly tonight?
- What would I tell my child to do?

If you are still not sure what to do, Lockheed suggests that you ask, and keep asking, until you are certain that you are doing the right thing.

Further discussion of the subject of personal ethical responsibilities unfortunately lies outside the scope of this book, although it was dealt with in my *Practical Computer Ethics* (McGraw-Hill, 1995).

Background to the examples

So far in this chapter it has been suggested that a personal definition of ethical conduct is essential, and that all potential problems with the appropriate use of office computer systems are first evaluated against this personal definition. Essentially, this means that it is never sufficient to assume that all is well just because you have been told so by someone in authority. If an action is, for you, personally unethical, then it does not and cannot become appropriate simply because someone else has issued an instruction.

When considering the following examples, we must therefore assume that the individuals concerned are not totally dependent upon an employer or manager for their definitions of what is appropriate behaviour. In evaluating what it is best to do, business computer people, like all other individuals within a business, should be able to draw upon their own perceptions of appropriate conduct rather than slavishly following the orders of officialdom.

This statement emphatically does not mean that all people will, or should, always act in the same way. Variance in views between human beings is crucial and is what makes people individuals. However, possession of a personal ethical standard *does* mean that an individual should possess knowledge of what is personally appropriate and then act in an ethically consistent manner. What, for them, is unethical today will remain unethical tomorrow – even if their line manager may disagree. Once an individual's general standards of ethical behaviour have been established, these personal standards should then be applied to every circumstance, including the business of everyday living – and business.

Business ethical code

It has been said that an individual's underlying ethical philosophy is applicable to all aspects of their life, including their business life, and consequently their experiences of business computing. To this extent, there can therefore be no special allocation of computing issues for judgement against some unique 'ethics of computing', because such a thing does not and cannot exist.

The use of business computers will be judged against what the society in which they are used considers are appropriate standards. This means that, to be effective, any code of professional behaviour, whether it is an internal company code or a professional code covering a whole industry, must be founded upon what are generally accepted standards of conduct and behaviour. Further, because it reflects and supports such external standards, a code of conduct can enhance, but not replace, the standards of society.

Finally, though, we must remember that the nature of modern computing is international. This fact inevitably brings the possibility of business computer operations effecting more than a single society. Consider, for example, a business that has subsidiaries in other countries, perhaps in the Middle East, Africa or the Pacific Rim. Clearly, when viewed from such disparate areas, the expectations of appropriate conduct may be radically different.

Even if a business does not have such widespread subsidiaries, however, ordinary business use of the World Wide Web means that there is still a real need for appreciation of cultural diversity in business computer systems use. A local site in the UK or USA intended to promote a company may certainly be seen from its electronic neighbourhood, but it may also be viewed from anywhere in the world. In such circumstances, it is clearly important to reflect on the appearance and attitudes expressed by a company web site.

What are ethical problems in business computing?

It is unfortunately necessary to begin this section with a brief warning. This concerns a hazard to be kept in mind when considering any list of ethical problems; in particular, ethical problems related to business computing. In my experience, when a list of examples is studied, there is often a real risk that the contents may be viewed as exclusive, or even, at the worst, definitive. In other words, if a particular action is not on the list, then it might be considered to be probably ethical and therefore potentially appropriate.

I must stress, therefore, that all the examples in this chapter – and indeed in the book as a whole – have been selected as representative examples, and in no way do they form a comprehensive list of all possible ethical problems. While it is clearly helpful to consider examples of real issues in business computing, particularly those issues considered by the business people directly involved as raising ethical problems, there can be no substitute for applying your own perceptions to the circumstances in which you work.

For purposes of analysis, I have divided the following examples into three groups, each group being intended to illustrate a different area of business responsibility. The first group is managerial; the second, technical; and the third, practical.

Managerial examples

Managerial examples are concerned with ethical problems that appear to be the primary responsibility of managerial staff. That is, they tend to affect a wider area of the business than individual use and require decisions that could well have longer-term effects. There is a further division to be made when considering managerial responsibilities: the need for managers to act both in advance of problems and in response to them.

Company A operates as a travel agency. Its computers are used to collect specific details, via network links, from firms offering travel and holidays, match these with customers' details, and present the results to clients. If the investigation does not result in a sale, should the details given by clients, and their requested choices for travel or holiday, be retained?

There are solid marketing reasons why this might be appropriate, and consequently Company A has an outstanding middle management request for official approval. But would such actions be ethical?

In this case, the senior management team at Company A spent a long time debating the issue before deciding that it was not appropriate to retain information. The situation was helped by a 'positive spin' from customers, who apparently felt more comfortable dealing with a firm that took their responsibilities for data protection seriously.

Incidentally, had the decision gone the other way, there might well have been problems with those companies that supplied data to Company A; the grounds upon which they supplied data could be said to have changed once long-term recordings of the information were made.

Company B, a long-established legal firm, replaced all its typewriters with networked word processors. It is possible for the new systems to record the actual amount of activity undertaken by members of staff – that is, how long they spend typing, at what rate, and what the eventual outcome is in terms of finished documents.

Such statistics would allow the office manager a much better insight into the way the office works and potentially result in substantial cost savings, too. But is it ethical? This is an interesting example for discussion, particularly as, in the event, there was no actual outcome to report. Debate within the firm was limited, and the issue was allowed to drop on the grounds that it was not worth spending valuable management time on a technical issue.

In the case of Company B, official permission to undertake recording of staff actions was not given, but it is easy to visualise a similar situation having a very different outcome. In these fairly typical business circumstances, what are the responsibilities of managers? Is it reasonable, as in Company B, for managers to refuse to make a decision – and what might comprise reasonable grounds for such a refusal?

It may be argued that Company B did, in fact, make a decision; it decided to refuse permission for recording to take place. That it did this by refusing to act, or even to consider the matter, was, in practical terms, irrelevant, although from an ethical perspective it was certainly unfortunate.

Of course, human nature being what it is, most managers would probably respond unfavourably if faced continually with a series of questions seeking rulings on such ethical matters. This supports a case for some form of company policy to be clarified rather than forcing individual managers to continue to seek resolution of issues on a case-by-case basis.

In contrast to the previous example, Company C had already developed an appropriate use policy for its computer systems. However, in business, conditions change.

Company C has just been taken over by a larger firm. Among many other requests, senior managers have been asked to institute new policies, involving their business computer systems: policies that fall outside existing definitions of appropriate use.

Should the existing policy simply be quietly modified to bring it into line with the new activities – or would this be unethical? How seriously should the potential effects of the proposed new policies be taken? The degree to which managers are prepared to allow their own views to be overtaken by those senior to them in the company hierarchy is clearly of central importance here. Anyone with business experience will have knowledge of what may seem to be a continuing conflict between what an individual may feel is appropriate and what those in more senior positions within the company decide must be done. Sometimes, a more senior manager may issue an instruction that is felt to be inappropriate, or even just wrong; but to question such instructions and, in particular, to refuse to carry them out, is not something to be done lightly.

However, while the instructions of a senior manager should always be taken seriously, this does not mean that it must always be necessary to follow such directions. On the contrary, it is essential for every member of staff to have a clear idea of what, for them, are appropriate instructions and appropriate actions. This limit should never be forgotten, or disregarded through expediency. Everyone should have awareness of a personal limit beyond which they are not prepared to move.

In the case of Company C, an executive team had previously been given responsibility for drawing up the company's appropriate use policy for its computer systems. The former members of this team felt a personal, as well as a professional, commitment to maintaining what had proved to be a solid and effective policy, and they regarded the proposed changes as unacceptable.

Technical examples

As is probably obvious, technical examples are concerned with those ethical problems that are the primary responsibility of technical staff. Such problems are potentially of considerable importance, as they may well be invisible to anyone who does not have technical oversight of a computer system. In particular, there is a real need for those non-technical staff who may be responsible for drawing up company policies concerning computer use not to overlook the technical aspects of such a policy.

To many people, the most typical example of problems concerning technical issues in business computing is probably what I call 'the case of the hushed-up hacker'. This is a well-known occurrence, although curiously difficult to pin down. In its essentials, a hacker, or perhaps a dissatisfied member of staff, manipulates an organisation's computers to embezzle a very large amount of money. The twist is that, because adverse publicity is to be avoided at all costs – because this would undermine commercial confidence in the company – the offending hacker is never prosecuted.

I felt that such a case would make an excellent illustration for this section, but unfortunately I was totally unable to find any reliable examples. Both large and small companies, perfectly prepared to allow suitably disguised examples of their experiences to be used in other areas of business computing, denied all knowledge of hushed-up hackers. No institution approached directly admitted, even under a promise of confidentiality, to ever having experienced such a thing.

Sadly, therefore, I feel unable to put forward the example of the 'hushed-up hackers' as a realistic instance of technically related ethical computer problems. However, there remain many others; the range of options is considerable.

Although the possibilities of technically related ethical problems may be substantial, in practice technical matters tend mainly to relate either to ways in which a business computer system may be inappropriately designed or, once in use, inappropriately manipulated.

Senior managers at Company D had decided to purchase a new computer system and chose an off-the-shelf package from a large supplier. When installed, the networked system appeared to work well and proved efficient and practical. However, after six months, it was accidentally discovered that there were substantial 'loopholes' in the system's protection from outside access. A default password (intended by the manufacturers to have been changed) had instead been left in place. It was perfectly possible for a 'hacker' to have gained access to the system by making use of the known default password. If this had indeed happened, such a hacker could easily have made changes to the system to totally obscure whether unauthorised access had taken place.

Large computers are normally delivered with default passwords in place, although most competent technical staff certainly make changes before the system is made 'live'. In this case, though, Company D's technical managers were apparently unfamiliar with the new system and had not appreciated the implications of leaving settings as they were. Non-technical staff, understandably, had not questioned the situation. The situation was clearly serious, especially as no one knew whether or not a hacker had actually accessed the system. The matter was finally resolved by the employment of an outside computer specialist, who was recommended by the manufacturer. Changes were made both in the system and in the nature of the technical support staff.

Not all technical issues are quite so major. Some deal in areas that might at first appear to be trivial, such as the precise ownership of a company word-processing application.

Company E had an extensive network of computers. In addition to other advantages, the network allowed individual members of staff to access commercial software, such as word processors and spreadsheets, from a company file server. The file server was basically a very large networked hard disk, containing applications that could be downloaded temporarily into the RAM of individual computers for staff use. This meant that many people might potentially use different copies of the same software package at the same time, but, to save money, technical staff at Company E had purchased only a single original copy of each application.

Here, although the issues might have seemed obscure to ordinary members of Company E's staff, the question is actually fairly clear. Copying commercial software without permission is wrong. It is therefore not appropriate to clone copies of a single software package, rather than buying a copy of the application for everyone who might need it. This does not mean a huge pile of floppy disks; software companies are normally happy to sell a licence to those needing multiple copies of their applications. However, it remains both illegal and unethical to simply 'pirate' additional copies, as Company E had done.

Interestingly, although the action was illegal, as well as unethical, at the time no one outside the technical staff of Company E had appreciated what was going on.

Finally, the work of a systems administrator is of crucial importance for the appropriate running of company systems. A systems administrator is responsible for the entire technical support of a networked computer system. However, a well-run system is one where systems administration is actually invisible – machines appear to run themselves, seamlessly and efficiently. For this reason, the business users of a company computer system may be unaware that the task of systems administration is far from easy.

Users may also not appreciate that, in order to do their job properly, administrators have to be allowed sweeping powers over a computer system. Indeed, the power of a systems administrator, as a 'super-user', over their machines is enormous. They can access, view, print and save any data held by their machines, even 'foreign' data that may just be passing through it by way of a network connection. They can monitor, create and destroy files, and they have the power electronically to 'become' any of their users, after which they are able to behave as if that person's data were their own. They can invisibly monitor the use of computers, the use of electronic mail, and even the use of a company link to the World Wide Web.

It is said that all power corrupts. In view of these awesome powers, it must be encouraging that systems administrators as a class generally seem to be aware and responsible people. Most are aware of the need to police themselves, since naturally even the most skilled user or external manager could not do so. Nevertheless, power and responsibility do not always automatically go together.

In many companies, it is traditional to ignore technically based ethical issues completely. At best, the technical aspects of company computer policy are left to *ad hoc* development by different administrators and managers. Of course, a practice of avoiding issues until they are undeniable, and then developing a piecemeal policy, may potentially work. However, such an approach has clear and obvious disadvantages.

Although little or no attention is normally given to the ethics of system management, I suggest that these points indicate that anyone taking responsibility for maintaining a computer network needs to be quite clear about what is expected of them ethically, as well as practically. It is understandably the case that, during the appointment of systems administration staff, most attention is given to clarifying their practical responsibilities. However, I suggest that there is just as much need to discuss the less easily defined ethical expectations. Defining the responsibilities of technical staff is at least as important as defining the responsibilities of anyone else.

It is clearly very important for the efficient and appropriate use of company computer systems that the technical guidelines for designing and particularly maintaining such systems are both defined and made clear to everyone – including their users.

Practical examples

In one Wall Street office, the normal practice for most members of staff arriving in the morning is to log on to their computer and then check out topical cartoons, such as *Dilbert*, from World Wide Web sites. Such use of an employer's computer undoubtedly takes time, as well as tying up company resources – but in this case, in the absence of a defined policy, there is no obvious way to know whether or not the company approves.

Many staff who have a computer connected to the Internet on their desktop spend time using it unofficially. However, what if one of those involved spent all day 'surfing' the Internet? Or, instead of checking out the latest *Dilbert* cartoon, checks out a pornographic web site? Would it be more or less appropriate if they did this during a lunch hour, or after the office closed?

Some guidance, if not definitive instructions, is clearly needed to ensure that networked computers are used appropriately. (The topic of Internet use is addressed in more detail in Chapter 8.)

Company F employed several hundred office staff, each having access to a computer and laser printer. After installation of a number of expensive new colour laser printers, it was found that running costs were unexpectedly high. Investigation uncovered at least one group of staff running a private typing service, operating on company equipment.

Company F was unwittingly subsidising private printing, and indeed had done so for a considerable time. If those involved had restricted themselves to printing black and white

copies, their actions would probably not have been discovered. This example of computer misuse is particularly relevant here, as the responsible line manager had turned a
'blind eye' to the situation, believing that, provided that use was not excessive, no harm
was being done. There were no guidance notes on computer use in force in Company F,
and no known company policy.

Expectations

It is clearly necessary for the efficient running of any business that all members of staff
understand exactly what is expected of them. This is particularly true when the business
systems to be used by staff contain the potential for widespread problems. It is consequently clear that company expectations of appropriate computer use should be made
explicit.

This inevitably means that a comprehensive 'appropriate use' document must be
developed and circulated. While such a document can prove invaluable in the event of
problems, once in existence it may, as discussed below, also prevent potential problems
even occurring.

Development of any company policy often tends to be circumscribed by internal
practice; however, while there may be many ways of producing an efficient and effective
appropriate use policy for business computer systems, I suggest that two aspects are
particularly important.

Involvement of staff at several levels

While it is tempting to set up a high-level working party to produce a suitable document,
or perhaps to delegate the task to a single executive, a policy is more likely to be generally
seen as appropriate if staff from different levels within the company play a part in its development. It is also more likely to prove effective if the contents have been considered from
a variety of different perspectives; after all, the view of those who will be carrying out a policy may be different from those responsible for seeing that it is implemented. Unworkable
demands need to be explored before, rather than after, a policy is introduced.

Much of this work is similar to the development of other internal company policies;
beyond the relevant technical aspects, there is nothing intrinsically different about the
development of a policy concerning the appropriate use of company computers.

Involvement of technical staff

As business computers must rely upon the support of technical members of staff, the
involvement of technical people in the development of policy is potentially very significant. There are two main reasons why this is so.

The first is that there are aspects of computer use that hold the risk of ethical misuse,
but which are not actually visible to anyone who does not possess relevant technical
knowledge – the intricacies of network security are a good example.

The second reason for the involvement of technical staff in policy development lies in
their ability to identify both practical and impractical suggestions. For example, one
company had to rapidly withdraw a new computer use policy after it had been expensively printed as a glossy booklet, because it had – wrongly – assumed that all company

access to the World Wide Web was monitored. Even had such monitoring been felt appropriate by the company – which it had not – at that time it was not technically possible to monitor such a high level of electronic traffic. The automatic involvement of technical staff in policy development should help to prevent such problems.

Practical suggestions

This section, aimed principally at managers, is intended to give a quick and basic summary of the essential points involved in dealing with computer systems 'appropriate use' problems. It can also be used as the basis for more general discussion.

Any business that uses computers should, at least, have

- A clear, preferably written, idea for what tasks their computers, and software, are intended.
- Defined appropriate tasks, in writing.
- Defined *inappropriate* tasks, again in writing.
- Combined these definitions into an 'appropriate use' policy.
- Made certain that all concerned members of staff are aware of the policy.
- Provide relevant staff education and training.
- Formally arrange to review the 'appropriate use' policy at regular intervals *and* when relevant circumstances change.

When facing problems

While it is clearly best to anticipate problems, this is unfortunately not always possible. However, anticipation of potential difficulties can certainly minimise them. Particularly when dealing with problems arising from the use of business computer systems, it can be a considerable help to be able to refer to a previously developed code of appropriate use, sometime referred to as a 'code of conduct'.

Such a code should deal with all aspects of normal business computer use and specifically detail those actions that are felt to be inappropriate. Prior knowledge of the code may head off some problems altogether.

If a code does not exist, then one should be developed as soon as possible after the resolution of the current problems. It is therefore important that any official actions – especially disciplinary actions – taken in response to the current difficulties will not be incompatible with a future code. A common mistake, often made at this time, is to assume that any computer-related problems are a one-off and will not be repeated.

Company G found that a member of staff had inappropriately gained access to a payroll record, although they had apparently not actually seen individual salaries. Called to account, the staff member apologised and explained that it was 'just a prank'. They were transferred to another section, but no further action was taken. Knowledge of the incident became known in the company. Two weeks later, someone else gained unauthorised access to the payroll.

It might have been better for Company G if it had been able to point to an appropriate use policy or, at least, if the first incident had led to the development of a policy, had one not previously existed. Using real incidents to shape a policy is an excellent idea; it not only brings actual risks into the equation but also allows those concerned to gain an insight into what may actually be potential problem areas for use of the company's computers.

One example of an acceptable use policy for computer systems is in Appendix 2. This is a high-powered document, the purpose of which is to regulate the backbone computer networks connecting all UK universities. Although most businesses may not need to include such depth of technical detail, the document itself provides an excellent example of a solidly constructed, comprehensive policy.

A final suggestion, which in practice has proved helpful, is to make sure that all computer-related problems are co-ordinated by a single individual or team. When, in a large company, individual incidents of computer misuse occur, there is otherwise a danger that any common risks or patterns of activity may not be seen. On a practical level, it is also true that evidence which can accumulate when this sort of co-ordination takes place may be of considerable help in convincing senior members of staff of the importance of an appropriate computer use policy, and of the issues generally.

Tasks within the business organisation

To draw together individual points made in this chapter, it may be useful to present the particular responsibilities of different levels of staff within a business:

Senior managers
- Should ensure that guidelines exist for the appropriate use of company computer systems.
- Should make certain that the job descriptions of staff – especially new technical managers – include appreciation of wider issues.
- Provide for regular monitoring and revision of computer use guidelines.

Middle managers
- Should confirm that a company policy on computer use exists, and, if not, lobby for one.
- Should ensure that all members of staff for whom they are responsible are aware of the policy, and that they follow it.
- Make senior staff aware of any deficiencies in the appropriate use policy, or of any changes that reflect upon it.

Employees
- Should make themselves aware of any company policy on computer use.
- Should ensure that all computer-related activities are in accordance with the policy.
- Should make their line manager aware of any deficiencies in the appropriate use policy.

In addition to their official roles as representatives of the company, all members of staff have a personal responsibility, which specifically requires them to act responsibly, regardless of the official policies of their employing company. In a worst-case scenario, they should be prepared to act as whistle blowers in order to publicise unethical or illegal company actions.

Clearly, in most well-regulated businesses there is very unlikely to be any need for an employee to step out of line to the extent of whistle blowing. However, it is essential for the corporate well-being of our society that, in extreme circumstances, individuals be prepared to do so.

Conclusion

This chapter began with examination of the possible definitions of 'ethical' problems in business computer systems, stressing that before attempting identification it was essential for an individual to first determine their own individual beliefs. After general discussion, the importance of what I called the 'feeling factor' was suggested; this proposed that inappropriate actions may be identified if they produce feelings of concern. More general business attitudes and policies were then considered, and the necessity for a business to reflect the attitudes of the society within which it operated was emphasised. The difficulties this involves for multinational concerns were pointed out, and it was stressed that the operation of a company World Wide Web site brought similar concerns rather closer to home.

Some potential 'ethical' problems were then examined from a variety of perspectives – the first managerial, the second technical and the third practical. The development of a code of appropriate computer use was discussed, and the importance of involving staff, particularly technical staff, at several levels in the development was stressed.

Finally, a series of practical suggestions intended to give a quick and basic summary of the essential points involved in dealing with computer systems 'appropriate use' problems were listed.

Discussion points

The following points are intended to form the basis for a class or seminar discussion on the issues raised in this chapter. They should not be considered until after the relevant examples have been read and thought through. As all questions have been carefully chosen to encourage debate, they are intended primarily to encourage thinking about the issues and are not necessarily capable of producing definitive answers.

1 What would you consider an 'ethical' problem in the use of an office computer or computer system? Make a short list, and then discuss the contents with a colleague. Compare items on your lists; are they similar, or different? How might you respond to items on their list? This exercise may also be undertaken at a seminar or class level, with lists either being interchanged or items selected from them for discussion by a seminar leader.

2 What, for you, is 'ethical' behaviour? This is not quite such an easy question to answer as it might seem at first.

3 Why might it be sensible to take time to consider a potential problem?

4 Your line manager tells you to access a colleague's hard disk and copy selected files. Under what circumstances do you feel that it might it be appropriate to question this instruction?

5 Why might it be appropriate to look more carefully at the assumptions underlying the presentation of your company's World Wide Web site? (Hint: who will see it?)

6 In what ways may managers carry a special responsibility for the appropriate use of company computers?

7 Consider and write down reasons why technical staff need to be involved in the development of an appropriate use policy. Compare your list with those of others. Are there similarities?

8 Had you heard of the 'hushed-up hacker' case? Do you believe it? Why might this example be so frequently repeated?

9 Have you ever copied commercial software, either personally or as an employee? What justification did you make? After reading this chapter, have your views changed?

10 How might you encourage a systems administrator to act ethically? How might their conduct be monitored?

11 If you are currently working within a company, or have had experience of doing so, are you aware of any company policy on how its computers should be used?

12 Have you seen either a paper or electronic copy of a company policy on appropriate use?

13 Who should be involved in construction of a company appropriate use policy? Why?

14 What items do you feel should be included in a company appropriate use policy? Write down your points, and compare your list with those of others. Are there similarities?

15 Why might it be appropriate for all computer-related problems to be co-ordinated by a single individual or team?

Notes

1 For the purpose of this discussion, I define an 'opinion' as a view that is lightly held, that is open to debate and that may change. A 'belief' is deeply held, is seldom open to debate and is unlikely to change.

2 Random access memory. The part of a computer that holds temporary information – that which vanishes when the machine is turned off.

7

Networking and the Internet

Most company systems are networked – but what does this mean in practice, and what implications are there for their appropriate use? This chapter looks at the technical aspects of both local networking and connection to the Internet, identifying potential problems and clarifying responsibilities.

It then moves on to consider how both the text-based and graphical aspects of the Internet might be used for commercial advantage, and identifies some of the consequent ethical problems.

Introduction

Today, most of the desktop computers and PCs used by business are networked: that is, they have the ability to link to other machines, usually to access data and other information held remotely. While such machines may sometimes just be connected directly to each other, as part of a local office or company computer system, more frequently networked computers are connected to other more distant machines, potentially at a considerable physical distance. Typically, such connection is through links to existing globally networked systems, such as the Internet, or World Wide Web (WWW). The networked machine itself may be anything from a powerful company computer with direct Internet connections to a single small business machine, accessing a bulletin board through telephone and modem.

It is important to remember that, whatever the type or the location of networked machines, their access to the network, and the network itself, was planned and constructed following deliberate design considerations. Apart from assessment of the obvious technical issues involved, such design considerations should specifically have included analysis of the appropriate uses of the future network. In practice, detailed task analysis of this kind will probably not have taken place. Such analysis is nevertheless important, as preliminary definition and clarification of appropriate tasks at the design stage of a computer system may well head off serious problems arising from inappropriate network use at a later date.

Once a computer network has been established, development is not over. The day-to-day operation of all networks must continue to take technical issues into account. However, it may be equally essential to continue to reflect on issues of appropriate usage.

This chapter discusses some ways in which the design of computer systems might appropriately be influenced by ethical issues and examines pressures on specialist staff and others to technically control network-related actions perceived as 'unethical'. After definitions and examination of the current technical situation, particular problems concerned with different types of network are clarified. Finally, the Internet is discussed, with particular emphasis on its commercial advantages and ethical problems. The chapter concludes by suggesting some ethically based recommendations for the future design and operation of networked business systems. First, though, let us begin at the beginning.

What is a computer network?

Consensus definitions in this field are sometimes difficult. For example, information systems specialists may argue that any computer network is an information system. Hardware engineers, approaching the same point from a different direction, might agree with a typical business view, and consider that *physically linking one or more computers in such a way that they can share data* will form a computer network automatically.

Computer networks themselves, of course, might be further technically classified according to their geographical extent: local area network (LAN), metropolitan area network (MAN), or wide area network (WAN). Networks may also be grouped according to the specific protocols used, and indeed by a wide variety of other measures. For our purposes, however, such specialist distinctions are an unnecessary complication. We may consider business computer networks as principally falling into just two groups, one a subset of the other. These divisions, discussed below, are known as *closed networks*, and *open* (or Internet-linked) *networks*.

To most business people, the networking design decisions that may have been made concerning the computer system they use are, almost certainly, functionally invisible. In ordinary business operations, user consideration of networked computer systems operation is almost certainly limited to visible problems – complaints about connection speeds being among the most common. Such an emphasis is quite understandable, because designers of networked computer systems have always been principally concerned with technical issues. Systems analysis provides explicit design criteria for the technical implementation of computer systems. It may potentially take on board user pressure for facilities, but traditionally – legal questions aside – designers of networked systems normally only respond to non-technical issues if such consideration is directly requested by a client. Such requests are not usual.

Technical focusing of this kind is certainly comprehensible. Limited budgets, together with heavy pressures on development time, combine to reduce space for the consideration of wider issues. This is especially true of problems that are not clearly an essential part of a technical specification. However, whether or not appreciated by client or development team, there *are* wider questions that have an important role to play in the development of modern networked systems. Increasingly, society is no longer prepared to allow the free development of networked computer systems – especially globally networked systems.

The definition of 'network design' used in this chapter is consequently broad. It covers not only the physical arrangement of connections and links but also the negotiated steps through which individual users must pass to obtain networked communication.

As an example, consider an office user connecting their desktop machine to a World Wide Web site located in a different country. To the users themselves, such connection is trivial – it is made by simply clicking an on-screen button. Nevertheless, such a simplistic view overlooks some significant issues. To obtain an accurate perception of what such apparently local facilities actually involve, normally hidden aspects, such as company cache utilisation, links to service provider, access links from service provider to Internet hub – and, of course, the Internet itself – all need to be examined. These areas, and their potential significance to business computing, are discussed later in the chapter.

My intention is to look beyond the immediate appearance of a networked system and to examine what lies behind it.

Closed networks

The simplest form of networking is probably micro–micro linking. This usually occurs in the form of an uncomplicated connection of one PC[1] to another so that each can exchange information and data. Further machines may be added, in the form micro–micro*N (where N is potentially a large number). The result is the linking of a *group* of computers together so that each can communicate and share information with any or all of the others.

Such a connection, which typically permits local e-mail (electronic mail) together with the exchange of data and files, is probably the most common type of office system. Figure 7.1 represents one typical way in which a closed group of computers can be linked. Frequently, such a closed system will have a large-capacity hard disk available to connected users, as is shown in Figure 7.2. A hard disk connected in this way is known as a 'file server', and software stored on it can normally be accessed from any of the connected machines.

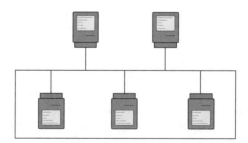

Figure 7.1 A typical 'closed' network

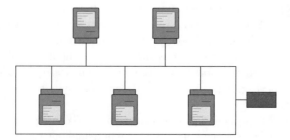

Figure 7.2 A 'closed' network with file server

The original small loop of cabling that joined company computers together may of course be extended, perhaps to take in further machines located elsewhere in the building. Additionally, a series of such network loops can themselves be linked together, or even (using telephone or other links) connected with machines and similar networks in different geographical locations. Although this wider connection may appear to be moving beyond the original definition of a closed network, the essential aspect of a closed system remains: how ever large a 'closed' system may become, no connection to machines outside the organisation is ever possible.

Information may also be made available on a closed network through utilisation of an *intranet*. A company intranet operates very much like a closed version of the World Wide Web in which an office computer running an ordinary Internet browser application (such as Netscape or Internet Explorer) accesses web 'pages'; in this case, however, all the available pages are maintained by the business network itself. Such an arrangement is of considerable potential value to a large business, for example in making up-to-date documentation readily available to large numbers of staff.

Both closed and open networks may need a 'server', which in this context is a dedicated computer used specifically to handle communications issues; the 'clients' are the individual desktop machines. Client–server communication is normally in the form of request and response messages – a client machine sends requests to the server and reads responses returned by the server. This dialogue permits, for example, the exchange of electronic mail, as well as other communications matters such as file transfers. For our purposes, the exact details of the request and response formats are of less importance than the fact that they occur. It is particularly important to note that in these circumstances communications are invisibly handled by a computer that exists outside the direct control of the user.

Closed networks, then, are those where anything from two to a potentially very large number of computers are linked together. The size of the network and the physical location of the involved computers are irrelevant, provided that no link has been made that extends communication beyond the limits of the organisation concerned.

Ethical issues in closed networks

As was discussed earlier, it must be remembered that, to ensure effective operation, all computer networks must be technically administered, or serviced. By definition, the individual carrying out such administrative duties has to be allowed complete control of 'their' system.

As was described in Chapter 6, the administrators of business systems can access, view, print and save any data held by their machines. They can monitor, create and destroy files, and have the power to electronically 'become' any of their users, after which they are able to behave as if that person's data were their own. These major, and generally unpublicised, administrator powers inevitably mean that any individual business user of a company network must be totally reliant upon the ethical views of their company's technical administrator. Regardless of the individual opinions of staff members, if the administrator holds a relaxed view on the examination of electronic data, for example, their invisible decisions can potentially mean that no company file can be private, and no electronic mail safe.

If an organisation has not established clear rules and guidelines, there is little beyond an individual sense of responsibility to prevent any network administrator misusing their privileges. It cannot be overemphasised that such misuse may always remain quite invisible to individual users and managers, who may continue to be quite unaware of any external interference with their data.

All networks need to be governed by a clear code of conduct that not only sets out the responsibilities of the users of business computers but also clarifies the accountability of those technical staff who have been given the task of maintaining the computer network.

Sometimes, however, a company may itself rely on unethical network systems administration:

A computer specialist was employed by a medium-sized company, principally to support its network and electronic mail. It became clear that the technical director, who had originally set up the mail system, maintained a log of all e-mail messages and made copies of all private mail of interest to him. The specialist learned that he was expected to continue monitoring mail (although, interestingly, he was told not to actually read it himself), and to pass on copies of mail from and to selected employees.

Monitoring of electronic mail of the sort experienced by the specialist in this case is extremely dubious. However, if in special circumstances it was felt to be essential, management should at least be open about the practice. Secret monitoring of network use is hard to justify ethically.

As was discussed in Chapter 5, networked computer systems in small companies may, in practice, actually be the responsibility of unqualified staff. Understandably, such staff may not possess detailed technical knowledge and may also have other obligations. In these circumstances, it may be difficult to ensure that company systems are administered appropriately. A smaller business may also find it hard to justify the need for any official policies on computer use. However, whatever the size of the company, the ethical issues concerned in computer use, and the responsibility of company management, remain the same. The appropriate use of company networks always needs to be considered.

It may be appropriate to state specifically that the ethical issues involved in monitoring of networks are clear – users of closed network systems need to be aware of any external oversight of their work. It is both insufficient and impractical to leave such issues undefined in the hope that the individuals concerned may eventually work something out for themselves. In all circumstances, it is the responsibility of management to clarify company expectations of employee behaviour.

Open networks

As would be expected, an 'open' network provides all the resources of a closed network system, but with a significant added link. This link, normally made through an Internet service provider (ISP), gives an additional channel allowing onward communication to the Internet – and hence to other computers and networks throughout the world.

Figure 7.3 illustrates a typical arrangement. The original computer (or closed network) located at (A) establishes links with a 'proxy server' (B). This server can act as a local store of external information to prevent frequent reloading of the same data. It is directly controlled by company (A), which may monitor and set limits on its use. The use of a proxy server has an additional positive role, in providing a 'fire wall', helping to prevent attacks by external 'hackers' on company systems.

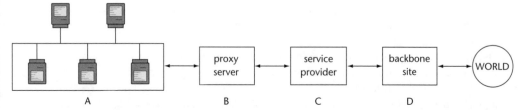

Figure 7.3 A typical 'open' network

In turn, this server is connected to an external 'service provider'. There has been an explosive growth in service providers – companies that exist in order to sell Internet connections. They are very roughly analogous to those businesses who sell portable telephones, and who, without themselves owning a telephone network, arrange connection to one of the mobile telephone networks. The activities of an external 'service provider' are beyond the immediate control of those individuals and companies who purchase their services, and even further beyond the individual user of a company computer.

All Internet service providers must make a further connection, to a national 'backbone site'; this site (which is under the control of a different set of administrators) is directly connected to the wider Internet. Except in the case of a single user, this series of network links is always followed. A single user is unlikely to have their own local network, so the proxy stage is often omitted. Personal computer and small company users instead normally establish a direct link to their service provider, generally by telephoning a special modem number. There are several important points to be made about such Internet-connected business systems.

First, all inherent problems and issues that were discussed in connection with closed network systems are equally valid here. Open network systems face additional problems, but all the original difficulties are still in place. Second, it is essential to appreciate that normal Internet connections – for example, those which take place between a desktop machine and a remote World Wide Web site – must *inevitably* mean that both requests and data pass through a whole series of different stages. At each one of these stages, there may potentially be interference with the transmitted data; it may be copied or distorted, and onward transmission may even be refused.

The principal important 'staging posts' for the transmission of electronic data are marked on Figure 7.3. They are:

- Internal company network
- Company proxy server
- Internet service provider
- Backbone site.

The technical implications that these stages have in the appropriate use of company computer networks are discussed below.

Ethical issues in open networks

Internet-linked business computers are used for many tasks. For example, we may often have a situation where an individual company user may wish to access and view a World

Wide Web site located in another country. Figure 7.3 shows the staging posts that request and data must pass through; but what does 'passing through' this succession of links actually mean in practice?

First, only the original desktop computer is under the direct control of the user. (In the case of a company computer network, even this may not be true.) All other stages in the connection of user to Internet are, inevitably, dependent upon others. This means that the stages through which data passes may be controlled and influenced by factors external to the user. Further, such control can be, and normally is, invisible. This is a central point of considerable significance and is worth emphasising. To a user, when 'their' computer requests and receives data from a remote machine, it may appear that the entire operation is under their personal control. It is not. Instead, the flow of data is invisibly controlled by others.

Second, because access to the Internet automatically involves access to, and distribution of, information and data, it is important to appreciate that a user's *specific* access may well be limited or controlled. This control may, again, be carried out invisibly – without the knowledge or consent of the Internet user.

Third, technical limitations inherent in a networked system can themselves restrict access. For example, there is a straightforward relationship between the volume of traffic carried by a network and its functional efficiency. The dramatic growth of Internet traffic has resulted in difficulties in speed and access for many users. Such problems – despite increases in network bandwidth – can only grow worse. The demands of increasingly large numbers of new Internet users are compounded by technical advances, such as the bandwidth demands of full-motion Internet video. Routing algorithms and hardware decisions taken to offset these problems must inevitably affect individual users.

Specific issues

So far, I have discussed the way in which a simple closed network is controlled and have examined the stages through which information must pass when a closed network becomes 'open' through an onward connection to the wider Internet. We will now look briefly at each of the four main levels of network control, at each stage identifying specific points that may repay further ethical investigation.

Local network management

A local network administrator has the ability to access, modify and delete all files of all local users. It is obviously important that the responsible company managers have clearly defined their expectations of their administrators, and that individual administrators are working within clear and understandable rules and guidelines. Further, it is essential that users of the networked system are aware of measures that are taken to control the system they use. This means that they should be told, for example, if specific monitoring procedures are in place. As discussed below, silently logging a list of World Wide Web sites accessed by staff members, for instance, is trivially easy. While it is reasonable for a company to ensure that its technical resources are not being used to support the private interests of its staff, secret monitoring and logging of staff access to web sites may be hard to justify ethically.

Proxy server

A proxy server is basically an electronic way of ensuring that a local site does not need to repeatedly request the same information from a remote computer. It does this by itself storing copies of everything requested by local users, and then, when further user requests are made, by checking to see if a copy of the required information is already available locally. The volume of information actually stored by the proxy server normally varies according to the size of the available storage. As well as providing rapid local access to frequently requested information, a proxy server may also act as a cut-out between a company network and the Internet, providing a secure line of defence against hacker access. A proxy server is normally under the control of local technical staff in exactly the same way that they oversee and maintain the local computer network.

The logging of staff access to web sites is possible because a local proxy server has the ability to keep a detailed log file of its operations – so that, as mentioned earlier, monitoring of the exact nature of Internet access made by company staff is consequently trivially easy. However, should employers monitor this information? James Derk works for the Indiana-based *Evansville Courier*. His views, posted to an Internet news group, are those of a concerned and informed professional:

> The original post [on the subject of newsroom Internet monitoring] said nothing about reading personal E-mail. It talked about looking in the Netscape cache, which I agreed was potentially slimy. However it is certainly less an invasion of privacy – on a company owned computer – than reading E-mail, which I can't condone under any circumstances. It's also dreadfully easy.[2]

Netscape is an Internet browser, that is an application used to access World Wide Web pages. Unknown to many users, Netscape (and other such browser applications) maintains its own version of a cache, essentially a disk directory, on the user's hard disk, where the browser keeps duplicates of all images requested by the user. Anyone with access to the application, or the disk, can potentially view this cache and is therefore able to find out exactly what images have been viewed.

Company oversight of employee network use, whether by studying a Netscape cache or local proxy records, is clearly an ethical issue; but there is an additional way in which a local proxy may be used to control individual users. This is by forbidding them access to certain sites that are felt 'unsuitable'. This restriction is directly comparable with the employment, by an individual user, of an application such as 'Net Nanny' (one of a number of commercial applications that interfere with the operation of an Internet browser). Individual network users may wish to prevent, for example, their children accessing pornography. Restriction of this sort, whether by employer or parent, is understandable, and may be perfectly justifiable, with certain provisos. Not the least important proviso is that the censoring process is 'open' and the justification for it made clear.

However, use of nanny-type applications may not be without further ethical problems. Recent disturbing allegations concerning the nature of these programs have emerged from the USA. Commercial gate-keeping applications must, inevitably, contain a list of 'forbidden' Internet sites and news groups, those which they consider should not be accessed. Although this information is coded, following a 'hacker' cracking, lists for most of the popular gate-keeping applications have been revealed. It appears that lists of forbidden sites may not be limited to pornography. Political and other censorship may also be taking place, censorship that is all the more disturbing because it is hidden.

Whether it is true or not – I have been assured of its truth by a respected US journalist – this case illustrates the relevance of ethical oversight. Use of guardian applications and control of local proxy hosts surely need informed consideration and evaluation.

Service provider issues

Internet service providers (ISPs) simply act as distribution points (and collection points) for Internet data. They are in effect acting as clearing houses for information, and, as commercial services, have to convince customers that their provision is preferable to that of another company. Because the service itself – Internet connection – is virtually identical, service providers have to maintain a distinction in other ways. The chief ethical problem that they face is probably that of the distribution of 'pornography' and other material perceived by some as inappropriate.

Here ISPs are in a classic cleft stick, bound to upset some customers whatever their choice. If they operate a restricted service, forbidding access to 'undesirable' web sites and refusing to relay 'inappropriate' Internet news groups (such as the infamous alt.sex. hierarchy), then a large proportion of prospective customers, aware of the free speech ethos of the Internet, will just go elsewhere. On the other hand, if such material is made freely available, then the provider is liable to be the focus of public anger, and perhaps legal action.

For example, in February 1996, the state prosecutors of Bavaria and Baden-Württemburg were concerned over Internet dissemination of neo-Nazi Ernst Zuendel's views. The major international ISP CompuServe, under threat for providing access, responded by preventing its German subscribers from viewing certain Usenet news groups. Unfortunately, as there was no easy way of screening out German users from everyone else, this action affected CompuServe's subscribers globally and resulted in massive protest. However, despite the enormous inconvenience that CompuServe's attempted censorship caused, the attempt to block access completely could not have worked without also closing down the whole of Deutsche Telekom. German users could otherwise just use ordinary modems and standard voice lines to access any alternative ISP, in any country.

Of course, viewing censorship as a solution to network information problems is not limited to sensitive German authorities. As *Guardian* journalist Jack Schofield put it:

> The problem with censoring the Internet is that somebody somewhere objects to almost everything. If local German authorities can remove all the right wing content, and all the pornography, then why shouldn't the Chinese remove all traces of capitalism? Why shouldn't American fundamentalist states ban any sites concerned with evolution? Why shouldn't the Vatican demand the removal of all references to birth control? Indeed, a few countries with radical views could quickly remove all religious, scientific and economic debate from the Internet, then all we'd need is a militant vegetarian state to finish things off.[3]

If outright banning is not possible, what about monitoring and checking data to ensure that no illicit material is being conveyed? Sadly, this too is impossible. Searching the enormous quantity of data that flows through an average ISP is not currently remotely practical – even expensive routers can hardly keep up with forwarding the data. There is certainly no spare capacity to comb traffic for suspect material, even if the inevitable delays that this would cause were acceptable. It is barely possible that this situation may change as technology develops further, although so far use of the Internet is increasing at a far faster rate than technological development.

A further ethical problem is related to the 'permission' that ISPs automatically give to their customers to use the Internet, more specifically the ability that this provides to send limitless quantities of electronic mail easily. Some of this mail is merely uninformed, and annoying to other users. However, some is intended purely for commercial purposes, and sent very widely – 'spamming', in netspeak. Traditionally, the Internet has had a non-commercial philosophy, but even the most tolerant of users can very rapidly grow tired of endless junk e-mail. Can such proliferation of mail be controlled? Perhaps not easily, although one contributor to a discussion on the UK government's ethics mailing list felt it might, by hitting the ISPs where it hurt:

> I do see a role for contractual sanctions after the event however. I would suggest that writing an enforceable contract with financial penalties for say, unsolicited commercial email, or commercial spam would be quite straightforward. If enough ISP's took the position that such activities were a no-no, those that continued to allow them could simply be declared rogue. If any one who connected through them couldn't access any major services, they wouldn't last long.[4]

Acting as the focus for users to obtain access to the Internet, ISPs perhaps inevitably provide a focus for ethical debate, too. Their responsibilities to the communities they serve, the wider population and the Internet itself have not yet been the subject of informed debate. Such debate is perhaps overdue.

'Backbone site' issues

All practical aspects of operating a national backbone site are related to keeping it operational. Several times, speaking to those involved I was told that the issue is not how to analyse or monitor transmitted data but how to keep the system running at all. Backbone sites are very much at the hard edge of technological network development and are even less open to monitoring and control than ISPs. As discussed above, the only viable option open to a government intent on control of the Internet would be to close down its entire communications system – an impossible choice, given the dependence of modern society on international networking thorough Internet links. Even then, the action would be comparable to sawing off a small branch in an attempt to fell a large tree.

Summary

Appreciation of technical issues involved in the connection of business computers to the Internet is important, not least because much of the mechanics is invisible to a typical user. In this section, I have therefore examined the stages through which an individual business user may obtain access to the Internet, discussing in particular the technical underpinning to Internet use by networked business computers. Looking first at the mechanics of setting up a 'closed' network, I urged that the role of a network administrator is considered carefully, and that their supervision of 'their' network is carried out under clearly defined rules and expectations. The particular importance of appropriate direction being given to those technical staff who have responsibility for developing and maintaining the system was emphasised.

I then looked at the expanding of 'closed' networks into 'open' ones – networks with an onward connection to the wider Internet. The part played by a proxy server, which provides an essential link between networks, was significant here. A specific issue was the use made of data passing through a company-owned server – particularly data monitoring by employers – and ways in which a proxy server might be used to monitor the use of a company Internet connection.

Finally, I looked at the part played in network communication by ISPs – Internet service providers. They admittedly have a difficult task, in facilitating their customers' access to Internet material while, potentially, limiting access too. The way in which this is done is clearly of importance. It is certainly ethically dubious to secretly restrict users from obtaining desired links, particularly if the censorship is carried out under a political agenda.

The technical background having now been established, we will now move on to look specifically at business uses of the Internet itself.

The Internet

Despite the incredible popularity of the World Wide Web, it is important to remember that there are two distinct – but relevant – aspects of the Internet. These are the Web itself and Internet *news groups*. Although the influence of the Web is now both significant and still growing rapidly, consideration of the far longer-established Internet news groups is also appropriate. Both areas are considered separately, before a concluding discussion.

Most business people today probably consider the 'Internet' to be very much the same thing as the graphically based World Wide Web. However, the Web is actually superimposed on another, long-standing aspect of the Internet. This is the original, text-based Internet, which has for many years offered a range of varied possibilities to business. For our purposes, however, it is reasonable to assume that business use of text-based Internet services will consist principally of news groups and electronic mail.

There are consequently at least four different potential business uses of the Internet:

- text use, though electronic mail
- text use, through postings to news groups
- graphical use, through access to the World Wide Web
- graphical use, through hosting of a World Wide Web site

The Internet is huge, the variety of information and opportunities that it offers is vast, and there are many more possibilities for business inherent in Internet use. However, these four aspects are likely to continue to be the most important, and analysis of their use will allow sufficient attention to ethical issues.

Text – electronic mail

'E-mail' is essentially an electronic message generated on one computer and transmitted to another. The two machines may be situated on adjoining desks, or, potentially, on different continents.

To employ e-mail, a user just needs a computer, connected with suitable software to a network. Normally, a person sending e-mail types a letter, which may possibly include other computer files as 'enclosures'. When finished, it is 'posted' (via a networked mail system) to the recipient's e-mail address. On a 'closed' business network, only local e-mail addresses, or addresses within that organisation, are valid. In contrast, an electronic message from an 'open' network may, literally, be dispatched to any suitable electronic address anywhere in the world, with no more difficulty than sending a message to the next office.

Potential problems with electronic mail

There are two possible areas of difficulty – problems caused inadvertently, and those caused deliberately.

Most inadvertent problems are caused by lack of thought and ignorance of the expectations of other Internet users. Electronic text has limited bandwidth – unlike other forms of human communication, there are no expressions, no tone of voice, no non-verbal cues, no handwriting style, and so on. The combination of the limited bandwidth allowed by electronic text and the casual nature of many messages can all too easily cause the recipient of a message to misunderstand its meaning. This is a particular risk if a message has been composed and sent quickly, or perhaps in a fit of annoyance. Electronic text gives little opportunity for feedback – unlike a verbal conversation, perhaps on the telephone, there can be no cue to the meaning of a message in the tone of voice of a caller, and initial misunderstandings cannot be corrected rapidly.

The immediacy of electronic communication also contrasts with the familiar experience of paper-based letter writing. The time and effort needed to prepare and send traditional paper-based messages tends to reduce the chance of accidental misunderstandings. For example, writing, addressing and mailing a paper letter in response to a temporary annoyance involves many more stages, and is far more difficult, than sending e-mail, while the rapid generation and dispatch of electronic mail inevitably means that misunderstandings are likely. It is therefore important that the sender of an e-mail message is always certain that the text actually reflects what they want to say, and that they are content to be associated with its style and manner – and sure that the organisation they represent would also be satisfied.

A business that gives staff the ability to send global electronic mail should give thought to the potential difficulties should the opportunity be misused. Written guidelines are clearly relevant here; a sample set of such guidelines is given later in this chapter.

Apart from those problems caused by a lack of knowledge in e-mail use, there is a further category of difficulties – those caused by a deliberate misuse of the facilities offered by electronic mail. Chief amongst these are security and 'spamming'.

Figure 7.4 User view of e-mail routing

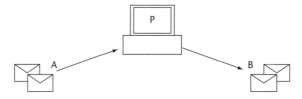

Figure 7.5 A typical e-mail routing

E-mail problems – security

Many business users of electronic mail treat its use as they would paper mail. Specifically, from years of Post Office experience, they believe that once a letter is sealed and posted, its contents will normally remain confidential. In electronic terms, this is not necessarily so. For example, consider the case of e-mail sent directly from one user to another. Such mail is, in theory, confidential to them both. While the superficial arrangements may differ for sender and recipients, e-mail appears to pass directly from one to the other, as in Figure 7.4. What actually happens, however, is normally slightly more complex: the electronic mail actually passes through at least one mail host or *mail server* – basically, a dedicated computer used to handle mail transfers. This gives a different picture of electronic mail distribution. In practice, in most company computer networks, distribution is more like that in Figure 7.5, where 'P' represents the mail server computer.

Should A and B actually be located in different companies, then mail will almost certainly pass through two mail servers; longer links may involve additional mail servers as well. This distinction is important because, once it is understood that there is always at least one *intermediary* stage between A and B, it can readily be appreciated that any message from A can in practice be intercepted. A message that is apparently from A can even be triggered by someone else, provided that they are able to persuade the relevant post machine to generate a suitable message header. A totally new message may thus be created, a message that looks to a recipient exactly as though it was created by a particular user, even though that user may never have seen it.

Interception and false generation of mail in this way can easily be done by anyone with the ability to carry out simple commands, and either the authorisation to do so or the ability to 'hack' access instead. It may happen at any point where the message from A is relayed to B through a mail host. (In the case of false messages, it can take place literally anywhere).

It is also true that electronic mail can be stored and referenced in ways that are impossible with paper communications. Potentially, this means that an unguarded piece of electronic mail can be circulated, or published, or even produced years later, at the most embarrassing time.

```
MSG FROM: NSOLN --CPUA TO: NSJMP --CPUA 06/16/86 23:21:27
To: NSJMP --CPUA
```

*** Reply to note of 06/05/86 15:15

NOTE FROM: OLIVER NORTH
Subject: HOSTAGES
It wd be helpful for you, I think, to hear from LtG Moellering and
Dewey on this before they do something rash and this thing leaks.
Had set a 15min mtg w/ you for last week and we had to scrub for
a conflict. Both Dewey and Moellering out of town after 1300 Weds.
Can Iset a time w/ Flo btwn now and then - 20min max? FOLLOW ON TO
OUR MARITIES[?] DISC.: Have just returned from 1 hr mtg. w/
McCurdy. Bottom line: All items negotiable except absolute minimum
on aid to CentAm Democracies will probably work out to abt. 300M
- well down from his earlier $500M. He agrees keeping NHAC will
not work and is willing to give on issues such as timimg of weaps
deliveries, etc. Basically he just wants someone to pay attention
to him. He wants to keep role as "broker" btwn conservatives/
liberals and Dems/Reps. At bottom is ego. It might be worth it to
have me tell him that a mtg w/ you might be possible if he becomes
more reasonable on things such as second votes, etc. pls protect
my mtg from our legislative folks. They will go crazy. Stay tuned
to Israeli TV - should be good if it lives up to advance billing.
Warm regards & good night.
North BT
HOSTAGES

Example of electronic mail – © 1995 The National Security Archive[5]

Clearly, while electronic mail may appear to be ephemeral, it is potentially extremely
long-lived.

E-mail problems – 'spamming'

Sending electronic mail is very easy, and costs are very low. It was probably not long after
the Internet was created before the commercial possibilities of the new electronic
medium became obvious and the first commercial postings were made. Today such postings are in their millions, and the selling of lists of e-mail addresses is a business in itself.

In strong contrast to the situation with postal charges and paper junk mail, the theory
runs that it is worth sending out 10,000 messages advertising your product, even if only
one recipient responds. If one person in 20,000 is stupid enough to send you money in
response to a pyramid scheme, the trouble caused to the other 19,999 is, in junk mailing
terms, well worthwhile.

Such bulk e-mailing is known in netspeak as 'spamming', after an old Monty Python
sketch. Spamming is very anti-social, and most Internet service providers are likely to
terminate the access of those who use it. However, the potential rewards are felt to be sufficiently attractive to encourage repeated bulk e-mailing; much Internet traffic is thus
composed of unwanted messages, which are inevitably to be thrown away. Legislation to
prevent commercial spam is being enacted in some areas, the most interesting so far
being the state of Washington.

The Washington anti-spam law prohibits 'the sending of commercial electronic mail messages that use a third party's Internet domain name without the third party's permission, misrepresent the message's point of origin, or contain untrue or misleading information in the subject line.' Messages must be sent from a computer located in Washington state or to a resident of Washington state, and the law places the burden of determining residency on the senders of unsolicited commercial e-mail.

It is very probable that other, similar, legislation will follow in other jurisdictions, but in the meantime, most users of the Internet will continue to be forced to cope with junk e-mail.

Essentially, e-mail needs to be used with care; and, in particular, it is very foolish to depend upon the security of electronic mail. If e-mail passes through public channels, it must have limited use for items like company-confidential materials. Furthermore, there can be no guarantees against external or even 'inside' snooping, for example by a competing member of staff in your office, or a rival division, or even by one's own management.

Sending commercial 'spam' e-mail may seem potentially attractive as a marketing tactic but is unlikely to prove a sensible longer-term option.

Text – news groups

Internet news groups are a long-established method of sharing information between interested individuals. News groups function in a similar way to electronic mail, in that 'messages' are sent to them; however, these messages (which may include encoded files and pictures) are not received as mail but instead deliberately accessed by interested individuals through a 'news reader' application. This application displays what is, in effect, an electronic 'bulletin board', where all available messages are displayed, arranged in specialised groups. Internet news groups really do cover the whole range of human activity, including every imaginable, and unimaginable, sexual variation. Posting of colour images, and even video, is common; once a news group is accessed, downloading information from it is very simple.

Not all news groups are available everywhere; indeed, virtually all ISPs forward only a subset of the tens of thousands of available groups to their downstream users – so a company may therefore wish to restrict those groups available to staff members by selecting an appropriate ISP. How many news groups exist? My university, Kent, currently offers only 4,349 groups, while a typical UK ISP offers 29,000. An attempt to determine (by asking Internet specialists throughout the world) exactly how many groups were currently available produced figures ranging from 30,000 to 100,000 – the reality is that no one is actually sure.

International Internet connections are complex, and news group messages are continuously circulated. When a site receives new messages, it checks to see if the news group is accepted locally, and if other details (such as the expiry date) are appropriate. If all is well, a copy of the data is made available to those using the site, while the same information is also passed on to 'downstream' Internet sites. Millions of messages are continuously being circulated around the Internet in this way.

As 'posting' an article simply involves sending mail to the electronic address of a relevant news group, there is no restriction whatever on what may be posted. Although some news groups are 'moderated', where a human acts as a filter for postings, the huge majority have no such control. Whatever is posted to a news group is therefore automatically distributed and is available at every Internet site subscribing to the relevant group. As I have said elsewhere, posting to an Internet news group is consequently the nearest thing on Earth to absolute free speech.

There are similar risks here to those discussed above in relation to the use of electronic mail. In particular, it is important that the wording of publicly posted items does not give offence. This is particularly important where the message originates from a known commercial organisation, which may otherwise be perceived as supporting the views expressed by a member of its staff.

It is possible to distribute junk postings to news groups in a way similar to the posting of 'spam', but for obvious reasons this is not normally seen as such a serious problem.

Posting guidelines

In sending electronic messages and news group postings[6]

1 Create single-subject messages whenever possible. This makes your meaning clearer, and if your message is to be forwarded, the process is simplified.

2 Assume that any message you send is permanent. How ever temporary you may consider your mail ought to be, you cannot dictate this view to your audience, who may keep it indefinitely.

3 Have in mind a model of your intended audience. Make sure that the language you use (for example, the use of slang) is appropriate; always keeping in mind the people who will read your e-mail helps in writing it.

4 Keep the list of recipients and cc's to a minimum. Do what you can to minimise unwanted e-mail.

5 Separate opinion from non-opinion, and clearly label each. If challenged, you should always be able to adequately defend what you have written. Unjustified speculation can be expensive.

6 If you must express emotion in a message, clearly label it.

7 Other content labels are useful. 'Spoilers' and 'smilies' help to indicate what you have in mind.

8 Think about the level of formality you put in a message. The importance given to a message by recipients is likely to be in proportion to the attention and care taken to produce it.

9 Identify yourself and your affiliations clearly. A message may come from virtually anywhere or anyone, so readers of your e-mail need to know who you are. The absence of a printed letterhead means that your message must contain sufficient data to 'place' you appropriately.

10 Be selective in broadcasts for information. Posting general queries to inappropriate news groups uses net bandwidth, annoys users and generally does not work. Select a news group carefully to obtain the best response to a query, and do not post unnecessarily – someone else may have just asked the same question.

11 Do not insult or criticise third parties without giving them a chance to respond.

Graphical – access to the World Wide Web

The World Wide Web (WWW), graphically based and consequently very visual in nature, is inherently easy to use. In structure, it can be considered as a static approach to service provision. Here, instead of the contents of a news group being constantly transmitted around the world, an individual uses freely available software to establish direct contact with a site containing desired information and specifically accesses it. A great advantage of this approach is that web sites are easily connected to each other. A user may, by clicking buttons on their personal computer's screen, move between the display of web pages in different countries – or different continents – without realising that they are doing more than accessing the next page of data. As is discussed below, communication may be two-way: companies and individuals can establish their own 'web sites'; any connected computer can then download and read the presented information. Access to web sites is very easy indeed – they form the simplest way of accessing electronic information and have played a large part in the recent enormous growth of the Internet.

Although their purposes – access to desired information – may seem similar, Internet web sites and Internet news groups are very different. The circulating messages that comprise a news group have no 'real' location and cannot therefore be said to exist in any one place, while a web site must, by definition, have a unique home address.

There are considerable commercial advantages to be gained by making good use of World Wide Web availability. It enables easy access to a huge amount of information, much of which would not normally be available at all.

Problems with World Wide Web access

Many tens of thousands of World Wide Web sites exist, and numbers are increasing exponentially. Most such sites are well designed and well conducted – but there are some web sites, for example, which exist to distribute pornography, both hard and soft, as well as those devoted to propagating extremist political views. All that is needed to view them is the correct electronic address.

The main problems for businesses in allowing their staff access to the World Wide Web are likely to be the issues of inappropriate access and an unacceptably large amount of time being devoted to Web 'surfing'. Clearly, the viewing of pornography is unlikely to be considered an appropriate use of business resources by most companies. However, as such viewing may be very easy, it is insufficient to simply assume that staff will not make use of company computer equipment to gain access. At least a definition of what the company considers 'appropriate' could be of help; a detailed conditions-of-use policy would be even more useful.

Graphical – hosting of a World Wide Web site

When a user is viewing a World Wide Web site, only the content and quality of the pages are visible, rather than the size of the supporting company. This means that, provided the quality of their Web pages is high enough, the use of a World Wide Web site gives even tiny companies the ability to compete on equal terms with major international businesses.

To 'host' a World Wide Web site, typically a company either uses space on the computers of its Internet service provider or it uses its own machines. Pages may contain full-colour photographs and illustrations, sound, and even video; the actual material consists of a mix of text and image files. The exact nature of these files will vary according to the sophistication of the site, but, although a full range of options can be expensive, a very acceptable appearance can be made with very simple tools. Once an attractive presentation has been developed, the principal need of a site is probably for speed of connection – the faster the connection to the Internet, the more rapidly potential customers and others may view material, and the more likely they are to visit the site again.

Unlike the distribution of similar material by traditional means, Internet publication costs are minimal, while, once connection has been obtained, 'transport' costs are virtually non-existent. It is also true that all Internet publication is, potentially, to the world.

The advantages of hosting a World Wide Web site are therefore considerable, and obvious. Advertising and direct interactive contact with clients and customers, actual and potential, is readily possible. Traditionally dull information, such as company reports, may be presented in an attractive format, and users may be given a choice of selecting their own paths through the data. Sales information may be kept not only highly visible but constantly up to date – and the Internet marketplace is automatically international. It is no surprise that today virtually every large business – and many smaller ones – advertise their presence on the Internet.

World Wide Web problems

As the Internet is an inherently international entity, it cannot be controlled by national regulation. There consequently may be no outside legal control of the contents of World Wide Web sites, and no international advertising standards authority to keep an eye on inappropriate claims or inappropriate material.

In practice, such lack of controls means, for example, that valuable company data, perhaps collected at considerable expense, may be 'pirated' for display on another site. The ability of international linking between sites can and does tempt unauthorised and unwanted links to company information – this is a particular problem for web-based news services but it is not restricted to them. Lack of external oversight and control can lead to many other potential problems.

Oversight is difficult, as World Wide Web pages are not distributed around the Internet in the same way as text messages – web pages must have a permanent physical location, and users must always have the specific address of a specific computer in order to access World Wide Web information. While initially this may seem to allow easy external oversight, there are overwhelming problems facing a would-be censor or legislator. While web pages can be accessed from anywhere in the world, they may be directly controlled only by the ISP that hosts them; and such hosting can be physically located anywhere in the world, too.

In practice, this means that it is trivially easy, for example, for a British or American company to have a World Wide Web site located on a computer in South America or Asia, and therefore subject only to local legislation. The actual content of the individual web pages may naturally be sent to the host machine electronically; there is consequently no need for the 'owner' ever to physically visit their site, or even to be on the same continent.

In the absence of international law, it will be seen that direct control of World Wide Web pages must rely on direct control of their host computers; so, unless these computers *physically* lie within the sphere of the concerned authority, no control is possible. A useful analogy is that of telephone sex lines. When banned locally, such lines do not vanish; they add several digits and become located elsewhere.

While there are signs that this state of affairs is changing, for technical reasons it is unlikely to change soon. In the meantime, users should be aware of the risks involved in establishing a World Wide Web site. These include, but are not limited to, the following:

1 Data piracy.
2 Publication of inaccurate or deliberately erroneous material.
3 Inappropriate linking.
4 Trademarks and domain name 'passing off'.
5 Wider issues.

Data piracy

Material included on a web site may be easily copied by others, and readily used or distributed without permission. This is a particularly sensitive issue when valuable copyrighted illustrations or even company trademarks are duplicated in this way. The experiences of the owners of newspaper cartoon strips, such as UFS's *Dilbert*, or photographic images, like those from Viacom's *Star Trek*, for example, show that the risk of such illegal use is very real.

Publication of inaccurate or deliberately erroneous material

As the act of setting up a World Wide Web site is very easy, it is open to individuals to publicise what they may see as their mistreatment by a large organisation by publishing information setting out their side of the case. Such data may well be inaccurate, but this will not prevent potential global distribution. Those businesses prepared to publish misleading claims, either in favour of their own products or in order to denigrate competitors, are able to do so. The general public may well be unaware of a need for caution in viewing such information.

Inappropriate linking

Once a World Wide Web site has been established, the expectation of its owners is surely that visitors will access the contained material. This is usually done in one of two ways: either through user location of the site via a web search engine, such as Alta Vista or HotBot, or by following a direct link from another web site. In the second case, it is technically easy for the displayed material of site B to appear to have been made available by site A. If a link to material on site B is surrounded by site A graphics and text, the real nature of the link may not be clear to a potential viewer. One interesting example consisted of two web-based newspapers; stories in one were accessible through headline buttons in the other.[7]

Trademarks and domain name 'passing off'

'Domain names' are used by all World Wide Web sites, and personalised versions are especially valuable to business. Such labels as <www.ford.com> or

<www.parliament.the-stationery-office.co.uk> make the identities of Web sites clear to a viewer. For some time, though, many companies did not appreciate that such domain names could be registered by individuals or companies unconnected with the named business. Such unconnected registration has led to many problems, and several court cases. For example, one dissatisfied customer of telecommunications giant BT – whose own web site was registered as <www.bt.com> – claimed that his company's telephones would not work and alleged that he lost business as a result. He subsequently established a new web site, registered under the domain name <www.british-telecom.com>, which not only contained content critical of BT but invited users to post negative stories about their experiences with the company. The reactions of some major companies to the activities of those whom they perceive as 'passing off' may sometimes seem excessive. See, for example, Appendix 3 for the 'Toys 'R' Us'/'Roadkills-R-Us' conflict.

Trademarks are used throughout the word to identify companies and products. Understandably, they are widely used on World Wide Web pages – not always by the company that owns them. This has led to a significant number of trademark allegations involving the Internet, perhaps because activity on the Internet and the World Wide Web is so easy to monitor. While previously the owner of a trademark in London would probably be unaware of what might be happening to their mark in Tennessee, the abilities offered by Internet search engines allow trademark owners to undertake a complete Internet search for users of their marks in a matter of seconds. Consequently, more trademark infringements (whether unintentional or otherwise) are being discovered by trademark owners.

It has been suggested[8] that this ease of discovery may be a two-edged sword for trademark owners, because one of the obligations of a trademark owner is to police use of their mark, so the ease of Internet searching may be placing the requirement on trademark owners to police the Internet routinely. If an infringer of a mark is known to the trademark owner (or should have been known through routine diligence) and is allowed to go unchallenged, the trademark owner could lose their trademark.

Wider issues

It is important to appreciate that although international regulation may not yet be a possibility, there are many legal safeguards on the use of the Internet within Europe and the UK. These aspects cover issues such as copyright and intellectual property rights, libel and slander issues, and data protection. Legal matters are addressed directly in Chapter 8.

Conclusion

This chapter began by looking at what computer 'networking' actually means in practice, studying in particular the technical aspects of computer networking. Moving from local ('closed') to Internet-connected ('open') networks, it examined just what is involved in the passing of data over networked links. This identified potential problems, especially of data security, and clarified the responsibilities of technical staff. The role and responsibilities of the local network manager, in particular, was considered especially significant.

Data moving from the Internet on to company machines is likely to pass through a company-controlled data store known as a 'proxy server'. Records automatically kept by this server potentially enable management to know exactly what uses are being made of Internet access by their staff. The ethics of such monitoring were considered in some detail.

Consideration of the role of an Internet service provider was then made, together with assessment of the thorny question of censorship, or blocking of materials considered inappropriate.

Discussion then moved from technical issues to the Internet itself. It was made clear that there are in practice both text and graphical aspects of the Internet, the text aspects principally consisting of electronic mail and news groups, while the World Wide Web contributes a graphical approach – which may also include text, sound and video.

The two aspects – text and World Wide Web – were then considered, first descriptively and then by looking at potential problems.

Electronic mail is not secure; this and other potential e-mail problems that might occur, such as the retention of ephemeral mail and the issue of 'junk mail', were also discussed. Text news postings broadly followed the same lines. The text section concluded with a list of suggested guidelines for text postings.

The final section of this chapter dealt with use of the World Wide Web, from the perspective both of a user and of a company wishing to 'host' its own World Wide Web site. There are very considerable advantages to World Wide Web use, but the difficulties resulting from a lack of effective international supervision do give rise to problems. These were discussed, and the section concluded with a short list of potential problems facing the managers of a company web site.

Discussion points

The following points are intended to form the basis for a class or seminar discussion on the issues raised in this chapter. They should not be considered until after the relevant sections have been read and thought through. As all questions have been carefully chosen to encourage debate, they are primarily intended to encourage thinking about the issues and are not necessarily capable of producing definitive answers.

1 Is the computer you use networked? If so, who do you think has access to your data? If you send e-mail to someone at the next desk, who could potentially view that mail?

2 Why does the administrator of a 'closed' company computer network need to be aware of ethical issues?

3 Does the situation change if the 'closed' network becomes an 'open' one? How?

4 Can you remember the stages through which data must normally pass from desktop computer to remote World Wide Web site? What particular issues might cause you concern over each of these stages?

5 What does a proxy server do? Why may its operation be of potential ethical concern?

6 Do you agree with company censorship of access to the Internet? If so, why? If not, why not?

7 What ethical problems can you foresee relating to the use of company electronic mail? Why is e-mail not necessarily secure?

8 The Iran hostages scandal, and the role of Col. Oliver North, were mentioned in this chapter. Why do you think Col. North used e-mail?

9 What is 'spamming'? What are your views on its business use?

10 Why are Internet news groups different from normal publishing media?

11 Do you feel that staff access to the World Wide Web should be limited? Provide support for your views, and, if possible, debate with someone who holds different opinions.

12 Why does a business 'host' a World Wide Web site? What are some potential problems?

13 A World Wide Web site contains false claims against your company's products. How might these claims be contested?

14 What does 'passing off' mean in relation to Internet domain names? What does the importance of Internet domain names signify to you? How, and why, might similar use in paper publication be different?

Notes

1 'PC' is used as a convenient shorthand to describe the typical business computer. As a confirmed Apple Macintosh user, I did not intend to imply an exclusive business use of IBM-compatible machines!

2 Investigative Reporters & Editors mailing list, <www.reporter.org>, 14 February 1996.

3 Guardian OnLine, 26 January 1996.

4 ethics@ccta.gov.uk, 26 April 1996.

5 This e-mail is taken from the fascinating book *White House E-Mail: The top secret computer messages the Reagan–Bush White House tried to destroy*, edited by Tom Blanton; The New Press, New York, 1995. ISBN 1-56584-276-6.

6 This list is adapted, with kind permission of the Rand Corporation, from the paper 'Toward an ethics and etiquette for electronic mail', Rand Corporation paper R-3283-NSF/RC, 1985. Despite its date, the paper is well worth reading in full.

7 The Shetland Times case. See, for example

`<http://www.news.com/News/Item/0,4,5924,00.html>`

or 'To link or not to link: Problems with World Wide Web links on the Internet' (1997) Akdeniz, Yaman, *Int. Review of Law, Computers and Technology* 11.

8 The Minnesota law firm of Beck & Tysver maintains a most interesting web site offering a comprehensive Internet resource on technology law issues. Recommended.

`<http://www.bitlaw.com/internet/trademarks.html>`

8

The law and business computer use

Within developed countries, uses of business computers are normally regulated by statute law, so it is clearly essential for companies to be aware of their legal responsibilities in the area of computing. Within the European Community (EC) there has been pressure for conformity in control over electronic business, culminating in the Data Protection Directive (95/46/EC). This directive was the driving force behind the UK's new 1998 Data Protection Act, as well as other national European legislation.

This chapter principally looks at regulatory law within the UK, giving attention to the 1984 Data Protection Act, the 1990 Misuse of Computers Act and especially the new 1998 Data Protection Act, which now largely replaces the familiar 1984 Data Protection Act.

Introduction

It is absolutely essential that both those responsible for the development and operation of business computer systems and those staff working with business computers have a good knowledge of relevant legislation. While such information may seem unnecessary or even irrelevant to some, there is an unanswerable justification – law breaking can, and almost certainly will, cause difficulties and expense for any business; and ignorance of the law has never been a defence against breaking it. For an individual, knowledge of relevant legislation is particularly important should a personal code of ethics cause conflict with others, perhaps with an employer. In order to decide if unlawful action may be appropriate, it is clearly essential to understand first exactly what is illegal and to appreciate possible consequences.

While, in most countries, much of the specialised use of computers in business is covered by a wide range of general legislation, specific computing laws are normally also in force. Within the United Kingdom, for example, there is a growing volume of specialised legislation relating to computer use. For those using business computer systems and working within the UK, some knowledge of the principal Acts of Parliament – the 1984 Data Protection Act, the 1990 Misuse of Computers Act and the 1998 Data Protection Act – is essential. European legislation in this area is becoming increasingly uniform, so knowledge of the latest UK legislation is normally a good guide to elsewhere in Europe. Nevertheless, appreciation of the appropriate European Union Data Protection Directives is also strongly advised. At the time of publication, the most recent EU directive is 95/46/ EC, and the (English language) text is accessible through the World Wide Web; this, and other relevant web addresses, are listed at the end of this chapter.

Development of new legislation

There is little practical purpose in legislating against activities that are only theoretically possible. Within the UK, therefore, activities not previously considered by legislators are consequently technically legal, whatever their unethical status might be. For example, while a vehicle pulled by horses was the standard, there were no speed limits. The spread of motor vehicles, far faster than horses, meant the eventual introduction of new laws restricting the speed of traffic. The advent and widespread use of computers within business led to the introduction of computer-related activities perhaps even less desirable than speeding.

The original 'number-crunching' uses of business computers were largely restricted to the replacement of existing time-consuming and labour-intensive manual systems, such as stock control and financial records. The first business computers were consequently being used in areas where the employment of similar manual systems had for many years been clearly understood, and there were correspondingly few problems. However, when in the 1960s the next generations of computers began to undertake and accomplish tasks that had not previously been practical, potential difficulties began to emerge. The growing availability of more affordable business systems additionally drew attention to computer-related actions that, although previously feasible, had until that time been both difficult and prohibitively expensive.

Consider, for example, the role of credit references in business. The credit-worthiness of an individual or company has always been of considerable importance to any business considering transactions with them. For centuries, the physical collecting and storage of credit information has been a widely used business resource; however, the manual collection, storage and subsequent analysis by hand of potentially huge volumes of relevant data is clearly difficult.

Originally, then, although the eventual results were of considerable inherent benefit to business, a credit-worthiness investigation was potentially very expensive and therefore normally limited in scale. Indeed, formal credit references were largely confined to large businesses; for others, 'bank references' were commonplace. In the case of a bank reference, the credit-worthiness of a company was essentially a simple function of the view that its bank took of it. Should this not accurately reflect the credit-worthiness of the business, it was unfortunate.

The widespread use of computer systems, and subsequent dramatic development of commercial databases, radically changed this situation. The possession of powerful computers allowed private companies to build and, more importantly, search, hundreds of thousands of individual records. Information from many different sources could be collected, stored and collated. Some of this data was understandably incomplete, some perhaps illegally obtained, some just plain wrong.

While similar sorts of data collection, using pen and paper, had undoubtedly taken place in the past, the focus and scale of manual systems were inevitably of much smaller dimensions than those of the new computerised versions. If credit rating by manual systems had not generally been perceived as a problem, in strong contrast the use of computers brought with it considerable associated difficulties. As it became simple to store and retrieve huge amounts of personal information, confidential references and similar private material could readily be collated, extracted and sold. Many companies understandably made use of this new ability, while specialist credit agencies were soon expressly formed to investigate and supply such data.

From an ethical point of view, the use of improperly obtained data – for instance, data that had been provided specifically for one purpose but used for another without the knowledge or consent of the person concerned – would normally be inappropriate, whether or not its use was illegal. However, before the introduction of legal restrictions, some business practitioners did not appear to feel constrained by either personal or business ethics. By the late 1970s and early 1980s, there was increasing public disquiet about the uses being made of electronically held personal data, both by specialised computerised credit reference agencies and by business generally. This disquiet, together with European political pressure, expressed in the 1981 Council of Europe Convention on Data Protection, was the immediate precursor of the 1984 Data Protection Act.

This new Act, the first ever UK legislation to deal expressly with the use of computers and electronically held data, reflected the government's desire to respond appropriately to electronic risks to individual privacy while supporting the free international flow of information within Europe. Interestingly, in the parliamentary debate on the Act (then a Bill), Lord Eton (under-secretary of state) said:

> The first [purpose] is to protect private individuals from the threat of the use of erroneous information about them, held on computers. The second is to provide that protection in a form that will enable us to satisfy the Council of Europe Convention on Data Processing so as to enable our own data processing industry to participate freely in the European market.[1]

Although most attention has always been given to the data protection components of the legislation, this two-pronged approach – both to encourage the use of international standards in information technology and to protect the individual from incorrect entries on personal data – underlies the 1984 Act.

It is unfortunately true that UK governments have not been notable for their concerns with computer-related risks. It is debatable whether much current computer-related legislation would actually have been introduced in the UK without European pressure; the 'freedom of information' aspect, for example, while popular in Europe, has seldom been given a high priority here.

Data Protection Act, 1984

While the 1984 Data Protection Act will be largely overtaken by the provisions of the 1998 Act, the later legislation incorporated and built upon the earlier, so understanding of the original legislation is still of benefit. For completeness, the substance of the 1984 Data Protection Act is included here.

The 1984 Act's primary purpose was to stop the misuse of computer files containing *personal data*. The concept of personal data is central to both the wording and operation of the Act, which, in Section 1, defines 'personal data' as:

... information which relates to a living individual who can be identified from that information (or from that and other information in the possession of the data user), including any expression of opinion about the individual but not any indication of the intentions of the data user in respect of that individual ... which is recorded in a form in which it can be processed by equipment operating automatically in response to instructions issued for that purpose.

The 1984 Act states that, with certain exceptions, everyone holding personal information on a computer (significantly, manual systems were not then included) must both operate within defined guidelines and register their system and its data use with a new authority, to be known as the Data Protection Registrar. It was the responsibility of the Registrar to ensure compliance with the Act.

Personal data is protected by the 1984 Act against three potential dangers:

- Against being incorrect, or incomplete, or irrelevant.
- Against being distributed to unauthorised users.
- Against being used for a purpose other than that for which it was originally collected.

The 1984 Act's main sections attempt to provide this protection by stipulating that the storing and processing of personal data should be in accordance with the following eight principles:

1 The information to be contained in personal data shall be obtained, and personal data shall be processed, fairly and lawfully.
2 Personal data shall be held only for one or more specified and lawful purposes.
3 Personal data held for any purpose or purposes shall not be used or disclosed in any manner incompatible with that purpose or those purposes.
4 Personal data held for any purpose or purposes shall be adequate, relevant and not excessive in relation to that purpose or those purposes.
5 Personal data shall be accurate and, where necessary, kept up to date.
6 Personal data held for any purpose or purposes shall not be kept longer than is necessary for that purpose or those purposes.
7 An individual shall be entitled:
    a) at reasonable intervals and without undue delay or expense:
        - to be informed by any data user whether he holds personal data of which that individual is the subject;
        - to access to any such data held by a data user;
    b) where appropriate, to have such data corrected or erased.
8 Appropriate security measures shall be taken against unauthorised access to, or alteration, disclosure or destruction of, personal data and against accidental loss or destruction of personal data.

Although the comprehensive right of a subject to view, and, if necessary, correct data that refers to them is clearly defined, the Act does nevertheless have limits in its application. Sections 27 to 34 detail data that may be legally excluded from its provisions. Broadly, these begin by excluding anything viewed by any minister as pertaining to 'national security' (S.27) and move on to exclude personal data held for:

- 'prevention or detection of crime', 'apprehension of offenders' and 'assessment of tax'   (S.28,i)
- 'discharging statutory functions'   (S.28,ii)
- data 'held by government departments or local authorities' for social work purposes   (S.29)
- data held for the regulation of financial services   (S.30)
- data held for the purposes of judicial appointments   (S.31)
- payroll and account data (with some restrictions)   (S.32)
- domestically held data (with some restrictions)   (S.33)

Other, specialised, exemptions are listed in S.34.

At the time, there were serious reservations about the contents of the Act – the omission of controls on paper documentation and the wide omissions relating to police and government-held data being probably the most significant. However, the 1984 Act was undoubtedly a significant milestone for UK electronic data protection.

It is important that subjects with personal information held on computer systems appreciate what information may be held about them, and for what purposes it is stored. There is both a legal and an ethical responsibility for a data holder to make concerned people aware of these issues.

A business organisation must consequently collect information both for its own needs and to comply with the legal requirements of the Data Protection Registrar. At the same time, it must make its data subjects appropriately aware both that this data collection is taking place and of the uses to which the collected information may be put.

A further check on the business use of collected personal data is made through the Data Protection Registrar directly. The questions posed by the Registrar to data holders are comprehensive and detailed. Some idea of their extent may be gained from Table 8.1, which shows typical question headings, together with the huge range of possible answers, required by the Data Protection Registrar under the 1984 Act.

Essentially, the 1984 Data Protection Act lays a legal duty on business holders of all electronic information that contains 'personal' data – in other words, electronically held information that concerns *people*. Such electronic data must not only be held for a specific and legal purpose but must also be both current and accurate. If requested by the person concerned, the accuracy of the data can be checked and corrected. Compliance with the Act is policed by the Data Protection Registrar, with whom data holders must register.

Computer 'hacking'

Computers are not simply passive stores of information. When connected through a network, they become potential targets for unauthorised access from a class of computer users known as 'hackers'. While early in the development of computer systems the term 'hacker' had a more acceptable meaning, today a hacker is usually defined as someone who accesses a computer system without the express or implied permission of the owner. Hackers may gain access remotely, by using a home or office computer connected, perhaps by telephone, to a computer network, or directly, by accessing a computer network through one of its terminals.

Table 8.1 Examples of personal data details, 1984 Data Protection Act

Purpose for collecting the data:
Personnel/employee administration

Types of individual about whom data is being held:

Current/past/potential employees	Current/past/potential retired persons
Trainees, voluntary workers	

Classes of personal data held:

Academic record	Allowances, benefits, grants
Career history	Current employment
Current marriage or partnership	Details of other family/household members
Disabilities, infirmities	Financial identifiers
Health and safety record	Identifiers issued by public bodies
Immigration status	Insurance details
Licences, permits held	Marital history
Membership of committees	Membership of professional bodies
Payments, deductions	Pension details
Personal details	Personal identifiers
Physical health record	Professional expertise
Publications	Qualifications and skills
Racial, ethnic origin	Recruitment details
Termination details	Trade union, staff association record
Training record	Travel, movement details
Work record	

Sources of data:

Data subjects themselves	Department of Education and Science
Department of Employment	Department of Health and Social Security employees, agents
Employers – past, current and prospective	Home Office
Inland Revenue	Trade unions, staff associations

To whom the data may be disclosed:

Banks	Building societies
Data subjects themselves	Department of Education and Science
Department of Employment	Department of Health and Social Security employees, agents
Education or training establishments, examing bodies	
Employers – past, current and prospective	Home Office
Inland Revenue	Insurance companies
Local authority housing departments	Local authority social services departments
Survey or research organisations, workers	Trade unions, staff associations

While vilified by the press, the vast majority of those considered to be hackers are probably merely computer enthusiasts, anxious to demonstrate their skills, rather than malevolent anarchists determined to overthrow governments. However, it must be kept in mind that even the most innocent *unauthorised* access to computer systems may inadvertently create damage and risk to life, while at best, a path may be cleared for other, less innocent access.

In the UK, hacking (defined as the accessing of computer information without permission) had been thought illegal, but in 1988 a House of Lords judgement following R. v. Gold, a famous case that arose from hacking the Duke of Edinburgh's Prestel mailbox, eventually decided to the contrary. Concern following this decision led to the Law Commission Working Paper on Computer Misuse (HMSO, 1988) and a series of private members' bills, culminating, in August 1990, in passage of the Computer Misuse Act. Incidentally, although the subsequent legislation incorporated recommendations from the Law Commission's 1988 paper, the penalties recommended by the Commission were greatly increased. As well as directly tackling the 'hacking' issue, the Computer Misuse Act took the opportunity to address other, wider, problems concerning the use of computers.

Computer Misuse Act, 1990

The Act introduced three new criminal offences:

1 *Unauthorised access to computer material.* Described by the Act's sponsor as 'simple hacking' – that is, using a computer without permission. This now carries a penalty of up to six months in prison or a £2,000 fine, and is tried in a magistrate's court.

2 *Unauthorised access to computer material with intent to commit or facilitate commission of further offences.* This section covers actions such as attempting to use the contents of an e-mail (electronic mail) message for blackmail. This is viewed as a more serious offence; the penalty is up to five years imprisonment and an unlimited fine.

3 *Unauthorised modification of computer material.* This section covers distributing a computer virus, or malicious deletion of files, as well as direct actions such as altering an account to obtain fraudulent credit (or, perhaps, an increased examination grade).

Both (2) and (3) are tried before a jury.

The Act also includes the offences of *conspiracy to commit* and *incitement to commit* the three main offences. This aspect of the Act makes even discussion of specific actions that are in breach of the main sections questionable practice. It is sufficient to be associated with an offender in planning their action, or to suggest carrying out an action that is illegal under the Act, to be in a position to be charged.

Finally, the Act attempts to cover international computer crime. An individual can be prosecuted in the UK under the 1990 Act as long as there is at least one 'significant link' with this country. For example, hacking into a computer in Paris from a terminal in London is illegal, as is hacking into London from Paris. Interestingly, using the UK as a staging post is also illegal under the Act – breaking into the Pentagon from Milan via a UK university is illegal, and could result in UK prosecution, even if the hacker has never been in England.

Interestingly, if a hacker (or anyone else, including a business) gained access to a system containing personal data, and then copied all, or even some, of that data on to their own computer system, they are likely to be guilty of breaking not just the 1990 Misuse

Act but also the 1984 Data Protection Act, as they would then be holding data that was unregistered. However, even if they *were* registered, obtaining data 'knowingly or recklessly' is an offence. Clearly, it is essential for a business to be absolutely clear about the provenance of all data that may be held on company computer systems.

Data Protection Act, 1998

The UK government was obliged to introduce enabling legislation in response to the EU Data Protection Directive (95/46/EC), which had effect in the UK from 24 October 1998. In order to implement the provisions of the EU Directive appropriately, it was decided that it was necessary to institute a new UK Data Protection Act. However, as there was need to allow time for a full period of public consultation on the effects of this new law, there was a short delay between the date for implementation of the directive and the new Act being brought into force. The new Data Protection Act received royal assent on 16 July 1998, but it was not anticipated that either the Act or the secondary legislation required to support it would be brought in before January 1999.

Producing detailed information on new legislation is not a trivial exercise; accuracy is vital. Much of the specialist information in the sections that follow is therefore based, with its kind permission, on material supplied by the Office of the Data Protection Commissioner (formerly the Data Protection Registrar); I am indebted to it for this text. I am also most grateful for help from the specialist UK data protection journal, *Data Protection News*.

Consideration of the Act begins with a synopsis, setting out a brief overview and summary. This overview is then followed by a more detailed discussion.

Summary of the 1998 Data Protection Act

While the Data Protection Act sets out the overall legal framework, much of the detail will be contained in secondary legislation. Under the new Act, some manual data will be covered, certain criteria will have to be met before processing can take place, particularly in the case of sensitive data, individuals' rights will be enhanced, and registration, called 'notification', will be simplified. Areas to be dealt with in detail through secondary legislation include the notification and fees regulations. The government amended the Act to include details of transitional provisions that provide for data users/controllers to have up to three years dispensation from adherence to the new law in respect of processing, which is already underway. There is also a further dispensation, until 2007, for some manual data.

Content of the Act

Preliminary

Part I of the Act begins with definitions of the main terms used and introduces the first four schedules, which deal with the data protection principles and interpretation of them; criteria to be met before processing may begin, particularly in the case of sensitive data; and circumstances in which transfers of personal data may take place to countries with 'inadequate protection'. The Act will apply to data controllers who are established in the United Kingdom or who use equipment in the UK for processing the data. The Data Protection Registrar will be renamed the Data Protection Commissioner.

Data subjects' rights

The individual's right of access to personal data will continue. The forty-day period for responding to a written request will commence on receipt of a fee, if required (maximum fee to be set by regulations), and any information necessary to identify the individual. A data subject will have the right to prevent processing for the purposes of direct marketing and, in certain circumstances, to prevent processing likely to cause him or her damage or distress. An individual will have the right to claim compensation where a data controller contravenes certain requirements of the Act.

In the case of inaccurate data, an individual will be able to apply to the courts for correction, blocking, erasure or destruction. Data subjects will have the right, subject to exceptions, not to have certain decisions made about them that are based solely on automated processing.

Notification

Data controllers are required to notify the Commissioner, before processing commences, although notification does not apply to manual records. The Act lists the broad categories of information to be notified. The register must be made publicly available. Exemptions from notification, in cases where processing is 'unlikely to prejudice the rights and freedoms of data subjects' – Clause 17(3) – are to be dealt with in the notification regulations. However, data controllers not required to notify may choose to do so in order to comply with the duty to publicise their processing activities. The Commissioner is required to submit to the Home Secretary proposals for the notification provisions.

Exemptions

Exemptions to certain parts of the Act, in limited cases (for example to safeguard national security, crime prevention, collection of tax or duty), are provided for in Part III. Personal data processed for journalistic, artistic or literary purposes will be exempt from certain provisions of the Act, (excluding Principle 7 on security, and certain of the subject access provisions) where the processing is 'in the public interest' – Clause 32(1)(b).

Enforcement

The Commissioner may issue an enforcement notice where a data controller has contravened the data protection principles. He/she may also issue an 'information notice' requiring the controller to provide him/her with information where he/she suspects that a principle has been breached. Failure to comply with either notice will be an offence. The Commissioner's powers and duties are set out in Part VI of the Act.

1998 Data Protection Act – detailed discussion

Introduction

In essence, the 1998 Data Protection Act is very close to the current law: at least 80 percent of compliance with the new Act flows from complying with the Data Protection Act, 1984. Key elements that will continue under the new law include:

- The data protection principles of good practice.
- Registration.
- An independent supervisory authority to oversee data protection legislation.
- The data subjects' rights to access their personal data, to correct inaccurate data, and to claim compensation for damage suffered in certain circumstances.

This section identifies aspects of the Act where it builds upon the 1984 Act, and where the way forward seems clear. It is also influenced by the Commissioner's initial interpretation of some areas that have yet to be clarified. In many areas, specific advice will need to be drawn from practical experience in interpreting the provisions of the new Act. This experience can only follow after a period of implementation. The current thinking on specific aspects, and the general progress, of the 1998 Act are always available through the World Wide Web home page of the Data Protection Commissioner, an address that is listed at the end of this chapter.

It is important to stress the three-year transition period for data controllers to bring 'processing already underway' into compliance with the new law, and, while data already held in manual filing systems is included in the Act, manually held data need not comply with many aspects of the new law until 2007. The government has said that it intends to ensure that data controllers can take full advantage of these provisions, so the effect of this transitional relief should be borne in mind when considering the changes, which are outlined below.

Registration/notification

The current 'registration' system will be replaced with a similar system of 'notification'. The new system should be simplified, and there will be some exemptions from the requirement to notify. The details of the notification regulations are not yet available and will be notified by the Registrar in due course. Until the notification regulations are finalised, it will not be clear exactly who will benefit from the exemptions.

A significant difference between the 1984 Act and the 1998 Act is that while the Commissioner cannot currently enforce the data protection principles against those who are exempt from registration, the Commissioner *will* be able to enforce the principles, which remain largely the same, against those who are exempt from notification. Data controllers will therefore need to consider how they will comply with the new law, even if they are exempt from the requirement to notify.

In addition, there is a requirement for controllers on request to make public the details of their processing. This will apply even where a controller has not been required to notify. The Registrar has said that there will be an opportunity for controllers to satisfy this requirement through voluntary notification.

Until the notification regulations have been published (probably in 1999), there is very little that data users can do to review their registration requirements under the new law. However, when the law has been finalised, the Commissioner will contact those data controllers already registered under the current scheme to advise them of any changes in the registration system.

The principles

The data protection principles are dealt with in Schedule 1 of the new Act; the data handling principles of the 1984 Act have been largely retained. Like the 1984 Act, the new Act states that personal data must be processed 'fairly and lawfully'. The 1998 Act expressly provides that personal data are not to be treated as processed fairly unless, as far as is practicable, certain conditions are met. These include informing data subjects of the identity of the data controller and any nominated representative as well as informing the data subject of the purposes for which their data is to be processed.

Conditions for processing

Schedule 2 provides that processing may only be carried out where one of the following conditions has been satisfied:

- the individual has given his/her consent to the processing;
- the processing is necessary for the performance of a contract with the individual;
- the processing is required under a legal obligation;
- the processing is necessary to protect the vital interests of the individual or to carry out public functions;
- the processing is necessary in order to pursue the legitimate interests of the business (unless prejudicial to the interests of the individual).

Stricter conditions apply to the processing of sensitive data. This category includes information relating to racial or ethnic origin, political opinions, religious or other beliefs, trade union membership, health, sexuality and criminal convictions. Where such data is being processed, not only must the controller meet the requirements of the principles and Schedule 2 but processing is prohibited unless at least one of the conditions in Schedule 3 can be satisfied.

The explicit consent of the individual will usually have to be obtained before sensitive data can be processed, unless the controller can show that the processing is necessary based on one of the criteria laid out in Schedule 3 of the Act. The important Schedule 1 of the Act, detailing the principles and their interpretation, is included in this book as Appendix 6.

Security

There is still a requirement for data controllers to take security measures to safeguard personal data (Principle 7, Schedule 1, Part I), but the Act states explicitly what precautions data users must take (Schedule 1, Part II). Under the Act, appropriate technical and organisational measures must be taken to prevent the unauthorised or unlawful processing or disclosure of data. There is also a requirement for data controllers to ensure that where a data processor processes data on behalf of the controller there is a written contract between the parties whereby the processor agrees only to act on the instructions of the controller and to abide by the provisions of the security principle.

The Data Protection Commissioner advises that data users should consider the implications of this requirement, and ensure that their existing security measures are appropriate for the types of data they are processing. (Reference to BS 7799 may help data users to assess the adequacy of their current security regime).

Data subjects' rights

Subject access

The subject access provisions under the new law have been enhanced (see Part II of the Act). Whereas under the old law the data subject was only entitled to have a copy of any data processed by reference to him/her, the new law states that a data subject is also entitled to:

- a description of the data being processed;
- a description of the purposes for which it is being processed;
- a description of any potential recipients of the personal data; and
- any information as to the source of their data (where available).

In addition, where the data is processed automatically and is likely to form the sole basis for any decision significantly affecting the data subject, then the data subject will also be entitled to know the logic involved in that decision making. The data subject will also be entitled to have all relevant information communicated on the payment of a single fee, as opposed to payment of one fee per register entry, as was previously the case.

The problem of enforced subject access, where data subjects are forced to obtain access to their information in order to provide it to third parties, such as prospective employers, is also addressed by the new law. Section 56 of the Act makes it an offence to require an individual to provide a record obtained by virtue of that individual's right of access, where the information is required in connection with employment purposes or the provision of services, and where the information would reveal prior conviction or caution details. The offence will not have effect until Sections 112, 113 and 115 of the Police Act, 1997 (which provide for the issue of criminal conviction and criminal record certificates, etc.) come into force.

Eligible data, which is data where processing is immediately underway prior to 24 October 1998, may benefit from a limited exemption from subject access during the transitional period. Subject access to eligible manual data held in a 'relevant filing system' is not likely to begin until 2001, although access to 'accessible' manual records, such as health records, will be available immediately. Eligible automated data will also be exempt from some of the new subject access requirements until 2001. However, data users should still clearly give consideration to what steps will be necessary to modify their existing subject access procedures to meet the new requirements.

New rights

Some new data subject rights are created under the new law. The data subject has

- the right to prevent processing likely to cause damage and distress;
- the right to know the logic behind automated decision making;
- the right not to have significant decisions based solely on the results of automatic processing – for example, psychometric testing for employment purposes.

There is also the specific right for the data subject to prevent processing for the purposes of direct marketing, a right that was indirectly provided for through the fair obtaining aspect of the old Principle 1 of the 1984 Act but that is now made explicit. The new legislation will provide for data subjects to be able to 'opt out' of having their data used (S.10(1)) for this purpose; explicit consent ('opting in') may be required where more sensitive data is concerned.

> 10. – (1) Subject to subsection (2), an individual is entitled at any time by notice in writing to a data controller to require the data controller at the end of such period as is reasonable in the circumstances to cease, or not to begin, processing, or processing for a specified purpose or in a specified manner, any personal data in respect of which he is the data subject, on the ground that, for specified reasons:
>
> (a) the processing of those data or their processing for that purpose or in that manner is causing or is likely to cause substantial damage or substantial distress to him or to another, and
>
> (b) that damage or distress is or would be unwarranted.

Part of Section 10 of the 1998 Data Protection Act, detailing 'opting out' rules.
© Crown copyright 1998

Data users clearly need to consider how they will be affected by the new rights given to data subjects.

Compensation

Under the 1984 Act, data subjects were allowed to claim compensation through the courts only where they had suffered damage as a result of inaccuracy or unauthorised disclosure. This right has been considerably extended to allow the data subject the right to claim compensation for damage caused by any breach of the Act, and in addition for 'distress', in certain circumstances.

Transfer of data overseas

In addition to the changes to the existing principles outlined above, there is also a new eighth principle, restricting the transfer of personal data outside the European Union.

> 8. Personal data shall not be transferred to a country or territory outside the European Economic Area unless that country or territory ensures an adequate level of protection for the rights and freedoms of data subjects in relation to the processing of personal data.

Principle 8 of the 1998 Data Protection Act, detailing data transfer limitations.
© Crown copyright 1998

It will be seen that there are to be no restrictions on the free flow of personal data between countries in the European Economic Area (this includes Norway, Iceland and Liechtenstein, as well as the fifteen member states of the European Union). However, personal data may be transferred to third countries only if those countries ensure an *adequate level of protection for the rights and freedoms of data subjects*. When determining adequacy, controllers should consider, for example:

- the nature of the data;
- the country of origin;
- the final destination country;
- the law, or any relevant codes of conduct, in force, both locally and in the destination country.

Adequate protection of personal data may not be required where certain criteria are satisfied. These include where the data subject has consented to the transfer; and where the transfer is necessary for the performance of a contract between the data subject and the controller (see Schedule 4 for other criteria). It is unlikely that adequate protection to European Union standards will be found widely outside the EU, and alternative safeguards are currently being evaluated. The development of model contract clauses to guarantee the protection of personal data is one possibility, but the obvious problem of enforcing such a contract to protect the data subject is still being considered by the Data Protection Commissioner.

Data users who transfer data outside the European Economic Area should consider whether or not they will be able to benefit from the transitional provisions, which provide an exemption until 2001 from compliance with the eighth principle for data that are subject to processing that is already underway. They should also consider whether they can satisfy any of the criteria set out in Schedule 4 of the new Act.

Manual records

While we are of course principally concerned with the use of computer systems and electronically held data, it is probable that most businesses will additionally hold some paper records. For this reason, the handling of paper records under the new Act is dealt with here, albeit briefly.

Information recorded as part of a 'relevant filing system'

The Data Protection Act 1984 only covers personal data held in an automatically processable form. The definition of data in the new Act has been extended so that it now includes information that is recorded as part of a 'relevant filing system' where the records are structured, either by reference to individuals or by reference to criteria relating to individuals, so that 'specific information relating to a particular individual is readily accessible.' This definition will clearly include some types of manual data.

The transitional arrangements will exempt manual records held in a 'relevant filing system' from compliance with much of the new law until 2007. However, data controllers should obviously consider taking steps now to ensure that all their information systems comply with the data protection principles of good practice, regardless of whether the data in those systems is processed by manual or automated means.

Accessible records

The definition of data in the Act is also extended to cover information forming part of an 'accessible record'. An accessible record is described in the Act as any health record, or any accessible public record defined in Schedule 11.

Some accessible records may be held manually, and these will also enjoy a period of exemption from many of the provisions of the new law until 2007. The transitional exemptions available for accessible records will not be as wide as that afforded to other exempt manual data.

Transitional arrangements

'Processing already underway'

The new law provides for a transitional period for data controllers to bring their processing in line with the new requirements. Until 23 October 2001, all manual data held in a 'relevant filing system', and, subject to certain conditions, backup data, data processed only for the purposes of payroll and accounts, producing mailing lists, or by unincorporated members' clubs will be exempt from compliance with the principles and Parts II (data subjects' rights) and III (notification requirements) of the Act.

In addition, all eligible automated data (i.e. data that is the subject of processing already underway before 24 October 1998) will be exempt until 23 October 2001 from many of the additional requirements of the new law (see Schedule 8).

As mentioned above, manual data held in a 'relevant filing system' will also enjoy a more limited exemption from some of the principles until 2007.

Accessible records

Data forming part of an 'accessible file', regardless of whether 'processing is already underway' before October 1998, will also enjoy an exemption from the data protection principles and Part II of the Act (except in so far as these provisions relate to subject access or the rights of the data subject provided for in S.12A or S.15 of the Act) until 23 October 2001. Data held in an accessible record will also have a further limited exemption from some of the principles until October 2007.

Data users should consider whether or not they can take advantage of the transitional provisions and whether any of the exemptions will apply to them. Further advice on what will be considered 'eligible data' and 'processing already underway' will be issued in the near future. It would be sensible for data controllers to ensure that they keep up to date with advice from the Commissioner on the transitional arrangements.

The 1998 Data Protection Act will undoubtedly create problems for those responsible for business computer systems – the provisions relating to data subject access and the transfer of data overseas, in particular, will need very careful attention.

Other legislation

There is a great deal of other legislation relevant to computer users in the UK. This includes:

- For copyright issues – Copyright, Designs and Patents Act, 1988.
- For improper electronic claims, including for example the transfer of electronic funds – Forgery and Counterfeiting Act, 1981; Theft Act, 1968 (S.25).
- Trade Descriptions Act, 1968.

Other, more general, laws may also apply. For example, as discussed in Chapter 3, it is necessary to ensure that all software being used by a company has been obtained legally.

For further information concerning these Acts and other legal aspects of computing, reference to specialist books listed in the Bibliography – for instance Bainbridge's *Introduction to Computer Law* – is highly recommended.

Relevant DTP World Wide Web addresses

Visiting the Data Protection Commissioner's World Wide Web site is very strongly recommended. The Commissioner's site contains much helpful information and guidance notes, together with many specialist papers and reports.

```
<http://www.open.gov.uk/dpr/dprhome.htm>
```

The actual texts of the two UK Data Protection Acts are available electronically:

Data Protection Act, 1998

```
<http://www.hmso.gov.uk/acts/acts1998/19980029.htm>
```

Data Protection Act, 1984

```
<http://www.open.gov.uk/dpr/dprhome.htm>
```

Useful further information is also available:

EU Data Protection Directive (95/46/EC)

```
<http://www2.echo.lu/legal/en/dataprot/dataprot.html>
```

Data protection: the government's proposals

```
<http://www.homeoffice.gov.uk/datap1.htm>
```

Notes

1   Hansard, Lords, 5th ser, v.443, col.50.

9

Support for appropriate behaviour

What can be done by a responsible business organisation, concerned to ensure that its computer systems are used efficiently and appropriately? How might an individual, working within a business organisation, ensure that their computer-related behaviour is appropriate?

This chapter examines the availability of both formal and informal support, including professional codes of conduct. It looks at developing a formal ethical computing policy within a company, as well as considering the role of a concerned individual member of staff. It then moves to consideration of practical issues, including questions such as what to do about unethical staff and the problems of ethical working within an unsympathetic company environment. The importance of education and training is stressed, and the chapter concludes with some practical strategies for ethical survival.

Introduction

So far, we have dealt with a wide range of potential uses of business computers and have discussed many related difficulties. In order to respond adequately to problems associated with computer use, it has been emphasised that preparation is essential. Development of an 'appropriate use' policy was discussed in Chapter 6; it was stressed that leaving production of a policy until problems actually occur has many practical disadvantages. Such emergency policies also carry a high risk of failure.

Apart from analysing the benefits of an effective appropriate use policy, we have also examined the legal position, particularly the new data protection laws. It may perhaps be assumed that most businesses will be concerned to act within the law, but not every inappropriate action is necessarily illegal, and legality does not automatically grant ethical merit.

This chapter draws together many of the themes discussed so far and looks at potential practical responses that might be made to a variety of different situations. Beginning with an examination of formal and informal support for appropriate conduct, it then considers responses to issues of concern to senior managers, such as the development of an ethical computing policy. It also considers the personal role of a computer-using individual within an organisation before addressing ethical problems that may arise following management conflict. The chapter concludes with a description of the development of strategies for ethical survival, both corporate and individual.

Formal support

While we have so far considered the regulation of business computer networks only through the proposed establishment of an internal company code of conduct, it is important to appreciate that a number of external agencies may also offer support and guidance.

The use of business computers should not be approached in isolation and therefore needs to be considered in relation to other areas of business ethics. For example, a company that has an appreciation of the ethical implications of business computer use is also likely to appreciate the importance of other business behaviour; the opposite may also be true.

Where might an appreciation of the ethical implications of business activities actually originate? It is obviously not appropriate or even possible for every company to be continually forced to 're-invent the wheel' of appropriate conduct. Although local problems may at first appear to be totally individual, it is probable that at least some other companies have previously experienced similar difficulties, and, if so, their accumulated knowledge is likely to be both helpful and relevant.

As well as much else, the collective experience of other companies is available to the corporate members of 'professional' business organisations. Such organisations, developed in response to a common need, normally offer appropriate information and support to business as their primary aim. It is from these professional business organisations that concerned managers can learn of the broader ethical risks of modern business and discover potential solutions.

Professional codes

While the term 'professional' is today used fairly freely within business, for our purposes it can essentially be held to refer to a group of individuals who work in a similar area, who have undertaken specialist training, and who share a common goal of maintaining high working standards. Historically, such professional groups have included those working in the fields of medicine and law. Today, there are many more professional bodies, including organisations dealing specifically with the professional use of computer systems.

One of the definitions of a 'profession' is that it defines appropriate standards of behaviour for those working in its specified field. Normally, to ensure that these standards are maintained, professional organisations will provide for regulation of their members. Professional codes of conduct are the formal expression of these expectations and requirements. All professional organisations tend to develop such codes, and adherence to them is generally an important condition of membership.

There are several important reasons why professional codes of conduct exist, including:

- To allow those inside and outside a profession – including members of the general public – to evaluate exactly what may be appropriately expected from members of that profession.

- To provide clear and *public* definitions of what is – and what is not – viewed as acceptable professional behaviour.
- To allow the profession as a whole to support an individual who is maintaining an agreed viewpoint.

The written expression of an 'official' view of professional behaviour has several very real advantages. Setting out a detailed written code makes it much easier for an individual who is new to the field to understand and appreciate the full range of circumstances that might potentially be met in their future professional life, and thus to gain an appreciation of what may actually be involved in their work. Knowing what is considered relevant by experienced specialists allows appropriate planning on both personal and professional levels. It is perhaps important also to stress that such planning is not simply concerned with uncommon problems. Some difficult situations in business may be extremely familiar, but this need not mean that they are consequently unimportant.

In summary, a comprehensive range of events and activities, well beyond the scope of even a very well-informed individual practitioner, may need to be anticipated for even an expert to feel professionally secure. The pressures of modern business, and barrage of day-to-day demands, mean that it is all too easy to lose sight of the wider perspectives of professional work and the potential longer-term effects of behaviour. Also, the nature of business specialisation is inherently likely to obscure the more extended implications of professional actions.

Following an amalgamation with another firm, a senior manager of a transport company was given the job of co-ordinating computerised records, which basically organised the movement of vehicles, drivers and loads. Because he was intent on solving a difficult technical computing problem, necessarily defined in units rather than people, the personal effects of changes on company drivers were totally overlooked.

In the UK, the professional body for computer scientists is the British Computer Society (BCS), while in and beyond the USA the Association for Computing Machinery (ACM) is regarded as the principal professional organisation for those who work with computers. Many other concerned organisations also exist: two of the largest are, in the UK, the Institute of Electrical Engineers (IEE), and in the USA, the Institute of Electrical and Electronic Engineers (IEEE). All these organisations are well aware of the need to develop and use computer systems responsibly, and all have worked hard to produce codes of conduct to determine exactly what the 'appropriate use' of computer systems means in practice.

On a much wider scale, the generation of industry-wide codes of conduct allows the greater weight of collective views to be felt. Publication by professional bodies means that the general public may be reassured that those working within a field are also concerned with its standards. Closer to home, individual commercial decisions by clients and customers can undoubtedly be enhanced by the confidence engendered through adherence to a well-publicised professional code.

Codes of conduct developed by professional organisations may not refer just to the behaviour of their members. While a code of conduct may have been drawn up by a particular specialised professional body, this does not automatically mean that the contents of the code are consequently of relevance *only* to members of that particular association. The conclusions of a relevant professional body are of concern to everyone working within that area. Whether an individual working in a particular field is a member of several relevant organisations, or one, or none, they need to be aware of what the relevant professional organisations consider to be appropriate – and inappropriate – behaviour. Such individuals also have a legitimate interest in knowing about attempts to codify behaviour in their particular business area. I have suggested earlier that it is appropriate for individuals to develop *for themselves* a concept of what is, and is not, appropriate conduct.

While members of a particular professional organisation may follow the official code because it is required of them, what of concerned individuals who are not members of a professional body? They may well decide that it is appropriate to incorporate all or part of an 'official' code into their personal ethical beliefs, and to use this specialised information to maintain appropriate standards in their work.

It is relevant here to suggest that those professionals who are exercising their skills appropriately have a responsibility to cascade down information on what constitutes good practice. Others in the organisation may also use computers but may not be as aware of relevant issues. This educative role, in which an informed professional helps in spreading a wider awareness of good practice, may be of considerable benefit to a company.

Quite apart from those specialised codes developed by organisations particularly concerned with computer use and with the professional use of computer systems, as business professionals we also need to be aware of additional resources that are open to us. These come from codes and guidelines developed by those specialist organisations who are *generally* concerned with ethical business practice.

One such specialist organisation is the European Business Ethics Network, established in 1987 and supported by many of Europe's leading companies. A not-for-profit association of increasing influence, it has branches throughout Europe and in the UK.[1]

The Business Ethics Network takes an interesting, no-nonsense approach; the following series of questions and answers (reproduced, with permission, from its material) provides a very effective summary of the importance of ethics to modern business.

What value can a business ethics approach add to good management?

- opens up communications throughout the organisation
- identifies problem areas
- ensures that the right decisions are made – more quickly
- improves team working
- motivates and empowers staff
- protects the corporate reputation

Good business ethics do not require companies to get it right all the time. Good business ethics require companies to try to get it right all the time and to ensure that they have structures in place that will enable them to deal quickly and ethically with the situation at any time they get it wrong.

What about the law? If we keep within the law, surely we're being ethical?

There is a clear distinction between obeying the law and ethical behaviour. It is normally ethical to obey the law, but obeying the law alone does not produce a guarantee of ethical merit. The law and regulatory processes can only ever be a baseline – a minimum standard of behaviour that society considers acceptable. Ethical behaviour takes obeying to the law as a starting point. Ethical behaviour is concerned with the grey area above that baseline, between the black area of 'always wrong' and the white area of 'always right'.

But of course we're ethical, aren't we?

Many companies believe themselves to be ethical and hold this belief on the basis of the understanding and consensus among senior management about proper behaviour. If, however, there is no regular scrutiny of values and behaviour at all levels in the company, both customers and shareholders may legitimately question the effectiveness of the ethical stance. Openness is crucial to ethical behaviour. For a company to claim to be ethical and then refuse to permit shareholders or customers – perhaps by means of independent auditors – to validate this claim is not consistent. And if a company is going to make ethics a selling point (whether to sell services, goods, shares or itself as an employer), it needs to define and clarify just what it means when it calls itself ethical.

The Business Ethics Network makes solid points, which are well worth consideration; other business organisations offer similar help. Appendix 4 lists a number of professional business organisations that maintain an electronic presence on the World Wide Web and are therefore easily accessible. Checking these web sites directly is likely to be informative.

Code of business ethics

While a specialised code of appropriate conduct for the use of company computer networks is particularly recommended, its integration into the development of a comprehensive code of business ethics is strongly advised. Organisations such as the Institute of Business Ethics offer support for companies in the development of a code of business ethics; its twelve steps[2] form a very solid foundation for most businesses:

1 *Integration*   Produce a strategy for integrating the code into the running of the business at the time that it is issued.

2 *Endorsement*   Make sure that the code is endorsed by the chairman and CEO.

3 *Circulation*   Send the code to all employees in a readable and portable form and give it to all employees joining the company.

4 *Breaches*   Include a short section on how an employee can react if he or she is faced with a potential breach of the code or is in doubt about a course of action involving an ethical choice.

5 *Personal response*   Give all staff the personal opportunity to respond to the content of the code.

6 *Affirmation*   Have a procedure for managers and supervisors to state regularly that they and their staff understand and apply the provisions of the code and raise matters not covered by it.

7 *Regular review*   Have a procedure for regular review and updating of the code.

8 *Contracts*   Consider making adherence to the code obligatory by including reference to it in all contracts of employment and linking it with disciplinary procedures.

9 *Training*   Ask those responsible for company training programmes at all levels to include issues raised by the code in their programmes.

10 *Translation*   See that the code is translated for use in overseas subsidiaries or other places where English is not the principal language.

11 *Distribution*   Make copies of the code available to business partners (suppliers, customers, etc.).

12 *Annual report*   Reproduce or insert a copy of the code in the annual report so that shareholders and the wider public know about the company's position on ethical matters.

As well as being appropriate for the construction of a broadly based ethical code for a firm, I suggest that these twelve steps are equally appropriate when considering development of a specialist company code for the appropriate use of business computer systems.

What formal help is available?

So far, we have discussed our original, internal, company 'appropriate use' policy, together with some external policies and additional availability of help. Professional organisations concerned with computing and computers such as the BCS and the ACM have developed codes of conduct that set out what tasks may be appropriately undertaken by their members; they have also specified computer-related tasks that they consider inappropriate. It is clearly sensible for managers who carry responsibility for company computer systems to have made themselves aware of the provisions of such 'specialised' codes. (Both the ACM and the BCS codes are reproduced as Appendix 5).

In addition to the specialist professional codes describing appropriate and inappropriate computer-related behaviour, there are also broader professional codes intended to ensure that all the operations of a business are carried out in an ethical manner. Development of such broadly based company codes are strongly recommended but lie beyond the scope of this book. However, those interested in the development of a company-wide code of business ethics can seek assistance from specialist business support organisations such as the Institute of Business Ethics.

Problems related to internal diversity

So far, we have discussed the concept of ethical issues within business computer systems as if there were only a single controlling power in every company, and that this central authority could be readily influenced. Such an approach, while helpful, is clearly an oversimplification. For those without an understanding of organisational theory, it may perhaps seems that it only needs action by an enlightened board of management for all problems to be resolved, and for all possible ethical concerns in the use of company computer systems to be eliminated.

While it is certainly to be desired, such an ideal state of affairs may not be easily achieved. Most businesses today have multiple influences upon their policies and practices. Even when a consensus agrees with changes, given the pressures on modern business, establishing a workable policy will not necessarily be effortless. For example, while the advantages and potential savings of a company-wide computer usage policy may well be evident to cost-conscious managers, so might expectations of additional expenditure and anticipation of possible practical limitations. The ethical intentions of some members of staff may, in practice, be opposed or undermined by the less scrupulous, and so on.

It is also true that not all companies are necessarily prepared to incorporate ethical business policies, so it is possible for an ethical individual to find themselves working within an organisation that appears intent upon unethical actions. They may consequently need additional help, and possibly even external support. These and other such problems are addressed below.

What needs to be done?

It may be easier to identify appropriate actions if we divide problems into a series of possible headings, describing situations that need to be addressed:

1 A company wishes to ensure appropriate future use of its computer systems and networks.
2 A company wishes to ensure immediate implementation of an appropriate computer use policy.
3 An individual within an ethical company wishes to work ethically.
4 An individual within an unethical company wishes to work ethically.

Appropriate future use of computer systems and networks

Let us assume a business that currently has no current code of conduct relating to any of its activities; for whatever reason, it has been decided at a senior management level that this state of affairs cannot be allowed to continue. Specifically, it has been determined that an ethical computing policy be introduced as a matter of urgency.

Here the need is for rapid development. Consequently, the principal risks are related to the likelihood of preliminary research into the precise needs of the company being skimped. Although it can perhaps be argued that any ethical use policy is better than none, there is a substantial body of empirical evidence to suggest that a policy introduced without adequate initial preparation is unlikely to succeed. The reasons for this are bound up in two important aspects of an effective policy.

The first is that an effective appropriate use policy needs to be 'owned' by those it covers; in other words, staff need to feel that they and their specific needs have been individually considered in the creation of the policy. Clearly, in a company of any size individual consultation is likely to be complex, but nevertheless a properly directed consultation process can allow individuals to feel that they are able to make contributions. Human nature being what it is, even an employee whose suggestions are not incorporated into a final policy is likely to feel more positive for being given the opportunity of making a contribution. It is also true that contributions of unexpected weight have been known to come from the most unlikely members of staff; one major US telecommunications company, for example, incorporated suggestions from an electrician into its effective use policy.

The second reason why adequate initial preparation is essential lies in the need to ensure that any policy concerns the individual needs of the company. One reason why I have not included an all-purpose ethical computing policy in this book is that such a policy is very unlikely to be suitable for more than a small number of firms; specific adaptations are almost certain to be essential. Implementation of a policy that does not fit the needs of a company will therefore lead inevitably to policy failure. Reasons for this are obvious – if there are instances where a supposed comprehensive appropriate use policy does not, or cannot, apply, then (even when it is applicable) staff are likely to consider it acceptable to disregard it. After all, if one aspect of a policy can be ignored, why not another? Given that local changes to any 'pre-cooked' policy will be made anyway, it makes good practical sense to base a policy on a firm foundation, one that is specific to the business concerned.

One area where this approach may cause problems, however, lies in the growing spread of multi-national companies. Here the establishment of a perfectly workable policy by the parent company's head office may well cause considerable problems if introduced in another division, situated in a country with different cultural norms. The extent to which a policy can be modified is clearly the responsibility of concerned management, but I would urge that an ethical policy not be watered down by external demands. A familiar example concerns corporate bribery in order to gain a contract. While such bribery is both illegal and unethical in most Western countries, there may be a very different philosophy in other parts of the world. In some markets, therefore, an international business may be forced to compete with less scrupulous rivals. Is it reasonable that an ethical business code be suspended in such cases?

Decisions concerning modification of an ethical business code, such as this one, are clearly of considerable importance. They should always be formally addressed at a high level of management and not left to informal activities. However, it is necessary to keep in mind that a company code created in the way I have suggested, especially one that is developed after drawing upon the collective knowledge and experience of staff members, is not to be casually and secretly discarded. A good rule of thumb is that if a change to an ethical computing policy cannot be made public, then it probably should not be made at all.

After a company code has been developed, it should be formally endorsed by the most senior member of the business – normally the chief executive, chairman or president. It should be widely distributed, and every member of the company should be considered an appropriate audience. New members of the company, joining after this initial distribution of the code, also need to be made fully aware of it.

Unfortunately, the development of a code does not automatically mean that it will be distributed. Even in companies where an excellent code of conduct has been in place for years, I have found employees who, far from being aware of its requirements, were apparently unaware that their company code even existed.

Immediate implementation of a computer use policy

It is likely that many businesses today have already developed a code of conduct and therefore carry an expectation that their staff will act in a responsible way. While preparation and development of a new code will hold the potential for publicity in itself, interest is likely to die down over a period, and awareness may dwindle seriously unless there are regular and deliberate efforts to promote knowledge of the company's code among staff. It may also be that there are changed circumstances, and that situations unforeseen at the time the code was originally developed now offer potential new risks.

Such problems provide justification for what is called an *ethical audit*, where the ways in which a company ensures that its staff act in an appropriate manner are checked and confirmed. An ethical audit of computer systems, for example, would normally be carried out by an outside consultant, who would be given the task of determining both in what ways the company computer systems are being used and how these uses might relate to the existing ethical use policy. Any changes that have occurred since the original appropriate use policy was created would be identified, and, if appropriate, consequent recommendations for changes to the policy made. Such an investigation may be carried out as an internal project, although in this case it is essential that the staff carrying out the examination are given sufficient authority to ensure that they are able to produce a dependable report. Once the firm is clear about its formal objectives, then the policy should, if necessary, be amended. It should then be actively promoted in a similar way to promotion of a new policy, described above.

Finally, it is essential that appropriate use policies are reviewed regularly, both for their content and to confirm that they are being actively followed. It is insufficient to stop once a policy has been created in the expectation that no more needs to be done. While asking firms about their approach to appropriate use of computer systems, I have had concerning experiences in this area. On more than one occasion, for instance, I have been shown an appropriate use policy, produced from a filing cabinet by a senior manager, who was probably the only person in the company to know that such a policy existed, and where to find it.

An ethical individual within an ethical company

This situation obviously appears to be the easiest to handle. However, while a company may be intending to operate in an ethical way, it is possible that there may be some slippage between the policy makers, operating at a high level, and policy implementers, who are probably somewhat lower in the hierarchy.

Ideally, an ethical individual will have determined for themselves what they consider to be appropriate conduct; this is not dependent upon outside demands but is a fundamental and personal belief. For example, an individual in a police state might feel that following state orders would breach their own beliefs, regardless of external rules or orders. While circumstances such as this are fortunately rare, it does demonstrate the need for individuals to maintain their own ethical standards. Even though an employer may say 'this is acceptable conduct', it is essential to measure the proposed actions against an internal monitor. If we assume that such a personal ethical code exists, then an individual would next draw upon professional codes, and the specific codes of conduct drawn up by their employer, before considering more local factors, such as the views of colleagues and friends.

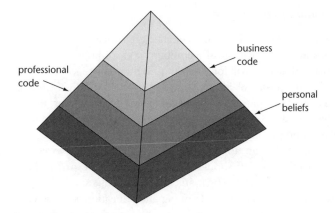

Figure 9.1 'Pyramid of support'

Consider Figure 9.1, which shows the 'pyramid of support'. This illustration is intended to show the various formal and informal influences that act upon an individual, ranging from the bedrock of personal beliefs through to the less formal influence of friends and colleagues. It is suggested that these levels of support are potentially available in most if not all business situations, and that a concerned individual will be able to draw upon them when confronted with a situation that may have ethical implications. The most important aspect of the figure is the order of the levels; it would not be acceptable, for example, to allow basic personal beliefs to be overruled by the imposition of a business code of conduct by an employer; or for the employer's code to be ignored in favour of the views of a friend.

It may happen that individual views within a company clash; for example, members of staff might disagree about the implementation of a policy, or perhaps even about the importance to be given to particular sections of it. In every case, it is essential for a dispute that cannot be resolved to be brought to the attention of a more senior staff member, preferably (in the case of disagreement about the implementation of an appropriate use policy) someone who has actually been involved in the development or promotion of the policy.

Quite apart from the need to resolve any dispute between two individual members of staff, such a disagreement may indicate areas of ambiguity in the policy itself, and monitoring of problems may lead to both resolution of a current problem and prevention of similar difficulties in the future.

Individual members of staff should therefore take the initiative in making themselves aware of company codes of conduct and in relating these requirements to their own personal beliefs. It is also appropriate to consider the views of any relevant professional organisations, such as the BCS or the ACM, which may well, through the collective experience of their members, be able to alert individuals to particular risks and potential problems. It is also sensible to be aware of any relevant legal requirements; even the most concerned of businesses may sometimes accidentally breach the law, and in such circumstances an informed staff member may be uniquely valuable.

What to do about unethical staff?

We have so far assumed that all members of staff are concerned to follow company rules and guidelines, and that knowledge of a company code of appropriate conduct is in itself sufficient to ensure that staff will follow its requirements.

However, this is not a state of affairs that can be automatically assumed. It is perfectly possible for an ethical company to discover that it employs members of staff who do not behave ethically and who cannot be trusted to follow an appropriate use policy, even if one is formulated and promoted. What then, should be done?

First, it is essential that an appropriate use policy *has* been developed and actively distributed. No member of staff should be able to claim ignorance of the policy, or of its provisions. There is often a case to be made here for specific staff education in the application and use of a code of conduct. Training and education is particularly appropriate where a company has not previously maintained an appropriate use policy.

Second, there is a particular need to make managers aware of the importance of following the policy. It is not sufficient merely to distribute paper copies; active supervision by line managers should ensure appropriate behaviour on the part of staff.

Third, there should ideally be a degree of external monitoring of policy implementation, preferably by those who are not themselves directly concerned with local management. Such external monitoring prevents cosy relationships developing, relationships that can lead to informal local agreements to ignore policy guidelines.

Finally, once a code of conduct has been developed, and staff educated in its use, it is essential for it to be appropriately enforced. When, for example, an infringement is discovered, it should be dealt with in such a manner that the problem is unlikely to recur. Staff need to be made aware of the importance given by senior management to the successful implementation of an appropriate use policy; ignoring or minimising breaches of the policy will not encourage future compliance. Publication of the consequences of ignoring the policy, subject to internal disciplinary procedures, may also encourage others to follow the code.

An individual within an unethical company

While it might make for easier analysis, it would be a mistake to consider that all businesses are either 'ethical' or 'unethical'. While seriously flawed companies do exist, they are very much in the minority. Far more common in practice is an unethical department, or division within a company. It should also be kept in mind that, although there are certain baselines, the precise definition of 'ethical' may vary in different locations and circumstances, and certainly in the beliefs of different individuals. As has been discussed elsewhere in this book, it is just not possible to define what ultimately is and is not ethical for everyone, everywhere. However, it *is* essential for individuals to have a solid knowledge of what they, and their employing organisation, consider to be appropriate conduct. 'Unethical' in this context may therefore mean either that the policies of a company violate the personal code of ethics of an employee or that they are in breach of accepted formal or informal codes of conduct.

We will assume that an ethical worker discovers, either after accepting a job or perhaps at a later stage, that they are employed by a company with a problem over corporate ethics. There are probably two immediate personal responses to this problem, with a more realistic third option that will become evident a little later.

The first, and most obvious, response is for the concerned employee to leave the company. For an ethical individual, working within an unethical setting is probably going to be extremely difficult, if not insupportable. Should the demands of a job place you in opposition with your personal beliefs, then some form of internal or external conflict is inevitable. In these circumstances, it may certainly make sense to abandon the job completely in order to move to more congenial surroundings.

While opting out of an unattractive situation in this way is certainly advantageous, it does perhaps beg the question of how to actually cope with unethical behaviour. A more dedicated individual, or one with a more crusading approach, might be tempted to remain in post in order to use their position to work for change within the company. The extent to which this 'working for change from within' approach actually forms a realistic policy almost certainly depends upon the seniority of the post, and the nature of the 'unethical' company. However, while a career of forcing issues is not a choice likely to be made readily by everyone, such efforts deserve support.

Useful approaches in such a situation would certainly include the threat of publicity, by making management formally and informally aware of the image problems consequent upon unethical activities, for example. The distribution of externally produced material, such as specialist codes of conduct from professional organisations, as well as the more general recommendations of external authorities, such as business advisory institutes, may help to alter the internal climate of a company. Direct involvement of professional associations may also be appropriate, but it has to be appreciated that without the support of senior management, institutional change is not a trivial task.

If a concerned individual does not choose to leave, or is not able to do so, and they have no appetite for personally taking on their employing organisation, a third option becomes clear. Here the member of staff does not leave, and does not campaign for change, but remains in post as an ethical individual, isolated in an unethical setting.

We are essentially considering strategies for ethical survival. Before looking at possible defensive strategies in more detail, let us briefly consider what relevant examples of computer-related unethical behaviour might exist. There are probably as many possibilities as there are users of business computers, but some main headings could include:

- *Inappropriate collection of electronic data or material*, where, for example, personal data is collected unnecessarily; or, as in the case of Company 'A', which was discussed in Chapter 4, when information irrelevant to immediate needs is collected for an inappropriate future use.

- *Inappropriate use of electronic data or material.* Here the possibilities are very wide. They could range from the concealed monitoring of staff's electronic mail messages to the case of one US company, which passed a list of staff to a political organisation for vetting.

- *Inappropriate modification of electronic data.* This covers most 'hacking' activities, where an individual gains unauthorised access to data; it also includes the creation of computer virus programs and other malicious activities. (For example, in one business a fake letter, claiming to be from an unpopular manager, was distributed electronically.)

- *Inappropriate use of technology.* Computers can be used to collect data from a wide range of different inputs. This may permit secret recording of staff activities, monitoring of their behaviour, and even electronically checking time spent in the toilet.

- *Inappropriate electronic access.* Where confidential material is viewed by those who have not been authorised to do so. An example is the viewing of electronically held personnel records by a dissatisfied employee.

As will have been seen throughout this book, the huge range of uses to which business computers have been put makes it impossible to do more than indicate broad areas where a particular focus may be necessary.

What, then, can be done by an individual faced with situations like these within their own company? The following proposals are based upon suggestions and contributions from business managers and employees who have personally experienced ethical difficulties within their working environment. While all contributors were involved in computer-related issues, their responses are probably also applicable to other problem areas within business. When considering the following proposals, though, it must be appreciated that they are not suggestions for standard business behaviour but are intended solely as practical suggestions intended to help personal survival in potentially intolerable circumstances.

Strategies for ethical survival

When faced with a business situation that conflicts with your ethical standards, this check list may be helpful.

1 *Is involvement necessary?* While the inappropriate activities within the company may not be compatible with a personal or professional code of ethics, are they actually close enough for you to affect them, or for them to personally affect you?

2 *Is it possible to withdraw from the risk area?* If the activities are too close to ignore, is it possible to relocate yourself to a safe distance from them? Requesting a move to a different division, for example, or perhaps taking on an appropriate task that will leave no room for the inappropriate activities.

3 *Establish the official position.* If it cannot be avoided, establish whether the inappropriate activity is actually supported by senior managers. Might it perhaps be the unauthorised ideas of someone at a lower level in the organisation?

4 *If officially supported, can this support be changed?* Should the inappropriate activities appear to have official support, might it be possible to widen the area of concern to involve other senior managers? For example, if the area is a technical one, could it be promoted as potentially benefiting from a wider perspective?

5 *Check the law.* It may be that the proposed activity is actually illegal. Making those responsible aware of this may be sufficient to head off an illegal inappropriate activity.

6 *Blow the whistle.* This is the more positive choice of two 'last ditch' activities. 'Whistle blowing' involves moving objections to an unethical activity to a higher level, or even outside the company, normally through the press or television. Making the world aware of your employer's lack of ethics in this way is certainly not a good career move, but it may prevent inappropriate activities from continuing.

7 *Quit.* This is obviously the negative choice, to be considered if all else has failed, and, for whatever reason, whistle blowing is not an option. Faced with being forced to participate in an activity that you believe to be unethical, then it may be appropriate to consider leaving. Annual leave or time to reflect may help; one computer manager, confronted with a policy he could not support, developed a bad back, and during a period away from work gained thinking time. Other such possibilities may suggest themselves, but I cannot recommend them.

Conclusion

In this chapter, we have looked at the development of corporate codes of conduct, beginning with consideration of the specialist codes of professional organisations concerned with computer use and moving on to consider the more widely ranging professional organisations, such as the Institute for Business Ethics, designed to assist business directly.

We then considered practical issues related to the implementation of a policy, looking in some detail at four important areas.

1 Appropriate future use of its computer systems and networks.
2 Immediate implementation of a computer use policy.
3 An ethical individual within an ethical company.
4 An ethical individual within an unethical company.

The chapter concluded by examining some strategies for ethical survival.

Discussion points

The following points are intended to form the basis for a class or seminar discussion on the issues raised in this chapter. They should not be considered until the relevant sections have been read and thought through. As all questions have been carefully chosen to encourage debate, they are primarily intended to encourage thinking about the issues and are not necessarily capable of producing definitive answers.

1 In the context of business computer system regulation, we have discussed 'formal support'. What do you understand by the term 'formal support'? How might it be implemented within a company?
2 How might 'formal support' be available from *outside* a company?
3 Do you consider yourself a 'professional'? What do you think are the criteria that might define a 'profession'?
4 Where do professional codes of conduct actually come from?
5 Who should be appropriately involved in drawing up a company code of conduct, for instance in defining the appropriate use of its computer systems?
6 Why might you need to consider the content of a professional code of conduct?
7 You join a new company as a middle manager; your staff use company computers. A code of conduct, covering the use of company computer systems, is not in force. What do you do?

8 You join a new company as a middle manager; your staff use company computers. A code of conduct, covering the use of company computer systems *is* in force. What do you do?

9 Why do multi-national companies need to take particular care in developing an 'appropriate use' policy?

10 You are responsible for developing your company's World Wide Web site. The business is (and will remain) purely local. What external factors do you need to consider in your content and design?

11 You are a senior manager. The company's chief executive tells you that it has been decided that the company code, governing use of computer systems, needs updating, and you have been given the task. What do you do?

12 What factors do you feel might *appropriately* lead to changes in a company code?

13 The 'pyramid of support' was described in this chapter. Match the 'pyramid' to your own circumstances, and identify how it might then appear.

14 What might you define as 'unethical use' of company computer systems?

15 You become aware of unethical use being made of company computers. What do you do – and why?

Notes

1 Details of Business Ethics Network UK from Laura Spence, Small Business Research Centre, Kingston University, Kingston Hill, Kingston-upon-Thames, Surrey, KT2 7LB.

2 *Twelve Steps*, © the Institute of Business Ethics, 12 Palace Street, London, SW1E 5JA. Reproduced with permission.

10

Summary and conclusions

This chapter begins by establishing the background to the appropriate use of company computer systems. It then describes the essential points that need to be covered by a business concerned with the appropriate use of its computer systems and networks. It stresses the importance of an awareness of the issues, clear definition by a company of expectations, and regular monitoring. It then looks specifically at actions appropriate for senior managers, before concluding with the role of the individual employee and a discussion of the importance of individual beliefs.

Introduction

The use of computers underpins modern business in the developed world. Much of what *makes* 'modern life' modern, from banking to air travel, from traffic management to shipping, would be quite impossible without the support of interlinked computer systems. As well as this pivotal role in automating and enabling business directly, computers also play a vital part in the internal operations of most companies by aiding internal and external interaction. Through the use of electronic mail and other links, today's 'closed' computer networks within business can now form a major part of internal company communications. In addition, 'open' company networks extend these communications links, literally, to the entire world. The electronic interchange of both specific data and general business information through local, national and international computer networks is continuing to increase dramatically, and there is every sign that this expansion will continue to accelerate.

The advent – and explosion in popularity – of the World Wide Web has brought many changes to business. In particular, the way in which modern business electronically presents itself to an increasingly global marketplace has, in the past few years, changed dramatically. The World Wide Web has spectacularly altered the way in which modern business is promoted. Previously, for instance, considerable capital was needed to obtain a broad availability of advertising material; today, even a small business is able to promote itself globally, at a surprisingly low cost.

While the use of computers and computer networks has changed, and is changing, monitoring and control of computer use may be lagging some distance behind. The original employment within business of specialist computer staff encouraged the devolution of wider accountability from business managers. As was described in Chapter 3, managers typically defined a task to be undertaken by company computers before passing it on to specialists for execution and operation. This early pattern inevitably meant that those whose prime concern was the creation and maintenance of computer hardware were additionally assumed to take responsibility for its appropriate use, a responsibility for which professional training at that time had not prepared them.

Today, many companies remain unaware of the often awesome power of their computer systems, and they may not have considered the potential for their misuse. Only recently has an appreciation of ethical issues entered a computer scientist's professional training, ironically at a time when the rapid expansion of individual computer possession and use inevitably means that most business computers are no longer under the immediate control of a trained computer specialist.

This combination of circumstances – widespread use, lack of informed oversight and distancing of trained specialists – may easily result in the misuse of company computers and computer networks. Misuse is also possible because, without external help, even well-intentioned staff may not appreciate how inappropriate use may be defined; and because, without a clear official definition of computer-related misbehaviour, it can become all too easy for less scrupulous members of staff to act inappropriately.

It is therefore clear that a responsible business organisation needs to take steps to determine exactly to what uses its computer systems are being put, and to clarify what it considers to be appropriate operations. Without such a considered overview, followed by the establishment of clearly defined and published guidelines, staff may well continue to act inappropriately and so risk bringing their employing company practical, legal and ethical problems.

What needs to be done?

In earlier chapters, we have looked at a wide range of situations and potential problems relating to the design and operation of business computer systems, and have discussed many possible responses to them. However, in order to examine in detail the position of computer systems management within a target firm, it is best first to consider the book as a whole and then to draw upon the contents as necessary.

While there can be no substitute for a broadly based investigation and early action, it is appreciated that in the 'real world' of modern business such a time-intensive approach may not always be possible. In this final chapter, therefore, we begin with the presentation of a concise practical response. This synopsis is not intended to replace but to supplement earlier material. It should therefore be of help both in summarising approaches previously discussed in this book and by providing a more succinct coverage of essential material.

The condensed approach that follows is therefore presented as covering essential points in the appropriate control and use of business computer systems. As will be clear from the content, the first summary is intended principally for senior company management, rather than for computer users; a second synopsis, directed at individual employees, will follow.

A practical summary for managers

Reduced to essentials, the three major points that need to be considered by senior managers concerned with the operation of their company computer systems are:

- awareness of the issues
- clear definitions
- monitoring.

Awareness of the issues

Before it is possible to develop any specific answers, it is necessary for a company to be aware of problems. For this reason, the first of the three major points in this section is concerned with establishing the circumstances of business computer deployment and use. While it is true that there are many broad similarities in the way that computers are employed within modern business, it is not necessarily easy simply to transfer a policy from one firm and impose it upon another. Preliminary research, intended to establish the way in which company computer systems are currently being used and to identify any perceived problems related to their use, is strongly recommended. Such an investigation is always likely to be beneficial, but it is *essential* if there should be no computer use policy currently in force. In this case, computer-related activities may bear little or no resemblance to the expectations of management. For management and staff, the baseline of appropriate use is inevitably uncertain, and the actual, as distinct from intended, uses of the computers remain undefined. Imposing any sort of coherent computer use policy in these circumstances is clearly likely to be troublesome and may indeed prove impossible.

The principal advantage of an investigation is that, if carried out well, it should ensure that any subsequent management decisions on computer use are taken in the light of relevant information. It is perhaps too easy, especially under pressure, for a senior manager to base a general view of employee behaviour on their own perceptions. In discussions with senior staff, I have several times been told that such an initial investigation can reveal practices that, while perhaps not that unusual within business, were literally unimaginable to the responsible executives. One example mentioned to me was of a company computer, taken home each night by a member of staff so that they might use it for private work. Had it been a laptop, or portable device, this might have been understandable; but the computer in question was actually a large desktop machine.

It might eventually prove difficult or impossible to actually legislate against all the apparent misuse revealed by an investigation. However, a final advantage of an inquiry is that the investigation and disclosure of particular local problems and issues can, in itself, reassure staff of a company's concern to establish appropriate working practices.

Essentially, then, before making any decisions or instituting a new or changed policy, research intended to produce a current picture of the working practices and technical management of company computer systems is necessary. The depth of this investigation should naturally reflect the topicality and relevance of information that may already be available.

Incidentally, it needs stressing that such a project should always start with a neutral agenda – restricting the investigation to seeking out evidence that supports a previously established position may not be unknown, but it is certainly not advised.

Clear definitions

While guidelines for other aspects of staff behaviour may already exist, in many businesses the use of computer systems has attracted few specific rules and regulations. However, once a company policy has been determined, it is necessary for all those who need to use or maintain company computers and computer systems to be adequately briefed. This means that staff should be aware, before using a business computer, of what the company considers is appropriate behaviour – and what the company considers is *inappropriate* behaviour. While such a proposal may be deceptively simple to suggest, ensuring that staff using computers are properly informed is, in practice, by no means an easy task. It may be especially difficult when the organisation is a complex one, and the management hierarchy may mean that direct involvement and direction by senior staff is not possible.

It must be admitted that, rather than spending time on developing and promoting an appropriate computer use policy, it is clearly far simpler to set the problem aside and instead to assume a common understanding on the part of personnel concerned. Many businesses have indeed taken this approach. However, as has been seen, this tempting alternative may well lead directly to serious problems. It is no substitute for accepting the hard work involved in designing and developing a detailed policy.

For these and other reasons, it may well be that a company has not previously made clear, even to senior managers, what expectations it may have concerning use of its computers. The company assumes, perhaps, that staff will always act responsibly, and that, even if they do not, a local line manager will act to keep their behaviour within acceptable limits. Even if this optimistic scenario is indeed the case, precise definitions of what is considered to be 'acceptable' can easily vary between offices and departments, while the interpretation that different staff members may place upon such casual control is very unlikely to be consistent. It is also true that, without appropriate external input, technical staff in particular may be genuinely unaware of the wider implications of their actions. If left to themselves, this innocence is likely to continue.

Even when a company policy has been developed and promoted, it needs to be continuously monitored and enforced. The passage of time will inevitably result in new members of staff joining the company, while knowledgeable older ones leave. Such changes mean that, without regular clarification, under pressure it is perfectly possible for even the most conscientious employee to lose sight of unfamiliar guidelines. In these circumstances, the effective enforcement of a computer use policy may be difficult. There can be no substitute for regular circulation of a clearly defined and solidly based code, setting out exactly what is officially considered as acceptable behaviour.

Nevertheless, as mentioned earlier, formal company expectations of computer use should not be limited to a description of suitable behaviour. As, with justice, it might be assumed by staff that everything not explicitly condemned is allowed, it is essential for company expectations of *unacceptable* behaviour to also be clarified. This not only has the obvious advantage of defining precisely what type of behaviour is considered unacceptable but also of emphasising a generally socially conscious attitude on the part of the organisation – a responsible view that in the memorable words of one senior US executive, 'always plays well with the stockholders'.

Monitoring

Regular monitoring

Let us assume that a broadly based investigation results in the production and distribution of a well-researched and well-defined company code of conduct. We will further assume that all concerned members of staff are made fully aware of the existence of the code, of its contents, and of its relevance to them. Is it safe to assume that our task is finally over?

Clearly, the answer is 'no'. The procedures outlined can, at best, provide only a snapshot of the computer use currently taking place and ensure that at the moment of implementation all is likely to be well.

Ethical monitoring of all computer-related activities can provide an on-going reassurance to management of the appropriate use of their company systems. As well as encouraging appropriate enforcement, it can additionally give an 'early warning' of the growth of potentially hazardous practices and ethically uncertain new technical developments. For such monitoring to be effective, it needs to cover all areas of business computer use, both internal and external.

Internal aspects of monitoring

Internal aspects might include the behaviour and attitudes of staff, and any information concerning current use of computers or computer networks that might lie outside existing policies. Such monitoring may be indirect, where the effects of computer-related actions are recorded, or direct, when a comprehensive 'sweep' of activities is undertaken regularly. When organising both an initial investigation and later monitoring, there may sometimes be a case for involvement of an external specialist or consultant. This may be especially relevant in smaller companies, where the services of specialist staff may not be available.

The concept of an 'ethical audit' of company computer systems is also relevant here. As was described in Chapter 9, an ethical audit would normally be carried out by an outside consultant. The consultant would be given the task of determining in what ways the company computer systems are currently being used, how these uses relate to any existing ethical use policy, and the relevance of any technical or managerial changes that may have been instituted since an existing ethical use policy was established or last revised. The advantage of involving an external consultant in this way is principally of increasing objectivity, although a report from someone with current specialist knowledge is likely to be more reliable than one carried out by staff members with other responsibilities. A regular ethical audit of business computer systems is not only an ethical insurance policy but it can also provide reassuring concrete evidence of actual current practice, while potentially also giving early warning of impending problems.

External aspects of monitoring

External aspects of monitoring have three principal targets: the development of computer technology relevant to business; the evolution of relevant national and international law; and changes in the expectations of wider society.

As was discussed in Chapter 4, the driving force of developing technology lies behind many decisions that are taken in the business use of computers. It is consequently essential for companies to monitor those technical developments, which may impinge on business computer use. An interesting recent example concerns confidential business data on a laptop computer being copied during routine airport data scans. While such a risk may at first seem remote, Vin McLellan, a US expert, makes a persuasive case for concern. It is detailed in Appendix 7.

Chapter 8 dealt with the principal current legislation relevant to the use of business computers within the UK; knowledge of such legislation is crucial to any business user of computers in the UK. However, the chapter also emphasised the growing trend for European national legislation to absorb the wider collective views of the European Union, as exemplified by EU directives. Concern about appropriate computer use is not limited to the EU; other countries, outside the EU, such as Australia and Canada, are also moving towards legislating about computer usage. Modern business with trade in and beyond Europe needs to keep a keen eye on moves by legislators that may impinge upon their business activities generally, and upon their business computer use specifically. Such active monitoring might, for instance, ensure that adequate and relevant information is given to legislators in advance of the drafting of legislation. It is of course clearly essential to continuously ensure appropriate business conduct, within the law.

Public expectations of business behaviour are notoriously hard to predict. While the popular press may give an aggressive slant to the issues, individual responses can cover a much wider range of reactions. One company, accused of misuse of its computer records, was 'pilloried' by a mass circulation newspaper – at least in the opinion of its management team. However, the same company also claimed to have received letters of support from individual members of the public. What actually happened is still under debate; but what actually *was* the 'public' perception of its behaviour? In such circumstances, it is almost invariably best to present a 'cleaner than clean' image.

The practice of collecting names and address details from those people responding to advertisements is widespread, but selling on the accumulated lists to direct marketing organisations without permission is harder to justify. However, what if a tiny box were printed on each advertisement, with, printed in minute letters, 'tick here if you do not wish to receive direct mailing'?

The practice is legal, but ethically dubious; in such circumstances, can respondents really be said to have made an informed decision? A wiser company might take a radically different course and instead publicise widely its refusal to pass on computer records.

It is difficult to illustrate all possible aspects of the wider monitoring of public opinion, particularly as the aspects that are particularly relevant to individual companies probably vary as much as does public opinion itself. Generally, though, a consistent approach, which emphasises a company's determination to act appropriately while avoiding even the appearance of misbehaviour, is likely to prove the most effective.

A practical summary for individuals

In the first chapter of this book, the relevance of ethical issues to business was demonstrated by reference to personal and professional codes of conduct. In this last chapter, it is well worth stressing that all appropriate business use of computers should be underpinned by an individual appreciation of what is 'right'. For this reason, it may sometimes be necessary to step outside an official role.

In Chapter 6, it was emphasised that, in addition to their official roles as representatives of their employing company, all members of staff have a *personal* responsibility. This responsibility specifically exhorts them to act in accordance with their beliefs, regardless of the official policies of their employing company. In a worst case scenario, they should be prepared to act as whistle blowers in order to publicise unethical or illegal company actions.

Individuals should therefore actively take steps to make themselves aware of appropriate use policies governing computer use that may be held by their company. For a personally ethical employee, it is not sufficient to passively await instruction in what should or should not be done with their allocated computer, or with the company computer network; if necessary, they should actively seek out the necessary information.

Once aware of the company code of conduct, a concerned individual should ensure that all their computer-related activities are in accordance with the policy, except in the event of an ethical conflict such as that described above. In such a case, it may well be necessary to make a line manager aware at an early stage of any perceived deficiencies in the company policy.

Conclusion

In this book, I have described the use of computers within a business setting and have emphasised their power, and the consequent importance of their appropriate use. Given the huge range of uses to which computers can potentially be put, my considered recommendation is that all companies making use of computers should formalise a computer usage policy. The purpose of such a policy would be to make clear to staff what are, and what are not, officially considered to be appropriate uses of company computer systems.

The responsibilities of senior managers are inevitably considerable, and it is perhaps not surprising that, when faced with the everyday pressures inevitable in modern business, the uses of computers may not previously have been given a high priority. However, while the power and ubiquity of today's computers and computer networks provide a powerhouse of business opportunity, they also carry an equal potential for harm. It is essential that the power of business computer systems is appropriately used and controlled, and that this control is exercised in a clear and consistent manner. The development and promotion of an appropriate use policy, together with regular monitoring to ensure its continued effectiveness, is therefore strongly recommended.

At the same time, for all company employees, whatever their level of seniority, underpinning the 'official' actions concerned with appropriate use of computer systems must lie the establishment of a personal code of ethics. Once such a code has been achieved, the individual becomes clear about what they personally believe is right and appropriate.

If the definitions of appropriate use are built upon the joint foundations of official codes and personal belief, both corporate and personal confidence in the use of company computers and computer networks must be stronger. Company machines can continue to provide an irreplaceable benefit to modern business practice.

Appendix 1: Network etiquette

It is essential that the users of networked company computers have guidance on how their employer feels their company's computers should be used. Production of a company document that clarifies an employer's expectations is both sensible and appropriate. Time should be given for employees to read it, and it is a good idea to request a signature confirming that they have done so.

As an example, this appendix contains the guidelines of the Oxford University Computing Services (OUCS). It is used with their kind permission. The original of this document is held electronically at

`<http://info.ox.ac.uk/rules/etiquette.html>`

Network etiquette – for e-mail and news groups

The following guidelines are derived from those in use at many locations on the Internet, and which OUCS strongly recommend all users of e-mail and news groups at Oxford University adopt.

In the established communication media (such as postal mail and telephone) certain widely observed conventions have emerged that help to promote a sound basis for communication between the relevant parties. Electronic mail and news groups are relatively new forms of communication, and consequently few people may be aware of appropriate conventions to use. These are gradually emerging, and the following set is based on advice being provided to network users at many sites around the world.

These conventions (often called 'network etiquette', or 'netiquette') recognise that it is very easy to dispatch e-mail messages or news group postings very quickly, and often little thought is given as to how the message will be received. For instance, if you had intended something in fun, will the humour be evident? If not, it could become quite offensive.

The following code sets out what is considered acceptable behaviour for network users. The guidelines apply equally to the use of e-mail, news groups and any other electronic communications media.

Daily routines and housekeeping

- Check your mail regularly; ignoring a mail message is discourteous and confusing to the sender.
- Always reply, even if a brief acknowledgement is all you can manage – there is still sufficient unreliability about e-mail transmissions to create doubt in the mind of the sender that you ever received it.
- Conversely, never assume that simply because you have sent a message it has been read.
- Reply promptly. E-mail systems often do not have the conventional 'pending' trays of the desktop, or secretaries to remind you, so it may be easier to forget an e-mail message.
- Treat the security of e-mail messages about the same as a message on a postcard; i.e. recognise that anyone along the chain of distribution could get to see what you have said, and it might even end up in someone else's hands. If you have sensitive messages to send, use some form of encrypting (known only to you and the recipient, such as PGP), or use some other more secure medium.
- Develop an orderly filing system for those e-mail messages you wish to keep; delete unwanted ones to conserve disk space.
- Make arrangements for your e-mail to be forwarded to someone to handle when you go away, or install an automatic reply system advising that you will not be able to respond.
- Encourage others to communicate with you by e-mail. Ensure you give them your correct e-mail address – include it on your business card and letterhead.

Writing styles

Be very careful how you express yourself, especially if you feel heated about the subject (for instance if you are shooting off a quick response to some issue). E-mail lacks the other cues and clues that convey the sense in which what you say is to be taken, and you can easily convey the wrong impression. If you meant something in jest, use a 'smiley' to convey that.

Remember that the message will be read by another person, who may not appreciate your 'personality'.

Do not reproduce a message in full when responding to it, especially if you are posting to a news group. This is hard on the readers and wasteful of resources. Instead, be selective in the parts that you include in your response.

Try to keep messages fairly brief. Most people would not choose a computer screen to read text on in preference to a printed document, and it can get very tiring for some users. Try to restrict yourself to one or two screens at most.

Message subjects

Make sure that the 'subject' field of your message is meaningful. Where someone receives many messages, it can be very confusing and frustrating not to be able to judge the subject matter correctly from its subject field. This is especially important when you are posting messages to news groups. When you use the 'reply' option, ensure that the subject field (usually filled in for you under those circumstances) still accurately reflects the content of your message.

Try to restrict yourself to one subject per message, sending multiple messages if you have multiple subjects. This helps recipients to use the 'subject' field to manage the messages they have received.

Do not broadcast e-mail messages unnecessarily. It is very easy to do but can be very annoying to recipients (and wastes resources). In particular, do not send or forward chain e-mail – it offends some people and is wasteful of network resources.

Other people's messages

Do not extract and use text from someone else's message without acknowledgement. This is plagiarism. You would not do this with conventional mail, so do not let the ease of being able to do it with e-mail lead you into bad habits.

Do not make changes to someone else's message and pass it on without making it clear where you have made the changes. This would be misrepresentation.

Be 'legal, decent, honest and truthful'

Do not pretend you are someone else when sending mail.

Do not send frivolous, abusive or defamatory messages. Apart from being discourteous or offensive, they may break the law.

Be tolerant of others' mistakes. Some people are new to this medium and may not be good typists, or they may accidentally delete your message and ask you to re-send it.

Remember that the various laws of the land relating to written communication apply equally to e-mail messages, including the laws relating to defamation, copyright, obscenity, fraudulent misrepresentation, freedom of information and wrongful discrimination.

And finally, your use of the university IT facilities and networks is restricted to academic, social and recreational use only. Remember that sending e-mail from your university account is similar to sending a letter on an Oxford University letterhead, so do not say anything that might discredit or bring embarrassment to the university.

Author: Alex Reid.
Copyright: Oxford University Computing Services.

Appendix 2: Example of an acceptable use policy

It is important that users of networked computer systems appreciate what behaviour is expected of them and are also aware of the purposes for which the systems they use were created and maintained. As described in Chapter 8, there is a legal and ethical responsibility for the owner of a computer network to make users aware of these issues. One good method of doing so is through the distribution of an appropriate acceptable use policy, which highlights areas of unacceptable behaviour.

This appendix contains a rather more heavyweight example of an acceptable use policy than that in Appendix 1, because it is a model for the appropriate use of a computer network rather than the actions of an individual user.

Universities in the United Kingdom have the advantage of electronic connection, to each other and to the wider Internet, through the provision of a special network (called JANET (**J**oint **A**cademic **NET**work), with a high-speed backbone known as Super-JANET). These are administered by the United Kingdom Education and Research Networking Association (UKERNA) on behalf of the Joint Information Systems Committee (JISC) of the UK Higher Education Funding Councils. The JANET Acceptable Use Policy (determined by the JISC) provides an excellent example of good practice.

This appendix reproduces (with permission) the complete text of the JANET policy. While most commercial organisations will clearly not require such a depth of technical material, many of the aspects of the policy are generally applicable to the provision of networked computer services at any scale.

JANET Acceptable Use Policy

Contents

Background and definitions.
Acceptable use.
Unacceptable use.
Passing on and resale of JANET service.
Compliance.

Background and definitions

1 'JANET' is the name given to the collection of networking services and facilities which support the communication requirements of the UK education and research community.

2 The Higher Education Funding Councils for England, Scotland and Wales are responsible jointly for the provision of JANET. They exercise this responsibility through their Joint Information Systems Committee ('the JISC') and any dispute over the interpretation of this Policy will be resolved by the JISC.

3 UKERNA (an acronym for the United Kingdom Education and Research Networking Association) is the trading name of the company contracted by the JISC, acting in the name of the Higher Education Funding Council for England, for the provision of the JANET service. This includes the day-to-day management of this Policy.

4 This Policy applies in the first instance to any organisation authorised to use JANET (a 'User Organisation'). It is the responsibility of User Organisations to ensure that members of their own user communities use JANET services in an acceptable manner and in accordance with current legislation.

5 It is therefore recommended that each User Organisation establishes its own statement of acceptable use within the context of the services provided to its users, and in a form that is compatible with the conditions expressed in this Policy. Such a statement may refer to, or include, this document. If material from this document is included, this must be done in such a way as to ensure that there is no misrepresentation of the intent of this Policy. UKERNA can advise on this aspect as and where necessary.

6 JANET is maintained to support teaching, learning and research. Only organisations whose predominant use of JANET falls into these categories, or whose use is approved by the JISC, will be permitted to make a connection to JANET, whether directly or via another organisation itself connected to JANET.

Acceptable use

7 A User Organisation may use JANET for the purpose of interworking with other User Organisations, and with organisations attached to networks which are reachable via interworking agreements operated by UKERNA. All use of JANET is subject to payment of the appropriate charges in force during the period of service. Any provision of service must be authorised in advance.

8 Subject to the following paragraphs, JANET may be used for any legal activity that is in furtherance of the aims and policies of the User Organisation.

Unacceptable use

9 JANET may not be used for any of the following:

   9.1 the creation or transmission (other than for properly supervised and lawful research purposes) of any offensive, obscene or indecent images, data or other material, or any data capable of being resolved into obscene or indecent images or material;

9.2   the creation or transmission of material which is designed or likely to cause annoyance, inconvenience or needless anxiety;

9.3   the creation or transmission of defamatory material;

9.4   the transmission of material such that this infringes the copyright of another person;

9.5   the transmission of unsolicited commercial or advertising material either to other User Organisations or to organisations connected to other networks;

9.6   deliberate unauthorised access to facilities or services accessible via JANET;

9.7   deliberate activities with any of the following characteristics:

- wasting staff effort or networked resources, including time on end systems accessible via JANET and the effort of staff involved in the support of those systems;
- corrupting or destroying other users' data;
- violating the privacy of other users;
- disrupting the work of other users;
- using JANET in a way that denies service to other users (for example, deliberate or reckless overloading of access links or of switching equipment);
- continuing to use an item of networking software or hardware after UKERNA has requested that use cease because it is causing disruption to the correct functioning of JANET;
- other misuse of JANET or networked resources, such as the introduction of 'viruses'.

10 Where JANET is being used to access another network, any abuse of the acceptable use policy of that network will be regarded as unacceptable use of JANET.

Passing on and resale of JANET service

11 It is not permitted to provide access to JANET for third parties without the prior agreement of UKERNA, with the exceptions in the following sub-paragraphs.

11.1 The JISC has resale schemes whereby certain types of User Organisation may sell on JANET services under defined circumstances. Details may be obtained from UKERNA.

11.2 It is acceptable for a User Organisation connected to JANET to extend access to others on a limited basis, provided no charge is made for such access. For example, it is acceptable that a visitor to the Organisation be permitted to gain access to JANET for the purpose of maintaining contact with his or her home organisation. It is intended that such use be regulated by the User Organisation in the same manner as it would regulate occasional use by third parties of its other facilities, such as its telephone and IT support systems.

12 A third party, where an individual, means someone who is not acting as a member of the User Organisation. Where it applies to a separate organisation, this is defined to be any organisation that is in law a separate entity to the User Organisation.

Compliance

13 It is the responsibility of the User Organisation to take all reasonable steps to ensure compliance with the conditions set out in this Policy document, and to ensure that unacceptable use of JANET does not occur. The discharge of this responsibility must include informing those at the Organisation with access to JANET of their obligations in this respect.

14 Where necessary, service may be withdrawn from the User Organisation. This may take one of two forms:

14.1 An indefinite withdrawal of service, should a violation of these conditions persist after appropriate warnings have been given by UKERNA. Such a withdrawal of service would only be made on the authority of the JISC.

Restoration would be made only when the JISC was satisfied that the appropriate steps had been taken at the Organisation involved to ensure acceptable behaviour in future.

14.2 A suspension of service, should a violation of these conditions cause serious degradation of the service to other users of JANET. Such a suspension would be made on the judgement of UKERNA, and service would be restored when the cause of the degradation of service to others had been removed.

15 Where violation of these conditions is illegal or unlawful, or results in loss or damage to UKERNA or JANET resources or the resources of third parties accessible via JANET, the matter may be referred for legal action.

16 It is preferable for misuse to be prevented by a combination of responsible attitudes to the use of JANET resources on the part of users and appropriate disciplinary measures taken by their Organisations.

Version: 4.0
Date: April 1995
Editor: R.A. Day

Trademarks

'JANET' and 'UKERNA' are trademarks of the Higher Education Funding Councils for England, Scotland and Wales, which have granted the JNT Association the right to use the marks.

Disclaimer

Neither the Higher Education Funding Council for England nor the JNT Association can accept any liability for any loss or damage resulting from the use of the material contained herein. The information is believed to be correct but no liability can be accepted for any inaccuracies.

Availability

Further copies of the JANET Acceptable Use Policy may be obtained from the JANET Liaison Desk, UKERNA, Atlas Centre, Chilton, Didcot, Oxfordshire, OX11 0QS.

• •

It is important that business users of the Internet appreciate the extensive acceptance there of the free speech ethic, having its roots in the academic nature of the early Internet.

'Passing off', where one World Wide Web site is felt to be assuming the identity of another, is clearly inappropriate. However, some reactions to a perceived instance of 'passing off' may be excessive.

• • • • • • • • • • • • • • • •

One large commercial company that vigorously defends its trademarks and company image is the toy giant 'Toys 'R' Us'. The following letter followed attempts by the company to silence the World Wide Web site 'Roadkills-R-Us', which was mentioned in Chapter 7. Full details are available on the (still unsilenced) Roadkills site:

```
<http://www.rru.com>
```

Roadkills-R-Us Does Not Exist
Rte 1, Box 558 / Johnson Rd / Leander, TX / 78641-9413
1-512-267-1063
1-512-343-6666

```
7 November, 1995

Mavis K. Fowler, Esq.
Toys 'R' Us
461 From Rd.
Paramus, NJ
07652-3524

Re: Your File No. TI95-082

Ms. Fowler:

This has gone on for too long. Toys 'R' Us has repeatedly refused
to answer my specific questions and objections. All good faith
attempts to clarify the situation have been ignored, except for my
```

offer to add a disclaimer to the Roadkills-R-Us web pages (which you referred to as "advertising"), which you rejected for no stated reason. Continued action of this sort on the part of Toys 'R' Us will be considered harassment.

I will respond one more time to your absurd demands. I expect you to respond to each of the following points fully and separately, showing any cause for your disagreement.

1 Roadkills-R-Us is purely a work of fiction for entertainment purposes – a satire of a number of things, one of which is the Toys 'R' Us name, and the courts have repeatedly upheld the use of satire in such cases.

2 Roadkills-R-Us does not exist as any sort of legal entity, and to the best of my knowledge, there never has been any such legal entity as Roadkills-R-Us. There is no corporation or other type of business associated with the name Roadkills-R-Us – or if there is, I am completely unaware of it and unassociated with it. Furthermore, since there is no company, there are no articles of incorporation, fictitious name certificates, or other legal forms to change. Therefore, Roadkills-R-Us was in compliance with your mandates before you sent them.

3 There is no Roadkills-R-Us building or physical entity, and hence, no sign outside it. Therefore, Roadkills-R-Us was in compliance with your mandates before you sent them.

4 There is no Roadkills-R-Us stationery. Therefore, Roadkills-R-Us was in compliance with your mandates before you sent them.

5 There are no Roadkills-R-Us business cards. Therefore, Roadkills-R-Us was in compliance with your mandates before you sent them.

6 There are no Roadkills-R-Us checks or bank accounts. Therefore, Roadkills-R-Us was in compliance with your mandates before you sent them.

7 There is no Roadkills-R-Us telephone or telephone number, and hence, no telephone directory entry. Therefore, Roadkills-R-Us was in compliance with your mandates before you sent them.

8 There are no Roadkills-R-Us trade directory entries. Therefore, Roadkills-R-Us was in compliance with your mandates before you sent them.

9 As I have stated before, there is almost no "likelihood of confusion" between the name Roadkills-R-Us and any actual business whose name ends in -R-Us. No reasonable person, person capable of reasoning, or even someone who followed the O.J. Simpson trial on national TV as if their own life depended on it, is any more likely to confuse Roadkills-R-Us with any actual business than they, or you, are likely to sprout wings and fly under their, or your, own power.

I request that I have your response to each and every point above within two (2) weeks from November 10, 1995, by which date you should have received this letter.

Sincerely,

Miles O'Neal

This letter is © Miles O'Neal and is reproduced with his permission.

Appendix 4: Professional organisations for management available on the World Wide Web

Business users of the Internet have the advantage of direct access to professional organisations through relevant World Wide Web sites. This list of professional organisations is based – with thanks – upon that drawn up by the the Institute of Management. To connect to one of these web sites, the url (universal resource locator) given in <angle brackets> is typed into a web browser, such as Netscape or Microsoft's Internet Explorer. Do not type the brackets.

UK professional organisations

British Institute of Facilities Management

<http://www.bifm.org.uk>

Provides details of BIFM membership, publications and training.

Business Clubs UK

<http://www.businessclub.co.uk/bcuk>

The federation of UK business clubs, groups and associations.

Chartered Institute of Management Accountants

<http://www.cima.org.uk>

Provides details of CIMA courses and publications and includes access to online mailing lists.

Chartered Institute of Marketing

`<http://www.cim.co.uk>`

Lists the activities of the institute and provides access to the library and an information service for members.

Chartered Institute of Public Finance and Accountancy

`<http://www.cipfa.org.uk>`

Includes a comprehensive listing of public service organisations in the UK.

Chartered Institute of Purchasing and Supply

`<http://www.cips.org>`

An international education and qualifications body for purchasing professionals.

Industrial Society

`<http://www.indsoc.co.uk>`

An independent UK training and development organisation.

Institute of Administrative Management

`<http://www.electranet.com/iam>`

Provides professional support for administrative managers.

Institute for Employment Studies

`<http://www.employment-studies.co.uk>`

Includes details of IES research, with summaries of research reports.

Institute for Fiscal Studies

`<http://www1.ifs.org.uk>`

A policy research charity that publishes all its work (including surveys and guides to taxes and pensions) in some form on the Internet.

Institute of Health Services Management

`<http://www.ihsm.co.uk>`

Provides details of events and publications and includes discussion forums for members.

Institute of Logistics

<http://www.institute-of-logistics.org.uk>

Provides details of services, publications and events.

Institute of Management

<http://www.inst-mgt.org.uk/institute/contents.html>

The mission of the Institute of Management is to promote the art and science of management.

Institute of Management Services

<http://www.imgtserv.co.uk/imgtserv>

Home page with details of the institute's services.

Institution of Occupational Safety and Health

<http://www.iosh.co.uk>

A professional body for individuals involved in occupational safety and health.

Institute of Personnel and Development

<http://www.ipd.co.uk>

Provides access to news groups and an online journal.

Law Society

<http://www.lawsoc.org.uk>

Primarily an information service for Law Society members, this site also contains public services such as advice on locating lawyers and solicitors.

Management Consultancies Association

<http://www.mca.org.uk>

Site includes an online directory of member firms and the services they offer.

Royal Society for the Encouragement of Arts, Manufacturers and Commerce (RSA)

<http://www.rsa.org.uk>

Charity carrying out research into economic and occupational issues. Current research includes the Redefining Work Project.

Non-UK professional organisations

American Institute for Managing Diversity

`<http://www.aimd.org>`

Details are given of research reports and other AIMD publications.

American Management Association International

`<http://www.amanet.org>`

Provides links to major AMA centres throughout the world, including the US head office, the Management Centre Europe, the Canadian Management Centre and Management Centre Mexico (see below for a direct link to Management Centre Europe).

Australian Human Resources Institute

`<http://www.ahri.com.au>`

Includes information resources for human resource professionals.

Australian Institute of Management

`<http://www.aim.com.au>`

AIM is introduced along with current activities and details of such services as training and information.

Canadian Institute of Management

`<http://www.cim.ca>`

Details of CIM plus some articles from *Canadian Manager* magazine.

European Institute for Business Ethics

`<http://www.nijenrode.nl/research/eibe.html>`

Site includes details of the EIBE and of the European Business Ethics Network.

Institute for Business and Professional Ethics

`<http://condor.depaul.edu/ethics/index.html>`

Based at De Paul University, Chicago. Site includes Online Journal of Ethics and a paper you may find interesting – 'Computer Ethics & Clothing' by Duncan Langford.

Institute of Management and Administration

`<http://www.ioma.com>`

An American site that provides articles, news, discussion groups and a list of over 600 links to other sites.

Irish Institute of Management

<http://www.imi.ie>

Details of the institute are given.

Management Centre Europe

<http://www.mce.be>

European office of the American Management Association International (AMA).

New Zealand Institute of Management

<http://nzim.co.nz>

Site contains details of NZIM and details of the Management Brief Abstracts journal summary service.

Project Management Institute

<http://www.pmi.org>

Leading international organisation that has established its own project management standards.

Singapore Institute of Management

<http://www.sim.ac.sg/simmain.nsf>

Non-profit organisation aiming to enhance managerial and organisational effectiveness in Singapore.

Society for Human Resource Management

<http://www.shrm.org>

Site includes a full-text online magazine and an extensive list of HR links.

Appendix 5: BCS and ACM codes of conduct

This appendix contains the text of the British Computer Society's Code of Conduct and the official summary of the Code of Ethics and Professional Conduct of the Association for Computing Machinery. Both of these professional codes of conduct are discussed in Chapter 9. The codes are reproduced with the kind permission of the BCS and the ACM.

British Computer Society Code of Conduct

Rules of professional conduct

As an aid to understanding, these rules have been grouped in the principal duties which all members should endeavour to discharge in pursuing their professional lives.

The public interest

1 Members shall in their professional practice safeguard public health and safety and have regard to the protection of the environment.

2 Members shall have due regard to the legitimate rights of third parties.

3 Members shall ensure that within their chosen fields they have knowledge and understanding of relevant legislation, regulations and standards and that they comply with such requirements.

4 Members shall in their professional practice have regard to basic human rights and shall avoid any actions that adversely affect such rights.

Duty to employers and clients

5 Members shall carry out work with due care and diligence in accordance with the requirements of the employer or client and shall, if their professional judgement is overruled, indicate the likely consequences.

6 Members shall endeavour to complete work undertaken on time and to budget and shall advise their employer or client as soon as practicable if any overrun is foreseen.

7 Members shall not offer or provide, or receive in return, any inducement for the introduction of business from a client unless there is full prior disclosure of the facts to that client.

8 Members shall not disclose or authorise to be disclosed, or use for personal gain or to benefit a third party, confidential information acquired in the course of professional practice, except with prior written permission of the employer or client or at the direction of a court of law.

9 Members should seek to avoid being put in a position where they may become privy to or party to activities or information concerning activities which would conflict with their responsibilities in 1–4 above.

10 Members should not misrepresent or withhold information on the capabilities of products, systems or services with which they are concerned or take advantage of the lack of knowledge or inexperience of others.

11 Members shall not, except where specifically so instructed, handle client's monies or place contracts or orders in connection with work on which they knowingly have any interest, financial or otherwise.

12 Members shall not purport to exercise independent judgement on behalf of a client on any product or service which they knowingly have any interest, financial or otherwise.

Duty to the profession

13 Members shall uphold the reputation of the profession and shall seek to improve professional standards through participation in their development, use and enforcement, and shall avoid any action which will adversely affect the good standing of the profession.

14 Members shall in their professional practice seek to advance public knowledge and understanding of computing and information systems and technology and to counter false or misleading statements which are detrimental to the profession.

15 Members shall encourage and support fellow members in their professional development and, where possible, provide opportunities for the professional development of new entrants to the profession.

16 Members shall act with integrity towards fellow members and to members of other professions with whom they are concerned in a professional capacity and shall avoid engaging in any activity which is incompatible with professional status.

17 Members shall not make any public statement in their professional capacity unless properly qualified and, where appropriate, authorised to do so, and shall have due regard to the likely consequences of any such statement on others.

Professional competence and integrity

18 Members shall seek to upgrade their professional knowledge and skill and shall maintain awareness of technological developments, procedures and standards which are relevant to their field, and shall encourage their subordinates to do likewise.

19 Members shall seek to conform to recognised good practice, including quality standards which are in their judgement relevant, and shall encourage their subordinates to do likewise.

20 Members shall only offer to do work or provide service which is within their professional competence and shall not lay claim to any level of competence which they do not possess, and any professional opinion which they are asked to give shall be objective and reliable.

21 Members shall accept professional responsibility for their work and for the work of subordinates and associates under their direction, and shall not terminate any assignment except for good reason and on reasonable notice.

22 Members shall avoid any situation that may give rise to a conflict of interest between themselves and their client and shall make full and immediate disclosure to the client if any such conflict should occur.

Association for Computing Machinery Code of Ethics and Professional Conduct – Summary

Adopted by the ACM council on 16 October 1992.

1 General moral imperatives

As an ACM member I will

1.1 Contribute to society and human well-being.

1.2 Avoid harm to others.

1.3 Be honest and trustworthy.

1.4 Be fair and take action not to discriminate.

1.5 Honour property rights including copyrights and patents.

1.6 Give proper credit for intellectual property.

1.7 Respect the privacy of others.

1.8 Honour confidentiality.

2. More specific professional responsibilities

As an ACM computing professional, I will

2.1 Strive to achieve the highest quality, effectiveness, and dignity in both the process and products of professional work.

2.2 Acquire and maintain professional competence.

2.3 Know and respect existing laws pertaining to professional work.

2.4 Accept and provide appropriate professional review.

2.5 Give comprehensive and thorough evaluations of computer systems and their impacts, including analysis of possible risks.

2.6 Honour contracts, agreements, and assigned responsibilities.

2.7 Improve public understanding of computing and its consequences.

2.8 Access computing and communication resources only when authorized to do so.

3 Organizational leadership imperatives

As an ACM member and an organizational leader, I will

3.1 Articulate social responsibilities of members of an organizational unit and encourage full acceptance of those responsibilities.

3.2 Manage personnel and resources to design and build information systems that enhance the quality of working life.

3.3 Acknowledge and support proper and authorized uses of an organization's computing and communication resources.

3.4 Ensure that users and those who will be affected by a system have their needs clearly articulated during the assessment and design of requirements; later, the system must be validated to meet [its] requirements.

3.5 Articulate and support policies that protect the dignity of users and others affected by a computing system.

3.6 Create opportunities for members of the organization to learn the principles and limitations of computer systems.

4 Compliance with the code

As an ACM member, I will

4.1 Uphold and promote the principles of this code.

4.2 Treat violations of this code as inconsistent with membership in the ACM.

ACM Code of Ethics and Professional Conduct is reprinted from Communications of the ACM, V. 36:2, February 1993, by permission.

Appendix 6: The Data Protection Act, 1998 Data protection principles and interpretation of principles

Knowledge of the new 1998 Data Protection Act is essential for those responsible for business computer systems. This appendix reproduces two of the most informative sections of the Act, those describing the Act's underlying principles, and how they should be interpreted.

This text is © crown copyright 1998, reproduced with permission.

Schedule 1 The data protection principles

Part I The principles

1 Personal data shall be processed fairly and lawfully and, in particular, shall not be processed unless
  (a) at least one of the conditions in Schedule 2 is met,
      and
  (b) in the case of sensitive personal data, at least one of the conditions in Schedule 3 is also met.
2 Personal data shall be obtained only for one or more specified and lawful purposes, and shall not be further processed in any manner incompatible with that purpose or those purposes.
3 Personal data shall be adequate, relevant and not excessive in relation to the purpose or purposes for which they are processed.
4 Personal data shall be accurate and, where necessary, kept up to date.
5 Personal data processed for any purpose or purposes shall not be kept for longer than is necessary for that purpose or those purposes.
6 Personal data shall be processed in accordance with the rights of data subjects under this Act.

7 Appropriate technical and organisational measures shall be taken against unauthorised or unlawful processing of personal data and against accidental loss or destruction of, or damage to, personal data.

8 Personal data shall not be transferred to a country or territory outside the European Economic Area unless that country or territory ensures an adequate level of protection for the rights and freedoms of data subjects in relation to the processing of personal data.

Part II Interpretation of the principles in Part I

The first principle

1 (1) In determining for the purposes of the first principle whether personal data are processed fairly, regard is to be had to the method by which they are obtained, including in particular whether any person from whom they are obtained is deceived or misled as to the purpose or purposes for which they are to be processed.

(2) Subject to paragraph 2, for the purposes of the first principle data are to be treated as obtained fairly if they consist of information obtained from a person who

   (a) is authorised by or under any enactment to supply it,
       or
   (b) is required to supply it by or under any enactment or by any convention or other instrument imposing an international obligation on the United Kingdom.

2 (1) Subject to paragraph 3, for the purposes of the first principle personal data are not to be treated as processed fairly unless

   (a) in the case of data obtained from the data subject, the data controller ensures so far as practicable that the data subject has, is provided with, or has made readily available to him, the information specified in sub-paragraph (3), and
   (b) in any other case, the data controller ensures so far as practicable that, before the relevant time or as soon as practicable after that time, the data subject has, is provided with, or has made readily available to him, the information specified in sub-paragraph (3).

(2) In sub-paragraph (1)(b) "the relevant time" means

   (a) the time when the data controller first processes the data, or
   (b) in a case where at that time disclosure to a third party within a reasonable period is envisaged
       (i) if the data are in fact disclosed to such a person within that period, the time when the data are first disclosed,
       (ii) if within that period the data controller becomes, or ought to become, aware that the data are unlikely to be disclosed to such a person within that period, the time when the data controller does become, or ought to become, so aware, or
       (iii) in any other case, the end of that period.

(3) The information referred to in sub-paragraph (1) is as follows, namely

   (a) the identity of the data controller,
   (b) if he has nominated a representative for the purposes of this Act, the identity of that representative,

   (c)   the purpose or purposes for which the data are intended to be processed, and
   (d)   any further information which is necessary, having regard to the specific circumstances in which the data are or are to be processed, to enable processing in respect of the data subject to be fair.

3 (1)   Paragraph 2(1)(b) does not apply where either of the primary conditions in sub-paragraph (2), together with such further conditions as may be prescribed by the Secretary of State by order, are met.
   (2)   The primary conditions referred to in sub-paragraph (1) are
      (a)   that the provision of that information would involve a disproportionate effort, or
      (b)   that the recording of the information to be contained in the data by, or the disclosure of the data by, the data controller is necessary for compliance with any legal obligation to which the data controller is subject, other than an obligation imposed by contract.

4 (1)   Personal data which contain a general identifier falling within a description prescribed by the Secretary of State by order are not to be treated as processed fairly and lawfully unless they are processed in compliance with any conditions so prescribed in relation to general identifiers of that description.
   (2)   In sub-paragraph (1) "a general identifier" means any identifier (such as, for example, a number or code used for identification purposes) which
      (a)   relates to an individual, and
      (b)   forms part of a set of similar identifiers which is of general application.

The second principle

5 The purpose or purposes for which personal data are obtained may in particular be specified
   (a)   in a notice given for the purposes of paragraph 2 by the data controller to the data subject,
      or
   (b)   in a notification given to the Commissioner under Part III of this Act.

6 In determining whether any disclosure of personal data is compatible with the purpose or purposes for which the data were obtained, regard is to be had to the purpose or purposes for which the personal data are intended to be processed by any person to whom they are disclosed.

The fourth principle

7 The fourth principle is not to be regarded as being contravened by reason of any inaccuracy in personal data which accurately record information obtained by the data controller from the data subject or a third party in a case where
   (a)   having regard to the purpose or purposes for which the data were obtained and further processed, the data controller has taken reasonable steps to ensure the accuracy of the data, and
   (b)   if the data subject has notified the data controller of the data subject's view that the data are inaccurate, the data indicate that fact.

The sixth principle

8 A person is to be regarded as contravening the sixth principle if, but only if

    (a) he contravenes section 7 by failing to supply information in accordance with that section,

    (b) he contravenes section 10 by failing to comply with a notice given under subsection (1) of that section to the extent that the notice is justified or by failing to give a notice under subsection (3) of that section,

    (c) he contravenes section 11 by failing to comply with a notice given under subsection (1) of that section, or

    (d) he contravenes section 12 by failing to comply with a notice given under subsection (1) or (2)(b) of that section or by failing to give a notification under subsection (2)(a) of that section or a notice under subsection (3) of that section.

The seventh principle

9 Having regard to the state of technological development and the cost of implementing any measures, the measures must ensure a level of security appropriate to

    (a) the harm that might result from such unauthorised or unlawful processing or accidental loss, destruction or damage as are mentioned in the seventh principle, and

    (b) the nature of the data to be protected.

10 The data controller must take reasonable steps to ensure the reliability of any employees of his who have access to the personal data.

11 Where processing of personal data is carried out by a data processor on behalf of a data controller, the data controller must in order to comply with the seventh principle

    (a) choose a data processor providing sufficient guarantees in respect of the technical and organisational security measures governing the processing to be carried out, and

    (b) take reasonable steps to ensure compliance with those measures.

12 Where processing of personal data is carried out by a data processor on behalf of a data controller, the data controller is not to be regarded as complying with the seventh principle unless

    (a) the processing is carried out under a contract

        (i) which is made or evidenced in writing, and

        (ii) under which the data processor is to act only on instructions from the data controller, and

    (b) the contract requires the data processor to comply with obligations equivalent to those imposed on a data controller by the seventh principle.

The eighth principle

13 An adequate level of protection is one which is adequate in all the circumstances of the case, having regard in particular to

(a) the nature of the personal data,

(b) the country or territory of origin of the information contained in the data,

(c) the country or territory of final destination of that information,

(d) the purposes for which and period during which the data are intended to be processed,

(e) the law in force in the country or territory in question,

(f) the international obligations of that country or territory,

(g) any relevant codes of conduct or other rules which are enforceable in that country or territory (whether generally or by arrangement in particular cases), and

(h) any security measures taken in respect of the data in that country or territory.

14 The eighth principle does not apply to a transfer falling within any paragraph of Schedule 4, except in such circumstances and to such extent as the Secretary of State may by order provide.

15 (1) Where

(a) in any proceedings under this Act any question arises as to whether the requirement of the eighth principle as to an adequate level of protection is met in relation to the transfer of any personal data to a country or territory outside the European Economic Area, and

(b) a Community finding has been made in relation to transfers of the kind in question, that question is to be determined in accordance with that finding.

(2) In sub-paragraph (1) "Community finding" means a finding of the European Commission, under the procedure provided for in Article 31(2) of the Data Protection Directive, that a country or territory outside the European Economic Area does, or does not, ensure an adequate level of protection within the meaning of Article 25(2) of the Directive.

Appendix 7: Risks to business from official inspections

Business people carrying laptop computers frequently pass through airport security. They may be unaware of the risks, graphically made clear in this news group posting from Vin McLellan, the Privacy Guild. It is reproduced with permission.

From: Vin McLellan <vin@shore.net>
Subject: Re: Computer hard disk scanning by HM Customs & Excise

Reading the comments of the UK Customs and Excise spokesfolk about their new policy of routinely scanning the digital memories carried by travellers, one is struck by their apparent naivete, e.g.[1]

Nothing bad could be happening since it is all done in the presence of the traveller. The traveller is allowed to watch. It's only a "scan" for appalling digital smut – although the process, as described, involves copying the disk (and almost any "scan" allows that, overtly or covertly.) It makes me wonder if they had any idea of what kind of Pandora's Box they were opening.

Two years ago, a gentleman at Hewlett-Packard Labs in California – the former head of R&D at Apple, as I recall – mentioned on one of the Internet newsgroups that senior HP executives had been warned by US intelligence agencies that big-number cash bounties had been posted (where and by whom, it was not clear) for anyone who could obtain the travel laptop of particular US computer industry executives. The targets were identified by name and position.

I suspect that the UK bureaucrats who thought up this search for illicit images never considered that the digital soup they were straining for porn in this low-level bureaucratic process might be worth $100K or $500K or $1M on the black market. (They may not have thought about how useful and productive their data-trap might look to Her Majesty's own Intel chaps either, although many suspect C&E's naivete in that regard was brief.)

Such casually intrusive and randomized search procedures are used for low-value valuables. (I suspect DeBeer's couriers don't get their wares pawed by junior staff who

174

can't tell a diamond from a rhinestone.) Information has always had potentially high value, of course – but even the post-industrial societies are still adjusting to the way computers concentrate and create such value in data. HM C&E is not likely on the cutting edge here. C&E officials have probably been amazed at anger and passionate resentment many knowledge-workers have shown toward their new policy.

The C&E baggage inspector who only barely computer-literate is not likely to realize how profoundly a traveller may feel violated by a process which, by it's nature, necessarily offers Her Majesty's government an opportunity to copy one or two gigabytes of personal and professional memories – with the traveller forced to open encrypted files as if they were just another "locked suitcase".

At least until this UK initiative raised the possibility of routine data searches, many of us typically travelled with almost all our personal messages, diaries, as well as all our professional work for the past two or three years in a laptop hanging from a shoulder strap. (With my RSA SecurPC, it seemed safe, as well as readily accessible.) My outrage at the invasiveness and indignity of such a search would probably shock someone who doesn't live and work online, the way I and many others do.

Corporate execs and couriers may have far more valuable files: business plans, negotiation options, strategic plans, industrial plans, prototype products, competitive analyses, corporate records of all types. (Old and deleted files – even unsaved data like remote-access passwords and encryption keys dropped in swap or temp files on a PC – are often retrievable from a copy of a hard disk.) A business traveller planning to negotiate a deal in the City, offer a contract to a British firm, or set up a plant or office in the UK, may now risk corporate treasure, as well as personal indignity, in subjecting himself to such a C&E search.

For some of us, a strip search and sodium pentathol session at the C&E post would be less invasive – but even the British bureaucrats who came up with this policy would probably consider routine truth-serum interrogations of travellers over the top: unreasonable, uncivil, disrespectful, and likely to drive off tourists, merchants, bankers, and traders who bring money and jobs to the UK.

Most of us, of course, will immediately jump to Cyberspace, where ready access to encrypted files on a server or website anywhere in the world leaves them available, but largely secure from government eavesdroppers (even when the recipient of the data transfer is in a London hotel!) It will be a very very stupid smut merchant who gets caught by C&E's memory trap. On the other hand, damage done to the British economy by C&E's routine searches of travellers' digital memories may be apparent rather quickly.

I know of several large multinational corporations that have regular couriers who (daily or several times a week) carry sensitive material – usually in digital form, on a laptop or Zip disks – from their Paris offices to London, where it is encrypted and transmitted to their corporate offices around the world. These firms, and others with similar requirements, restrict the size of their French installations (and investments) too.

This happens because French law forbids any firm, operating within France, from using strong encryption for either domestic or international data transfers – unless they give the French authorities the crypto keys that would allow the SCSSI to access, copy, and potentially exploit those messages or data files.

(French intelligence agencies – like their counterparts in most governments today – are widely suspected of trying to steal commercial and industrial secrets from non-French businessmen, and using them to benefit French industrial and commercial interests. France, not being a beneficiary of the Echelon net like the US and UK, maybe has to try a little harder. In recent years, rumours have also led many international flyers to believe, rightly or wrongly, that the first class seats on Air France are wired by those same French agencies for commercial espionage.)

Now, I wonder if those corporate couriers will be taking the Eurostar through the Chunnel next week? The couriers may lug briefcases full of paper (which C&E is unlikely to read, or Xerox) for a few days. I suspect, however, that many of those firms are even now urgently reviewing their telecom alternatives. As the recent GILC survey[2] and the EC's Copenhagen Hearings[3] make clear, more business-sensitive governments abound, even in Europe.

For the past two years, the dominant policies of the OECD and the European Commission have been to foster electronic commerce by respecting the legitimate needs of consumers and businessmen for crypto-enabled confidentiality. Some correlations between policy and investment have been reported. Ireland recently announced what appears to be one of the most liberal national policies, allowing for the use and trade in crypto-enhanced software, among the Wassenaar signatories.[4] At the time, a senior Irish official noted that his government believes that its progressive stance on corporate requirements for crypto-based confidentiality has led over 700 foreign firms to set up plants and offices in the Emerald Isle.

It makes you wonder at the cost–benefits of this British government campaign to nail a few closet perverts?

Vin McLellan + The Privacy Guild + <vin@shore.net>
53 Nichols St, Chelsea, MA 02150 USA <617> 884-5548

Notes

1   <http://www.open.gov.uk/customs/discscan.htm>

2   <http://www.gilc.org/crypto/crypto-survey.html>

3   <http://www.fsk.dk/fsk/div/hearing/krypt.html>

4   <http://www.irlgov.ie:80/tec/html/signat.htm>

Some books that may be helpful

At the present time, there are many more books for those concerned with business ethics than there are for those specifically interested in the appropriate use of business computers.

While the following bibliography is consequently biased towards business ethics, it nevertheless includes many texts of relevance and interest.

Abelson, R. (ed.) *Ethics for Modern Life*, 3rd edn; New York: St Martin's Press, 1987.

ACM (Association for Computing Machinery)/SIGCAS (Special Interest Group on Computers and Society) *Proceedings of the Conference on Computers and the Quality of Life*; New York: ACM Press, 1990.

ACM, 'ACM Code of Ethics and Professional Conduct', *Communications of the ACM* 36:2, February 1993.

ACM, 'Draft Software Engineering Code of Ethics', *Communications of the ACM* 40:11, November 1997.

Albrecht W., *Ethical Issues in the Practice of Accounting*; Cincinnati: South-Western Publishing Co., 1992.

Alexander, I., *Foundations of Business: Enterprise, Technology, Society*; Oxford: Blackwell, 1990.

Anderson, J. W., *Corporate Social Responsibility: Guidelines for Top Management*; New York: Quorum Books, 1989.

Anderson, R., Johnson, G., Gotterbarn, D. and Perrolle, J., 'Using the new ACM Code of Ethics in decision making', *Communications of the ACM* 36:1, February 1993.

Arnold, C. (ed.) *Yearbook of Law, Computers and Technology*; London: Butterworth, annually.

Axtell, R. E. (ed.) *Do's and Taboos Around the World*, compiled by the Parker Pen Company, 2nd edn; New York: Wiley, 1990.

Baida, P., *Poor Richard's Legacy: American Business Values from Benjamin Franklin to Donald Trump*; New York: W. Morrow, 1990.

Bainbridge, D. I., *Introduction to Computer Law*; London: Pitman, 1998.

Barry, V., *Moral Issues in Business*, 3rd edn; Belmont, Calif.: Wadsworth Publishing Co., 1986.

Bauer, R. A. and Fenn, D. H. Jr, *The Corporate Social Audit*; New York: Russell Sage Foundation, 1972.

Baumol, W. J. and Blackman, S. A. B., *Perfect Markets and Easy Virtue: Business Ethics and the Invisible Hand*; Cambridge, Mass.: Blackwell, 1991.

Bayles, M. D., *Professional Ethics*; Belmont, Calif.: Wadsworth Publishing Co., 1981.

Beardon, C. and Whitehouse, D., *Computers and Society*; Exeter: Intellect Books, 1993.

Beauchamp, T. L., *Case Studies in Business, Society, and Ethics*, 4th edn; Englewood Cliffs, NJ: Prentice-Hall, 1997.

Beauchamp, T. L. (ed.) *Ethical Theory and Business*, 5th edn; Englewood Cliffs, NJ: Prentice-Hall, 1997.

Bird, F. B., *The Muted Conscience: Moral Silence and the Practice of Ethics in Business*; Westport, Conn.: Quorum Books, 1996.

Birsch, D. and Fielder, J. H. (eds) *The Ford Pinto Case: A Case Study in Applied Ethics, Business, and Technology*; Albany, NY: State University of New York Press, 1994.

Black, A., *State, Community and Human Desire: A Group-Centred Account of Political Values*; Hemel Hempstead: Harvester-Wheatsheaf, 1988.

Blanchard, K. H. and Peale, N. V., *The Power of Ethical Management*; New York: W. Morrow, 1988.

Bok, S., *Lying: Moral Choice in Public and Private Life*; New York: Vintage Books, 1989.

Bowman, J. S. (ed.) *Teaching Ethics and Values in Public Administration Programs: Innovations, Strategies, and Issues*; New York: State University of New York Press, 1997.

Bowyer, K. (ed.) *Ethics and Computing: Living Responsibly in a Computerized World*; New York, IEEE Computer Society, 1995.

Brady, F. N., *Ethical Managing: Rules and Results*; New York: MacMillan, 1990.

Brown, D. and Crane, P., *Who Killed Alaska?*; Far Hills, NJ: New Horizon Press, 1991.

Brown, G., *The Information Game: Ethical Issues in a Microchip World*; Atlantic Highlands, NJ: Humanities Press Intl, 1989.

Brown, M. T., *Working Ethics: Strategies for Decision Making and Organizational Responsibility*; San Francisco: Jossey-Bass, 1990.

Brummer, J. J., *Corporate Responsibility and Legitimacy: An Interdisciplinary Analysis*; New York: Greenwood Press, 1991.

Buchanan, J. M., *The Economics and the Ethics of Constitutional Order*; Ann Arbor: University of Michigan Press, 1991.

Burrough, B., and Helyar, J., *Barbarians at the Gate: The Fall of RJR Nabisco*; New York: HarperCollins, 1991.

Burton, B. K., 'Estimating the incidence of wrongdoing and whistleblowing: Results of a study using randomized response technique', *Journal of Business Ethics* 14: pp.17–30, January 1995.

Bynum, T. W., Maner, W. and Fodor, J. (eds) *Teaching Computer Ethics*; New Haven: Southern Connecticut State University, 1992.

Callahan, J. C. (ed.) *Ethical Issues in Professional Life*; New York: Oxford University Press, 1988.

Cannon, T., *Corporate Responsibility: A Textbook on Business Ethics*; London, Pitman, 1994.

Carr, I. and Williams, K. S., *Computers and Law*; Exeter: Intellect Books, 1994.

Cavalier, R. J., Gouinlock, J. and Sterba, J. P. (eds) *Ethics in the History of Western Philosophy*; Basingstoke: Macmillan, 1989.

Cavanagh, G. F., *American Business Values: With International Perspectives*, 4th edn; Englewood Cliffs, NJ: Prentice-Hall, 1997.

Chakraborty, S.K., *Ethics in Management: Vedantic Perspectives*; New York: Oxford University Press, 1995.

Charkham J., *Keeping Good Company – Corporate Governance in Five Countries*; Oxford: Oxford University Press, 1994.

Christians C. and Traber M., *Communication Ethics and Universal Values*; Thousand Oaks, Calif.: Sage Publications, 1997.

Chrysides G. and Kaler J., *Introduction to Business Ethics*; London: Chapman & Hall, 1993.

Ciulla, J. B. (ed.) *Ethics, the Heart of Leadership*; Westport, Conn: Greenwood Publishing, 1998.

Clarke, M., *Business Crime: Its Nature and Control*; New York: St Martin's Press, 1990.

Clinard, M. B., *Corporate Corruption: The Abuse of Power*; New York: Praeger, 1990.

Clutterbuck, D. *et al.*, *Actions Speak Louder: Corporate Social Responsibility*; London: Kogan Page, 1992.

Collins, W. R. and Miller, K. W., 'Paramedic ethics for computer professionals', *Journal of Systems and Software* 17, pp.23–38, January 1992.

Comer, M. J., *Corporate Fraud*, 3rd edn; London: McGraw-Hill, 1998.

Cowan, J., *Small Decencies: Reflections and Meditations on Being Human at Work*; New York: Harper Business, 1993.

Cullen, F. T., Maakestad, W. J. and Cavender, G., *Corporate Crime Under Attack: The Ford Pinto Case and Beyond*; Ohio: Anderson, 1987.

Davies, P. W. F., *Current Issues in Business Ethics*; New York: Routledge, 1997.

De Mente, B., *Chinese Etiquette & Ethics in Business*, 2nd edn; Lincolnwood, Ill.: NTC Publishing Group, 1994.

De Mente, B., *Japanese Etiquette & Ethics in Business*, 6th edn; Lincolnwood, Ill.: NTC Publishing Group, 1994.

Dembo, D., Morehouse, W. and Wykle, L., *Abuse of Power: Social Performance of Multinational Corporations: The Case of Union Carbide*; New York: New Horizons Press, 1990.

DesJardins, J. R. and McCall, J. J., *Contemporary Issues in Business Ethics*; Belmont, Calif.: Wadsworth Publishing Co., 1990.

Donaldson, J., *Business Ethics: European Case-book*; San Diego: Academic Press, 1992.

Donaldson, T., *The Ethics of International Business*; New York: Oxford University Press, 1989.

Donaldson, T. (ed.) *Case Studies in Business Ethics*; Englewood Cliffs, NJ: Prentice-Hall, 1996.

Driscoll, D.-M., Hoffman, W. M. and Petry, E., *The Ethical Edge: Tales of Organizations that have Faced Moral Crises*; New York: MasterMedia Ltd, 1995.

Edmonson, W. F., *A Code Of Ethics: Do Corporate Executives and Employees Need It?: A Study of 100 Codes of Ethics from America's Largest Corporations*; Fulton, Mo.: Itawamba Community College Press, 1990.

Engerle, G., Almond, B. and Argandona, A. (eds) *People in Corporations: Ethical Responsibilities and Corporate Effectiveness*; Dordrecht and Boston: Kluwer Academic, 1990.

Erdmann, M. D. and Williams, M. B. (eds) *Computers, Ethics and Society*, 2nd edn; Oxford University Press, 1997.

Ettore, B., 'Whistleblowers: Who's the real bad guy?' *Management Review* 83: pp.18–23, May 1994.

Ezorsky, G. (ed) *Moral Rights in the Workplace*; Albany, NY: State University of New York Press, 1987.

Farbey, B., Land, F. and Targett, D., *How to Assess Your IT Investment: A Study of Methods and Practice*; Oxford: Butterworth-Heinemann, 1993.

Ferrell, O. C. and Fraedrich, J., *Business Ethics: Ethical Decision Making and Cases*; Boston: Houghton Mifflin, 1991.

Fidler, C. and Rogerson, S., *Strategic Management Support Systems*; London: Pitman, 1996.

Fishman, D. B. and Cherniss, C. (eds) *The Human Side of Corporate Competitiveness*; Newbury Park, Calif.: Sage Publications, 1990.

Forester, T. and Morrison, P., *Computer Ethics: Cautionary Tales and Ethical Dilemmas in Computing*, 2nd edn; Oxford: Blackwell, 1993.

Frankel, M. S., 'Professional codes: why, how, and with what impact?' *Journal of Business Ethics* 8 (2 & 3): pp.109–116, 1989.

Frederick, W. C. and Preston, L. E. (eds) *Business Ethics: Research Issues and Empirical Studies*; Greenwich, Conn.: JAI Press, 1990.

Frederick, W. C., Davis, K. and Post, J. E., *Business and Society: Corporate Strategy, Public Policy, Ethics*, 9th edn; New York: McGraw-Hill, 1998.

Freeman, R. E. (ed.) *Business Ethics: The State of the Art*; New York: Oxford University Press, 1991.

French, P. A., Nesteruk, J. and Risser, D. T., *Corporations in the Moral Community*; Texas: Harcourt Brace Jovanovich, 1992.

French, W. A. and Granrose, J., *Practical Business Ethics*; Englewood Cliffs, NJ: Prentice-Hall, 1995.

Gambling, T. and Karim, R. A. A., *Business and Accounting Ethics in Islam*; London; New York: Mansell, 1991.

Giacalone R. and Greenberg, J., *Anti-Social Behaviour in Organisations*; Thousand Oaks, Calif.: Sage Publications, 1997.

Gilbert, D. R., *Ethics Through Corporate Strategy*; New York: Oxford University Press, 1996.

Ginzberg, E. and Vojta G., *Beyond Human Scale: the Large Corporation at Risk*; New York: Basic Books, 1987.

Goldberg, M. (ed.) *Against the Grain: New Approaches to Professional Ethics*; Valley Forge, Pa.: Trinity Press Intl, 1993.

Goodpaster, K. E., Nash, L. L. and Bowers, J., *Policies and Persons – A Casebook in Business Ethics*, 3rd edn; New York: McGraw-Hill, 1997.

Gotterbarn, D., 'Editor's corner', *Journal of Systems Software* 17: pp.5–6, January 1992.

Gould, C. (ed.) *The Information Web: Ethical and Social Implications of Computer Networking*; Boulder, Colo.: Westview Press, 1989.

Goyder G., *The Just Enterprise: A Blueprint for the Responsible Company*; Twickenham: Adamantine, 1993.

Green R., *The Ethical Manager – A New Method for Business Ethics*; London, Macmillan, 1994.

Hartman, E., *Organizational Ethics and the Good Life*; New York: Oxford University Press, 1996.

Higginson, R. and Moore, G., *Apocalypse: The Business Ethics Game*; Chichester: John Wiley & Sons, 1998.

Hodapp, P. F., *Ethics in the Business World*; Melbourne, Fla.: Krieger Publishing Co., 1994.

Hoffman, W. M. and Moore, J. M. (eds) *Business Ethics: Readings and Cases in Corporate Morality*, 3rd edn; New York: McGraw-Hill, 1994.

Hoffman, W. M., Frederick, R. and Petry, E. S. Jr (eds) *The Corporation, Ethics, and the Environment*; New York: Quorum Books, 1990.

Hopkins, W., *Ethical Dimensions of Diversity*; Thousand Oaks, Calif.: Sage Publications, 1997.

Hosmer, L. T., The Ethics of Management; Homewood, Ill.: Irwin, 1987.

IEEE Computer Society Press, *Computing Curricula 1991*, Report of the ACM/IEEE-CS Joint Curriculum Task Force, Los Alamitos, Calif.: IEEE Computer Society Press, 1991.

Ince, D., Sharp, H. and Woodman, M., *Introduction to Software Project Management and Quality Assurance*; Burr Ridge, Ill.: McGraw-Hill, 1993.

Information Technology Law Group/Europe, *European Computer Law*; Hudson River Valley, New York: Transnational Publishers, 1996.

Johnson, D. G. and Snapper, J. W. (eds) *Ethical Issues in the Use of Computers*; Belmont Calif.: Wadsworth Publishing Co., 1985.

Johnson, D. G., *Computer Ethics*, 2nd edn; Englewood Cliffs, NJ: Prentice-Hall, 1993.

Jones, D. G. and Bennett, P., *A Bibliography of Business Ethics 1981–1985*; Virginia: Edwin Mellen, 1986.

Kidder, R. M., *How Good People Make Tough Choices*; New York: W. Morrow, 1995.

Kitson, A. and Campbell, C., *The Ethical Organisation*; Basingstoke: Macmillan, 1996.

Kizza, J. M., (ed.) *Ethical and Social Issues in the Information Age*; Heidelberg: Springer-Verlag, 1997.

Kling, R. (ed.) *Computerization and Controversy: Value Conflicts and Social Choices*, 2nd edn; San Diego: Academic Press, 1996.

Knight, P. and Fitzsimons, J., *The Legal Aspects of Computing*; Wokingham: Addison-Wesley, 1990.

Koocher, G. P. (ed.) *Ethics in Cyberspace: A Special Issue of Ethics and Behavior*; Mahwah, NJ: Lawrence Erlbaum Associates, 1996.

Kuhn, J. W. and Shriver, D. W., *Beyond Success: Corporations and their Critics in the 1990s*; New York: Oxford University Press, 1991.

Langford, D., 'Ethical issues in business computing', in *Ethics and Information Technology*, Collste, G. (ed.); Delhi: New Academic Publishers, 1998.

Langford, D., *Practical Computer Ethics*; London: McGraw-Hill, 1995.

Levy, S., *Hackers – Heroes of the Computer Revolution*; Delta Books, 1994.

Lewis, A. and Warnery, K.-E. (eds.) *Ethics and Economic Affairs*; London and New York: Routledge, 1994.

Liebig, J. E., *Business Ethics: Profiles in Civic Virtue*; Golden, Colo.: Fulcrum Publishing, 1991.

Mackie, J., *Ethics – Inventing Right and Wrong*; London: Penguin, 1991.

Manley, W., *Executive's Handbook of Model Business Conduct Codes*; Englewood Cliffs, NJ: Prentice-Hall, 1991.

Manley, W., *Handbook of Good Corporate Practice*; London: Routledge, 1992.

Marks, R. and Minow, N., *Power and Accountability*; New York: HarperCollins, 1991.

Mars, G., *Cheats at Work: An Anthropology of Workplace Crime*; Dartmouth Publishing Co., 1994.

Marshal E., *Business and Society*; London: Routledge, 1993.

Martin, C. D. and Martin, D. H., 'Comparison of ethics codes of computer professionals', *Social Science Computer Review* 9, 1: pp.96–108, 1990.

Messick, D. M. and Tenbrunsel, A. E. (eds) *Codes of Conduct: Behavioral Research into Business Ethics*; Chicago: Russell Sage Foundation, 1997.

Michalos, A. C., *A Pragmatic Approach to Business Ethics*; Thousand Oaks, Calif.: Sage Publications, 1995.

Monks, R. and Minow, N., *Corporate Governance*; Oxford: Blackwell, 1994.

Morgan, P. W. (ed.) *The Appearance of Impropriety: How the Ethics Wars Have Undermined American Government, Business, and Society*; New York: The Free Press, 1997.

Myers, C., Hall, T. and Pitt D. (eds) *The Responsible Software Engineer*; London: Springer-Verlag, 1997.

Myers, C. (ed.) *Professional Awareness in Software Engineering: Or, Should a Software Engineer Wear a Suit?* London: McGraw-Hill, 1995.

Nader, R. (ed.) *The Consumer and Corporate Accountability*; New York: Harcourt Brace Jovanovich, 1973.

Nader, R. *et al.* (eds) *Whistle-Blowing – The Nader Report*; New York: Harper & Row, 1975.

Nash, L. L., *Good Intentions Aside: A Manager's Guide to Resolving Ethical Problems*; Boston, Mass.: Harvard Business School Press, 1993.

Natale, S. M. and Wilson, J. B. (eds) *The Ethical Contexts for Business Conflicts*; Maryland: University of Maryland Press, 1990.

Newton, L. H., 'Taking sides: clashing views on controversial issues', in *Business Ethics and Society*, 5th edn Newton, L. H. (ed.); London: McGraw-Hill, 1998.

Nielsen, R. P., *The Politics of Ethics: Methods for Acting, Learning, and Sometimes Fighting with Others in Addressing Ethics Problems in Organizational Life*; New York: Oxford University Press, 1996.

Noll, J. W. (ed.) *Taking Sides: Clashing Views on Controversial Social Issues*, 9th edn; Guilford, Conn.: Dushkin Publishing Group, 1997.

Olive, D., *Just Rewards: The Case for Ethical Reform in Business*; Toronto, Canada: Key Porter Books, 1987.

Persig, R. M., *Zen and the Art of Motorcycle Maintenance*; New York: Vintage Press, 1986.

Ponemon, L., 'A proactive whistleblowing process', *Management Accounting* 77: 16, February 1996.

Prindl, A. and Prodhan, B., *ACT Guide to Ethical Conflicts in Finance*; Oxford: Blackwell, 1994.

Reder, A., *In Pursuit of Principle and Profit: Business Success through Social Responsibility*; New York: G.P. Putnam's Sons, 1994.

Reed, C. (ed.) *Computer Law*, 3rd edn; London: Blackstone Press, 1996.

Richardson, J. E. (ed.) *Business Ethics 96/97*, 8th edn; Madison, Wis.: Brown & Benchmark, 1996.

Rion, M., *The Responsible Manager: Practical Strategies For Ethical Decision Making*; San Francisco: Harper & Row, 1990.

Robinson, D. and Garratt, C., *Ethics for Beginners*; London: Penguin/Icon, 1996.

Rosenberg, R. S., *The Social Impact of Computers*, 2nd edn; Boston, Mass.: Academic Press, 1997.

Rothery, B., *BS 7750 – Implementing the Environment Management Standard and the EC*; Aldershot: Gower, 1993.

Russell, S. and Wefald, E., *Do The Right Thing: Studies in Limited Rationality*; MIT Press, 1991.

Shaw, W. H. and Barry, V., *Moral Issues in Business*, 7th edn; Belmont, Calif.: Wadsworth Publishing Co., 1997.

Shaw, W. H., *Business Ethics*, 2nd edn; Belmont, Calif.: Wadsworth Publishing Co., 1996.

Singer, P. (ed.) *Ethics*; Oxford: Oxford University Press, 1994.

Smith K. (ed.) *Business Ethics and Business Behaviour*; London: International Thomson Business Press, 1997.

Snell R., *Developing Skill for Ethical Management*; Norwell, Mass.: Kluwer Academic Publishers, 1994.

Solomon, R. C., *Ethics and Excellence: Cooperation and Integrity in Business*; New York: Oxford University Press, 1992.

Solomon, R. C., *The New World of Business: Ethics and Free Enterprise in the Global 1990s*; Lanham, Md.: Rowman & Littlefield, 1994.

Sorell, T. and Hendry, J., *Business Ethics*; Oxford: Butterworth-Heinemann, 1994.

Stackhouse, M. W. (ed.) *On Moral Business: Classical and Contemporary Resources for Ethics in Economic Life*; Grand Rapids, Mich.: W.B. Eerdmans Publishing, 1995.

Steiner, G. A. and Steiner, J. F., *Business, Government, and Society: A Managerial Perspective*, 8th edn; New York: Random House, 1996.

Sternberg, E., *Just Business: Business Ethics in Action*; London: Warner, 1995.

Stoll, C., *The Cuckoo's Egg: Tracking a Spy Through the Maze of Computer Espionage*; London: Pan Books, 1991.

Sturdivant, F. D. and Stacey, J. E., *The Corporate Social Challenge: Cases and Commentaries*, 5th edn; Homewood, Ill.: Richard D. Irwin, 1994.

Vallance, E., *Business Ethics at Work*; Cambridge: Cambridge University Press, 1995.

Van Luijk, H. and Ulrich, P. (eds) *Facing Public Interest: Ethical Challenge to Business Policy and Corporate Communications*; Norwell, Mass.: Kluwer Academic Publishers, 1995.

Velasquez, M. G., *Business Ethics: Concepts and Cases*, 4th edn; Englewood Cliffs, NJ: Prentice-Hall, 1997.

Wallace, J. (ed.) *Sex, Laws, and Cyberspace: Freedom and Censorship on the Frontiers of the Online Revolution*; New York: Henry Holt, 1997.

Walton, C. C., *Corporate Encounters: Ethics, Law, and the Business Environment*; Fort Worth, Texas: The Dryden Press, 1992.

Watson, C. E., *Managing With Integrity: Insights From America's CEOs*; New York: Praeger, 1991.

Weckert, J. and Adeney, D., *Computer and Information Ethics*; London: Greenwood Press, 1997.

Werhane, P. H., Freeman, R. E. and Freeman, E. (eds) *The Blackwell Encyclopedic Dictionary of Business Ethics (The Blackwell Encyclopedia of Management)*; Cambridge, Mass.: Blackwell, 1997.

Index

Introduction

The index covers Chapters 1 to 10 and Appendices 1 to 7. Index entries are to page numbers. Alphabetical arrangement is word-by-word, where a group of letters followed by a space is filed before the same group of letters followed by a letter, eg 'network etiquette' will appear before 'networked computers'. Initial articles, conjunctions and prepositions are ignored in determining filing order.

Learning Resources
Centre